Revolution and Papacy

MAP OF ITALY SHOWING THE PAPAL STATES

REVOLUTION
AND PAPACY
1769 – 1846

E. E. Y. HALES

Author of PIO NONO *and*
MAZZINI AND THE SECRET SOCIETIES

LONDON
EYRE & SPOTTISWOODE
22 HENRIETTA STREET WC2

TO HELEN ASQUITH

First published 1960
© 1960 E. E. Y. Hales
Printed in Great Britain
by Billing & Sons Ltd
Guildford and London
Cat. No. 6/2409

Contents

5

Illustrations

Preface

My *Pio Nono* (1954) was concerned with the political and religious events of Pius IX's long pontificate (1846–78). This book is about the similar events during the three quarters of a century before Pius IX was elected. I have chosen the pontificate of Clement XIV (1769–74) as the starting-point because that Pope's suppression of the Jesuits may be taken, as Ranke took it, to mark the first major retreat of the papacy before that Enlightenment which preceded the Revolution.

In a Europe politically experimental and increasingly secularist Rome was on the defensive. The popes were trying to defend two things: their traditional spiritual claims and their traditional political claims. On the whole, despite disasters, they succeeded; but unfortunately they were more successful in their secondary (temporal) aim than they were in their primary (spiritual) one. Only in 1870 would this unfortunate disproportion be reversed, the spiritual claims becoming irrevocably defined, and generally accepted by Catholic Europe, and the temporal claims being over-ridden. Not that Pius IX or his successors abandoned the temporal claims; that had to wait upon Pius XI in 1929. But it was in Pius IX's pontificate that, contrary to the will of the Pope, the burden of an impossible temporal care was at last wrenched from hands quite unsuited to carrying it.

While it is difficult to exaggerate the harm done to the papacy, particularly in the pontificate of Gregory XVI (1831–46), by its temporal preoccupations, it is possible to exaggerate their in-fluence in shaping papal policy. Those historians, for instance, who believed that Clement XIV was bribed into suppressing the Jesuits in 1773 with the promise of the return of Avignon and Benevento to Rome, or who attributed, as did Albert Mathiez, Rome's whole opposition to the French Revolution to her desire to recover her position in Provence, are assuming a scale of values which no Pope of the period adopted and which they denounced, when it was suggested to them, as simoniacal. Neither Clement XIV, at the

7

beginning of our period, nor Gregory XVI at the end of it (the
two popes whose motives have come, with some reason, under
the most serious suspicion) took so low a view of their exalted
office as to try to trade spiritual concession, in that way, for temporal advantage.

Yet we may also be making a mistake if we imagine that men
distinguished very sharply, in this period, between matters spiritual
and matters temporal; certainly the distinction was not sharply
focused in the minds of the rulers of the time, whether they were
laymen or bishops. The Emperor Joseph II saw no reason why he
should not initiate liturgical reforms, nor did Napoleon expect to
be rebuked for his Feast of Saint Napoleon or his 'Imperial Catechism'. And a similar confusion existed in the Papal States, where
the perspicacious Cardinal Giovanni Sala lamented: 'we have often
confused the spiritual and the temporal, sacrificing the one in our
desire to sustain the other, and thereby losing both'. Admittedly,
nobody who has read the legal opinions of the various commissions
(*Consultas*) set up in Rome during this period to examine difficult
issues will suppose that the Curia was blind to the distinction; and
when Sala said that the spiritual function of the papacy was
'essential and inherent in its character', whereas its temporal
function was only 'accessory and accidental', he was only quoting
the common opinion of the Sacred College. But it was also their
common opinion that Cardinal Consalvi was right when, at the
Congress of Vienna, he insisted that it was vital for the Pope to
remain a substantial temporal prince or the Church would never be
taken seriously by the other princes of Europe. The Temporal
Power might be only accessory but Consalvi – even Sala – thought
the papacy could not manage without it.

It seems strange to the modern critic that the papacy clung so
tenaciously to its temporal dominion. Even after he has allowed for
the fact that European government was monarchical, that it was
important to be a monarch if you were to argue with monarchs, and
that a monarch must be seen to have the resources and court proper
to his state, it still seems strange that nobody at Rome who mattered
drew a moral from Pius VII's experience between the years 1809
and 1814. For it was when Pius VII was without a state, and without

revenue, 'the poor monk Chiaramonti', Napoleon's prisoner, that he won the Church's greatest spiritual victory of modern times, and thus engendered the ultramontane revival. In the middle of the sorry story of papal concessions to the powers, from 1769 to 1846, and the tragi-comic efforts of cardinals to save the Papal States from invasion and revolution, there emerges the serene and saintly figure of a Pope who didn't mind that the Romagna was ruled by the French, who rather preferred an elected Emperor to a Hapsburg, who was happiest when in prison, but who met the claims on his spiritual independence with firm but courteous refusals. No doubt Pius VII, like the other popes, fought to retain his temporal sovereignty, and he excommunicated Napoleon for seizing it. No doubt, too, he was acutely sensitive about Rome, and insisted he must return there. But he showed that a Pope could be a Pope even in solitary confinement, and he showed his readiness, if need be, to sacrifice his temporal sovereignty for the sake of the papacy and the Church. Though physically Napoleon's prisoner he was never any ruler's prisoner in the sense that Clement XIV was the prisoner of the Bourbons or Gregory XVI of Vienna.

Only the first part of the story, the pontificates of Clement XIV and Pius VI (1769-99), has been told in any detail in England – in the translation of Pastor's *History of the Popes*. The period between 1800 and 1846 is the subject of Jean Leflon's *La Crise Révolutionnaire* and of Joseph Schmidlin's *Papstgeschichte der neusten Zeit*, of which there is a French translation. To these and many other continental historians I am naturally indebted; but I have often gone back to the sources, particularly to those at the Vatican.

My thanks are especially due to the staffs at the Vatican, Vallicelliana, Sapienza, British Museum, Cambridge University, and Yale University libraries and to the Librarian of St Edmund's College, Old Hall. Also to Mr M. W. Hutt of Leeds University, Mr J. M. Roberts of Merton and Mr J. D. Walsh of Jesus College, Oxford; to the Rev. B. FitzGibbon, S.J., Lady Helen Asquith, and Mr C. W. Baty; and to my publishers for their patience.

E. E. Y. HALES,
Fair Green,
Sawbridgeworth.

January 1960.

The Climate of Opinion in 1769

The temper of the later half of the eighteenth century in Europe, it is well known, was hostile to the claims of the papacy, as they had been handed down from the middle ages, and as they had begun to be codified by the Council of Trent and by the ultramontane theologians. In enlightened circles, and within the royal courts of the great capitals that temper was commonly opposed to the idea of any dogmatically defined revealed religion, resting on authority, and maintained by exclusive privilege and political sanction. No society in which the writings of Rousseau, Voltaire and the encyclopaedists were fashionable could well do other than smile at the papal claims, just as it was beginning to smile at a literal acceptance of those beliefs which the papacy existed to defend.

By the year 1769 the Roman claims were called in question not merely by the Protestant Churches or by those who openly adopted rationalist, naturalist or deist ideas, or by voluntary groups like the lodges of the freemasons; they were looked at askance by those who regarded themselves as orthodox Catholics but who felt that the royal power had a larger part to play than had the papacy in the reform and the control of the Church. Gallicans, Jansenists and Febronians, despite their other differences, held this belief in common.

This change in the climate of opinion towards Rome was to be reflected, in the sphere of government, in an advance in the claims of the temporal rulers at the expense of the spiritual ruler. The Tsarina Catherine, the Emperor Joseph II, Frederick the Great and the Bourbons of Spain and of Naples were rulers with a strong sense of the enlightenment which it was their duty to spread for the benefit of their subjects; and if the Bourbon at Versailles was less messianically minded that was not for want of enlightened principles at Paris.

It has often been noticed that the Catholic Church of this time stood in need of reform on account of her worldliness – the wealth of her bishops, and their preoccupation with political affairs. But it is equally necessary to notice how lacking she was in unity of faith. Had the Church in the year 1769 been more united as to what she believed, religiously speaking, or in her views on the right relations between Church and State she might, perhaps, have been less woefully worsted by the enlightened rulers, or by the revolution, or by Napoleon. But in fact she could scarcely be said to have known where she stood whether in regard to her own spiritual authority or in regard to her right relations with the State.

On the role of the State, in matters religious, the divergences were fundamental and a prime source of the violent polemics between Jansenist and Jesuit, Gallican and Ultramontane, or Febronian and Papal Nuncio. But interwoven with these differences were divergences of religious belief wider than had existed before or than would exist again after the ultramontane revival of the following century. There existed, for instance, quite widely amongst the clergy, especially in France, a vague and secularist outlook introduced from the contemporary deism or naturalism. No doubt the *Testament* of the notorious curé Meslier, who denied the existence of any intelligent God, represented an exceptional view; but there were many of the clergy who had absorbed, at the universities, the fashionable philosophy of the times – so much more compelling than the definitions of the schoolmen – and with it ideas which sometimes leant towards a Rousseauistic sentimentality, sometimes rather towards rationalism, but always away from a literal acceptance of traditional Christian beliefs. Such clergy preferred to talk about the Supreme Being rather than about God, and to find the Holy Spirit in nature rather than at Pentecost. But their chief difficulty came with the Second Person of the Trinity. His incarnation, crucifixion, resurrection, and ascension were apt to offend them. These fundamental beliefs of the Church seemed to them too concrete, literal, anthropomorphic. It embarrassed them to talk about such things; they preferred the abstract language of the philosophers, the analogies drawn from the seasons or the soil.

It should not be supposed that this deistic deviation within Catholicism was an attribute of cruder or less sensitive souls. On the contrary, it was the reaction of refined minds against what was regarded as the crudity and the literalness of the 'Jesuitical' approach to religion, with its emphasis on the personal and the particular, on the Rosary, on the human personality of Our Lord or of His mother, or on the saints. It was also a reaction against the placing of emphasis on dogmatic theology, and against precise devotions – especially the Exercises of Saint Ignatius.

A deism which 'played down' the Second Person of the Trinity was clearly misnamed in being called Christian. More recognizably Christian were the perfectionist groups which deplored most of the popular aids to devotion, and despised most that had happened in the Church since the first six centuries. Such 'puritan' aspirations were becoming common in the eighteenth century within the Church as well as having led to the formation of numerous groups outside it. Those Catholic clergy who embraced them, and who sought to give expression to their views in new catechisms or commentaries, and those members of Religious Orders (especially the Augustinians) who lent them their support were usually either openly or tacitly supporters of the Jansenist party.

It is easy to forget that, although in its later days the great convent of Port Royal housed only a handful of nuns, and although Louis XIV razed it to the ground, and although Pope Clement XI in *Unigenitus* (1713) condemned the principal ideas of the Jansenist prophet Quesnel, the Jansenist ideas lived on. They lived on at Utrecht, centre of a schismatic Jansenist Church where, six years before Clement XIV's election, and in the same year (1763) as most of the Jesuits were suppressed in France, a synod was summoned to give them greater precision. They lived on in Tuscany where, as late as the year 1786, a similar and more celebrated synod assembled at Pistoia. They lived on amongst isolated French bishops, such as Fitz-James of Soissons, but much more evidently amongst the lower clergy in France, the Netherlands, Germany, and Italy.

The Jansenists, like most reformers, invoked a greater simplicity, a stricter morality, universal study of the scriptures, less frequent communion (with a longer period of penance), and a readiness to

resist authority – especially the authority of Rome – when it con-
flicted with private judgement. They called for a return to what
they regarded as the attitude of the Early Church and they welcomed persecution as a sign that they were right. Only the earlier
Councils of the Church did they regard as valid; the later aggran-
disement of the Papal power, the Lateran Councils, the Council of
Trent, and worst of all the Jesuits represented 'something unclean
which had crept into the Church later than the first six centuries'.[1]
They preached an Elect – themselves. And by exaggerating the
teaching of Saint Augustine on the power and necessity of God's
grace for any efficacious act, and man's helplessness either to gain it
or to act aright without it, they made themselves not only into an
Elect but into a predestinate Elect, like the Calvinists.

Although the 101 censures of the Bull *Unigenitus* condemned
almost every known Jansenist tenet the authority of Rome was insufficient in France to ensure that Jansenist ideas were not taught in
seminaries or even approved by some bishops. They lived on to
nourish a movement whose antagonism to the papacy, and still
more to the Jesuits, had been aggravated by Clement XI's Bull, and
which found expression in France in a pamphlet warfare[2] directed
against *Unigenitus* and in a weekly periodical which appeared
regularly from 1728 to 1793, entitled *Nouvelles Ecclésiastiques, ou
Mémoires pour servir à l'histoire de la Constitution Unigenitus*. This
paper was ultimately succeeded by the *Annales de la Religion*, the
organ of the Constitutional Church under the French revolution –
a genealogy which suggests that a road did lead from Port Royal to
the revolutionary Civil Constitution of the Clergy.

Jansenism, then, in the eighteenth century, was still attacking the
constitution and teaching of the Church from within; only in the
case of the Utrecht schism did it operate from without, and even
that schism argued that it was within the fold. It was this Catholic
attitude of the Jansenists that made them dangerous. If Clement

[1] R. A. Knox *Enthusiasm*, O.U.P., 1951, p. 188.
[2] In the *Collection Languet* of the *Bibliothèque Municipale* of Sens is a quantity of
pamphlets, with some letters, on *Unigenitus* and Jansenism, made by Bishop
Languet (who was concerned to defend *Unigenitus* and orthodoxy) in the first half
of the eighteenth century. The collection extends from Vol. 1 (writings of 1705) to
Vol. 48 (writings of 1742).

XIV had only been confronted, at his accession in 1769, by a party numerically small, concerned to insist upon heretical opinions about grace, communion, or the criteria to be used in confession, he would have had no greater cause to be perturbed by it than the papacy had always been by any heresy. If the worst came to the worst the group could be expected to form a new sect, thus adding to the many which had already been founded upon similar principles. But the eighteenth-century papacy was confronted, in Jansenism, by something different from that and more dangerous. It was confronted by a movement which had no intention of making itself into a sect. The Jansenists intended rather (like the later Modernists) to reorder the Church, Catholic and Roman, from within. They clung tenaciously to the idea of a visible unity for the Church and they could perceive the need for a centre for that unity – a Holy See. They distinguished, however, between the Holy See and Rome. For the Holy See in principle they professed respect, but for the actual Rome, the Rome of *Unigenitus*, and still worse the Rome of the Jesuits, they felt nothing less than hatred.

The Jansenists were in love with their own idea of the Church and with their own idea of her unity. It was in this, as well as in other matters, that their position contrasted so sharply with that of the Jesuits, who were the champions of no mere idea of Christian unity, no impersonal concept of a Holy See. The Jesuits served actual Popes, an operating Church. They believed in a faith which had been most recently and fully defined in the sixteenth century at Trent. No special sanctity attached, for them, to the first six or to any other centuries of the Christian era. There was one Church, divinely established, which included saints and sinners, tares and wheat, foolish virgins and wise, and in that Church the supreme authority was the Pope. Only he – with or without the aid of a General Council – could define dogma. And as for pious practices, new rules for life in communities, special devotions, and the like, the Society of Jesus accepted them as elements in the developing life of the Church, but only to be embraced as orthodox, and recommended to the general use of Christians, if they received the sanction of Rome – as, for example, approval had been given by

Innocent III to the rules of the Franciscan Order or as the Institutes and Spiritual Exercises of Saint Ignatius himself had been approved.

The fact that the Jansenists were thwarted by Rome in their purposes for the reform of the Church led them, in the eighteenth century, to seek friends in other directions, and especially amongst the lower clergy. And in that down-trodden group they found many friends, if only because they developed the flattering theory that, if the bishops were the descendants of the twelve apostles, the parish priests were the descendants of the seventy-two, sent out by Our Lord; they were therefore entitled to their voice in the defining of dogma and in serious disciplinary measures such as excommunication. To the latter point the Jansenists attached particular importance, having been specially incensed by article 90 of *Unigenitus* which condemned their proposition that the consent of the whole body of the clergy was necessary to make an excommunication valid. Their ultimate aim, under the leadership of the See of Utrecht, became a General Council of the Church, at which the parish priests should be represented, the Bull *Unigenitus* quashed, and some measure of reconciliation with the Protestants and schismatics achieved. Their vision of Catholic unity was, indeed, none other than the administratively awkward one of the agreement of Christendom freely reached and continuously maintained by the parish priests of the whole Christian world. At the synods of Utrecht and Pistoia they attempted to put religious authority into the hands of the lower clergy within the area of a single diocese; in some French dioceses, notably those of Soissons and Auxerre, there were strong movements for similar synods.

Like Luther, the Jansenists were strong conservatives, politically speaking; they too would tie their reformation to the chariot wheels of the princes. But so far as authority and organization within the Church were concerned they tended to become democrats, in the sense that they hoped to find a more effective place for the parish priest; and on this side, in the eighteenth century, the movement is more properly known as Richerism,[1] because it claimed to inherit from the 'democratic' theologian Edmond

[1] See Appendix I, p. 296.

Richer (1560–1631) its zeal for the cause of the lesser clergy. Amongst the parish priests this egalitarianism found fruitful soil in regions as widely separated as the valleys of the Yonne, the Scheldt, and the Arno, and its spread may be accounted for, at least in part, by the widening gulf which yawned between the influence and condition of life of the lower clergy and those of the higher. A significant recommendation of the Synod of Pistoia was that parish priests should be given precedence over cathedral canons; as a class they had become depressed by the gradual elimination of the local patron and by the increasing control over the avenues of patronage and promotion enjoyed by the bishop. The parish priest had come to find that, in order to secure his advancement, he must at all costs please his ecclesiastical superiors.

But if the priest must please his bishop the bishop must please his king. Not only in great kingdoms like France, where the Pope scarcely ever refused to institute to their Sees the bishops nominated by the king, but also throughout the electorates, grand-duchies, and principalities of Europe generally it had become customary, by the year 1769, for Rome to approve the choice of the ruler. It was this custom which lay at the root of those essentially secular loyalties amongst the higher clergy which in France showed themselves in Gallicanism, in Germany showed themselves in what was beginning to be called Febronianism, and in Austria would soon be called Josephism, three terms which described, in different contexts, a closer association between Church and State which, in greater or in lesser degree, was widely accepted by the ecclesiastical hierarchies. The opposite tendency was called ultramontanism, or sometimes just Romanism or Papalism, and its main support came from the Jesuits. The long and unresolved struggle, inherited from the middle ages, between the spiritual and the temporal power, the struggle between Pope and Emperor, Archbishop and King, ecclesiastical court and royal court, was still very much in evidence, but everywhere it was going against the Church, and that was largely because her leaders so often saw themselves first as the king's men. The powers whose ambassadors and court cardinals pressed so hard upon the Conclave which elected Pope Clement XIV were in the ascendant, and with the election of a Pope of their

B

choice they believed, with some reason, that they had clinched their victory.

The Gallicans, though the eighteenth century was their heyday, by no means conceived of themselves as innovators. Like everybody else they appealed to tradition, and she did not let them down. In their more menacing moods they would remind Rome how Philip the Fair had treated Pope Boniface VIII, or how the papacy had been removed to Avignon. With a better show of right they harked back to the Pragmatic Sanction of 1438, which had asserted the superiority of General Councils to the Pope and had forbidden appeals to Rome. But the really relevant legal document was the Concordat of 1516, signed by King Francis I and Pope Leo X, which gave the king the right of nomination to French bishoprics and abbacies (taking it away from local chapters) and secured to the Pope the right to reject clearly unqualified nominees and to enjoy, in the form of annates, the first year's income of the new incumbent. In a soil so prepared there had grown up the powerful political cardinals and the nationally minded court bishops of the seventeenth century, while those who aspired to the French priesthood were taught at Saint-Sulpice doctrines never accepted at Rome, and summarized in the 'Four Propositions' of 1682: that the Church had no right to interfere in French civil and political affairs; that General Councils were superior in authority to the Pope; that Papal intervention by briefs or bulls in French affairs was subject to Gallican tradition (i.e. to the *placet* or *exequatur* of the monarch) and that even in matters of faith the Pope was not infallible save by the consent of the Church. By these propositions the French Church protected herself against the Pope, but only at the price of subjecting herself to the monarchy.

Yet in practice these propositions, though the Popes never ceased to protest about them, do not loom so large in the quarrels between Rome and Paris in the eighteenth century as Napoleon's Organic Articles (which embodied the same principles) do in the nineteenth, or when the issue of Conciliarism versus Papal Infallibility came to a head at the time of the Vatican Council. So long as the French king nominated bishops whom the Popes could conscientiously invest with their spiritual authority – as they normally did – and so long as Papal documents were accepted at Paris and published there – as they normally were – it was not in the interests of either the French monarchy or the papacy to press the issue about where the ultimate authority resided. Broadly speaking, the French monarchy, the French bishops, and the papacy were in working alliance in the eighteenth century. Amongst other bonds which united them was their mistrust of Jansenism; indeed the Bull *Unigenitus* itself bore witness, in its preamble, not only to the anxieties of the French hierarchy but to Louis XIV's personal desire that Rome should intervene to quieten the quarrels raised by the Jansenists:

> '. . . not only the aforesaid (French) bishops', says Clement XI, 'but even chiefly our most dear Son in Christ, Lewis the most Christian King of France . . . has often made protestation to and importunately solicited Us . . . that We would provide for the pressing necessity of souls by forthwith issuing the censure of the Apostolical Judgment'.

In short, despite the Gallican theory, to which both the French king and the French bishops adhered, relations between Rome and Paris were comparatively harmonious at the time of the Conclave of 1769. The really severe pressure was being put upon Rome by the Spanish Bourbon, Charles III, rather than by his French cousin. But when Charles III, and soon others in Germany and Austria, sought to restrict the traditional rights of Rome the Gallican theory provided them with a convenient set of principles to which they could appeal. They might have no belief in the notion of the innate superiority of the French theologians, still less in any peculiar authority in the sphere of Church affairs belonging as of right to His Most Christian Majesty of France; but they were beginning to see that the special powers claimed for the French monarchy by Gallicanism might just as properly be claimed by other monarchies. In the pontificate of Clement XIV's successor, Pius VI, such theories would find their fullest and most practical application in the projects of the Emperor Joseph II of Austria, so that his control over the Church went to lengths which demanded and were given a new name – Josephism. But already, nearly six years before

Clement XIV's election, a German bishop, Hontheim, suffragan of Treves, had published anonymously his *Book of Justinus Febronius* whose effect in Germany and Austria was so great as to give a particular colour to a whole anti-Papal movement within the German Church called Febronianism.

Febronius argued, in the manner of the sixteenth- and seventeenth-century reformers, that the authority of the Pope was an usurpation and was the source of most of the ills from which the Church was suffering. A disciple of Locke, he wanted to see Church government turned into a limited monarchy, with separation of powers between the executive power, the Pope (who need not necessarily be always the Bishop of Rome), and the legislative power, the bishops in council (to whom belonged the infallibility promised by Christ to His Church). So far he was only making an extreme statement of the traditional conciliar position. But he went on to attribute to the State (which he generally called the Prince) very extensive powers for the guidance and reform of the Church, arising from its position as her protector. It is for the Prince to protect the Church in his territories, even from the Pope, and his best means of doing so is by a rigorous use of the *placet*, of the right, that is, of accepting or rejecting papal injunctions, even on matters of spiritual purport. This right was traditional in the Gallican Church and had recently been claimed, when Hontheim was writing, in Spain. Moreover Hontheim put the ruler above his own bishops, even in spiritual matters. He should consult with the more enlightened amongst them, when the question is purely spiritual, but he will always make the decisive decisions himself.

Hontheim was as earnest, as devout, and as anxious for Catholic unity, which he hoped to see restored all over the world, as were the Jansenists. He had no doubt that the Church must rest upon the basis of a universally held dogma. But, extraordinary as it may seem, he supposed that the teachings of Luther and of the other Protestant reformers would easily be 'corrected', and that the unity of christendom would be restored, once the arbitrary absolutism of Rome was out of the way. The man who, more than any other after Luther, taught the rulers to settle Church affairs as they deemed best in their different states, whose theory so admirably suited the absolutist ambitions of the Bourbons, of Frederick the Great, of Joseph II, supposed, in all earnestness, that he was restoring the unity of the Church by encouraging the princes to subject her to their rule, and by denouncing the one power whose *raison d'être* was the maintenance of that unity. Protestant critics of the book, whilst welcoming its attacks on the papacy, made nothing of its plans for Christian reunion.

The reception accorded to Hontheim's work, and the personal fate of its author, throw interesting light on the confusion of ecclesiastical and secular opinion in the seventeen-sixties. Not unnaturally his book was placed on the Roman Index. But that did not prevent its running into new editions, or its being translated from its original Latin into German, French, Spanish, and Italian. Nor did it prevent its receiving considerable support from the Catholic clergy of the Rhineland, and very tardy and qualified condemnations from the Ecclesiastical Electors of that region, the archbishops of Mainz, Treves, and Cologne. Indeed Hontheim's own prince, the Archbishop of Treves, Klemens Wenzeslaus (a splendid example of political ecclesiasticism, having previously been 'Prince of Saxony and Poland', and having been elected Bishop of Freising and Regensburg before being ordained priest) thought nothing of entrusting Hontheim, five years after he had published the *Febronius*, and after his authorship of the book had become generally known, with responsibility for relations between Treves and the Papal Curia. It was only with difficulty that Pope Clement XIII succeeded in getting this insulting situation altered, and the general problem presented by Hontheim, who went on publishing volume after volume, was inherited by Clement XIV, and after 1775 by Pius VI.

It was a part of the purpose of Hontheim's *Febronius* to attack the Religious Orders. Since these Orders owed their recognition and support to the Papacy, and were independent both of the secular clergy and of the princes, they naturally came within the scope of the author's censure. But the Jesuits, being a Society founded to serve the Church under the direction of Rome, met with his special animosity. It was this which gave the *Febronius* particular popularity in those states which were engaged, at the very time that the book appeared, in expelling the Jesuits. Portugal had already done so, and had broken off her relations with Rome; in an edict denouncing the Society of Jesus her king, Joseph I, quoted the *Febronius*. In Spain the Council of Castile defrayed the cost of a new edition of Hontheim's classic. In France the enthusiasm of the Jansenists for the book tempered the enthusiasm of crown and hierarchy; but it circulated freely in several editions. In Austria, where the Jesuits still survived, it was well received, and the most important reply to it, the Jesuit Zaccaria's *Antifebronius*, was banned.

In the form of Febronianism, then, Clement XIV was confronted, at his accession, by the rapid spread in governmental and intellectual circles, and even within the hierarchy itself, of a theory of Church government closely related both to Jansenism and to Gallicanism but, from the Roman point of view, more dangerous than either. What was lacking on the institutional side in Jansenism, and on the moral side in Gallicanism, was made good in Febronianism. Europe was being taught to conceive of the Pope as an elective executive officer, responsible to General Councils; of the Church as a department of State for moral affairs; and of dogma as the highest common factor which either the clergy of the world (Jansenism) or the bishops and their princes (Febronianism) could agree had been made manifest in the first six centuries.

To the Jesuits, agents of a living and infallible Church, the prospect of such teaching could hardly seem attractive. But then it is arguable that the great popularity of Febronianism was precisely due to the great unpopularity of the Jesuits. Whatever else Hontheim had done he had provided the enemies of the Jesuits, who had become very numerous, with a theory of Church government which made the Society of Jesus both unnecessary and pernicious. Since there were so many who, on different grounds, were anxious to be rid of it, Hontheim was sure to have a hearing.

Because they defended the traditional teaching of the medieval theologians on the papal prerogatives the Jesuits laid themselves open to the fullest risk of the displeasure of temporal rulers. It is indeed hardly so surprising that they were constantly being expelled from the states of Europe as it is that, for lengthy periods of time, they were allowed to survive and to carry on with their work. Possessed of an authority which rivalled that of kings, *parlements*, universities, or colonial viceroys, they were always in danger from those rivals. Two assets only did they enjoy in their struggle to maintain their position in the popular estimation. The first and more important was that, so long as the generality of educated people believed, as they still did believe in Louis XIV's day, that the way to salvation lay through the Roman Church, so long the Jesuit missions, their teaching, their preaching, and their constant criticism of the secular authorities were stomached because they were worth stomaching. It was worth putting up with their pretensions if they brought with them eternal salvation. And their other asset was that they provided certain services, especially education, cheaply. They could run a good school, or a good college – often the best available – for very little, because they expected very little in return. This was a virtue which endeared them especially to Frederick II of Prussia and to Catherine of Russia, both of whom were sceptical about the power of the Jesuits to save souls but were impressed by their power to educate the young inexpensively.

At the time with which we are first concerned in this book, the pontificate of Clement XIV, the Jesuits were not only everywhere under fire but had already been expelled from Portugal and Spain, with their immense overseas possessions, as well as from France, Naples and Parma. The chief agents of their expulsion had been the rulers of the House of Bourbon, who reigned over all those countries except Portugal, and who, by a family compact, tried to keep their policies in harmony. Yet it would be wrong to see the Bourbons as personally inspiring the policy. The expulsions started in Portugal, where they were inspired by the free-thinking 'enlightened' minister the Marquis Pombal, for whom everything the Jesuits stood for was anathema. And King Charles III of Spain, whose kingdom on both sides of the Atlantic housed more than four thousand Jesuits (roughly two thousand in each of the two worlds) and whose sudden and ruthless expulsion of them, in the year 1767, was the most dramatic proceeding of its kind, had only slowly been converted to this line of policy. He had been persuaded by the enlightened theories of his friend Bernardo Tanucci, the Chief Minister of Naples, who had been his tutor when he had been ruler of that kingdom. And in France, though Louis XV suppressed the Society, the real agencies of the suppression were the Jesuits' age-long enemies, the *Parlement* of Paris and the provincial *parlements*, whose various edicts against the Society the king rather reluctantly ratified.

However, had the Bourbons been possessed of a more traditionally Roman or ultramontane view of religion they would not have lent their support to the expulsions. Prince Kaunitz, the Austrian Chancellor, was as much a man of the fashionable enlightenment of his age as were Pombal or Tanucci. He admired the contemporary rationalism of London and Paris and he disliked the Jesuits. But the Society was not expelled at this time from the Austrian Empire because his Empress, Maria Theresa, did not wish it. She held the Society in respect, and she knew that its expulsion from her dominions would not be generally popular and that it would give rise to serious practical problems in the field of education.

Louis XV of France was also personally well disposed towards the Society having found, as had Louis XIV and Henry IV before him, that it could be a useful ally to the crown against the *parlements* or against the Jansenists. But in the seventeen-sixties Louis' position was not a strong one. His insolvency had been made worse by the expenses of the Seven Years' War, which had made him more subservient to the *Parlement* of Paris, while his affections still made him subservient to Madame de Pompadour, who was incensed by Jesuit criticism of her conduct. When, therefore, the financial failure of a Jesuit trader in Martinique was followed by a foolish appeal by the French Jesuits to the Paris *Parlement* against a ruling that the Society as a whole was responsible for the trader's debts, the *Parlement* took its chance. It ruled not only that the whole Society was responsible for the debts of its individual traders but that, with its cosmopolitan constitution, at the head of which stood a foreign general, it was contrary to the laws and liberties of France. The Paris *Parlement* therefore suppressed the Jesuits within the area of its jurisdiction, and the other *parlements* for the most part

followed suit. Louis XV, after he had made various attempts to save
it by securing that the Society in France should be separated from
the World Society (attempts which were defeated by the Jesuit
General Ricci in Rome), endorsed, in January 1764, the ruling of
the *parlements*. During this crisis the French bishops lent more
support to the Jesuits than might have been expected from a body
possessed of Gallican traditions, and one which resented having no
jurisdiction over members of the Society and which found them,
in their capacity as confessors and spiritual advisers, dangerous
rivals in important matters such as influencing the court or the
government. These considerations had, however, become out-
weighed, in the minds of many of the French bishops, by the use-
fulness of the Society as an ally in curbing some of the more
eccentric off-shoots of Jansenism, such as the antics of the con-
vulsionaries of *Saint-Médard*, or in checking the egalitarian
'Richerist' ambitions of the lower clergy.

It would be unfair to the opponents of the Jesuits not to recognize that they based their dislike of the Society on the best moral
principles. They talked much about Jesuit immorality, and about
abuses arising from their penitential principle of probabilism (a
theory of penance which tended to give the penitent the benefit of
the doubt, where a reasonable doubt existed). They believed that,
with their famous casuistry, the Jesuits could argue, at choice, that
black was white or that white was black; and as long ago as the
middle of the seventeenth century, when Pascal had written his
fifth Provincial Letter, the opinion was already being expressed
that the Society used different yardsticks, in measuring different
cases, with the sole aim of aggrandizing its influence by gaining the
ear of every class of the community and every country of the
globe. Madame de Pompadour, however, knew to her cost that
merely to be a 'useful catch' was not a sufficient qualification to
secure absolution from the Jesuits; it was necessary also that she
should renounce sin, which was a higher price than she was
prepared to pay.

Isolated cases of laxity, or worse, existed amongst the Jesuits as
they must always exist in a society more than 20,000 strong and
composed of human beings. But the elaborate proceedings enter-

tained against them in the various countries from which they were expelled in no case brought to light any general condition of corruption. Nor did they bring to light, as it was confidently expected that they would, hidden reserves of wealth; no aspect of the expulsions caused more surprise and concern to the governments than the discovery that there was almost nothing to confiscate.

It is also important, in fairness to their opponents, to recognize that there was an element of genuine fear in their hostility to the Jesuits. For one thing, there was the traditional talk about tyrannicide. The fact that some Jesuit writers, for instance Suarez, had argued that, in certain circumstances, a ruler could or even should be disobeyed; that all political loyalty might be withdrawn from him; that ultimate authority, under God and the Church, rested with the People; led individual Jesuits to justify tyrannicide and, on occasion, to enter into political plots. None of the celebrated assassinations of the seventeenth or eighteenth centuries was in fact proved to be planned by the Jesuits, and the Generals of the Society reiterated their prohibitions against the teaching of tyrannicide; all the same, whenever an attempt was made against the life of a king they were the first to be suspected, if only because they seemed to be the men most obviously possessed of the daring and determination necessary for the enterprise.

Once the movement for the suppression of the Jesuits had started it seemed self-evident to their enemies that any attempt upon the life of a ruler must be laid at their door. When, in September 1758, such an attempt was made on the life of King Joseph I of Portugal, who had already begun his attack upon the Society, the proceedings undertaken against the Provincial and nine others, arrested for complicity in the plot, stated that, since no man 'would commit a great misdeed without having a great interest in it, it is also to be assumed that the man who has an interest in the deed must be he who committed it . . . unless he can clearly prove that someone else committed it . . . this legal presumption alone would be enough for it to be considered on the basis of the law as a clear proof that they (the Jesuits) have had responsibility for this accursed deed'.[1] Such

[1] Article 25 of the Proceedings, quoted Pastor, *History of the Popes*, Vol. XXXVI, p. 314.

were the grounds on which the Portuguese minister Pombal saddled the Jesuits with responsibility for the attack upon the king, which led to their expulsion from Portugal in the following year.

In the same way Charles III of Spain made the Jesuits responsible for the riots in Madrid in the spring of 1766, and this enabled him to expel them from his kingdom in 1767, though neither in this case nor in the Portuguese case was any concrete evidence ever laid against them and their innocence is now widely accepted. To accusations that they were potential assassins were added accusations, by the Spanish Bourbons, that they were in league with the enemy, namely England. Here again proof was lacking, and the fact that the English victory inevitably brought total disaster upon the Jesuit missionary endeavour both in North America and in the West Indies suggests that if, indeed, they were aiding the English, it was a suicidal policy. There were, however, numerous occasions for quarrel between the Jesuit missions in South America and the Portuguese and Spanish viceroys. In great territories of the interior, and notably in the famous Reductions of Paraguay, the Jesuit missionaries were operating in lands which no European civil administration had reached and were organizing the entire life of the native populations without outside help, and often in a manner more humane and more conducive to native prosperity than either the Spanish or the Portuguese had achieved in the regions which they ruled directly. This was not likely to dispose either of the Iberian governments in their favour, and when the Jesuits began to raise armies these governments, not unnaturally, determined that the time had come to humble them.

Lastly, it was held against them that they engaged in trade. This was true. The scale on which the Jesuits were trying to work in the Americas, the West Indies, Africa, India and the East made it difficult for them to avoid entering into the economic life of regions where they were often the only white men; this was appreciated at their headquarters and, with the permission of their General, they were allowed to trade. But their doing so gave a handle to their enemies, who were often also their competitors, and who were not slow to accuse them of exploiting native populations or of amassing fortunes for themselves. When their affairs came to be examined in detail at the time of their suppression it was realized that the accusations were ill founded; but in the seventeen-sixties they were generally believed even by intelligent critics like Voltaire, who was as unreasonable in what he wrote in *Candide* about the Jesuits in Paraguay as was Burke, speaking in London, about Warren Hastings in India.

Political and economic jealousy, which had earlier been insufficient to bring down the mighty Society, proved to be sufficient, in an age which had become so unsympathetic with the spiritual purposes of the Jesuits, to bring about their downfall. Their suppression in France and their expulsion from Spain, Portugal and Naples, serious enough in themselves, were less serious in the long run than was the ruin of their work in the mission fields of those vast territories of America, Africa and Asia which depended on the European colonial powers.

So long as the Society was still patronized by Maria Theresa, Frederick the Great and Catherine of Russia, together with many of the smaller princes, its fortunes might easily be restored; it was not the first time it had been suppressed in France, and had later returned there. This point was appreciated by the Bourbon powers, and they determined to safeguard their achievement by bringing about the suppression of the Society everywhere, which was something that could only be done by the papacy. When Cardinal Ganganelli was elected Pope in 1769 everybody knew that the issue which he would be forced at once to face was this one with which the Bourbons were confronting him. Would he come to the defence of his own defenders, or would he sacrifice them? And if he sacrificed them would the papacy, faced by the spread of Rationalism in intellectual circles; of Jansenism, Pietism, Deism and Naturalism in religious thought; of Richerism among the lower clergy of France and of Gallicanism among the higher; of State control over the Church, taught by *Febronius* and developing in Germany, Austria and northern Italy – would the papacy, confronted by this rising tide of opposition to its ultramontane pretensions, find that it had appeased its opponents by sacrificing the Society, and that henceforth there would be better harmony between Church and State, between Church and secular society?

Or would she find that, by sacrificing the Society, she had sacrificed the first and best line of defence of the ultramontane position, and that the very centre of her citadel was now threatened?

CHAPTER ONE

Clement XIV and the Suppression of the Jesuits

At 2.30 a.m. on May 18, 1769, after a wearing Conclave which had lasted since February 15, the cardinals of the Bourbon courts kissed the hands of Cardinal Ganganelli who had secured the necessary number of votes for election to the papacy. It was fitting that these cardinals should be the first to kiss the new Pope's hands for it was very certain that, humanly speaking, he owed to them his election. But after 3 a.m. the rest of the Sacred College attended on him for the same ceremony, and on June 4 he was duly crowned in Saint Peter's, taking the name of Clement XIV.

The delay of more than two weeks before he was crowned was partly caused by his having first to be consecrated bishop. For Giovanni Vincenzo Antonio Ganganelli was a Conventual Franciscan. He might, indeed, have been General of the Franciscan Order, but this advancement he had twice declined. It is said that he declined it because it would have prevented his becoming a cardinal; if so, his forbearance was duly rewarded for Clement XIII conferred the red hat on him as a reward for his good work as First Consultor to the Congregation of the Inquisition, a post for which his scholarly theological mind had well suited him.

At the time of his election as Pope Ganganelli was 63 years old – a good age, neither too advanced nor too immature. It was an age which could be expected to give him anything from ten to fifteen years on the throne of Saint Peter, long enough for him to achieve what those who had supported his election were determined he should achieve and not too long for those who were looking for a different policy to have one more chance before they died of securing the election of somebody different.

The Jesuit question dominated all minds at the time of the Conclave; everybody was interested in securing either a Pope who would suppress or else a Pope who would defend the Society. After the many expulsions they had suffered during the previous decade it was obvious that the pressure which would be brought to bear upon Rome to secure their suppression would be enormous; yet if the Pope chose to stand firm, at whatever cost, such pressure could not prevail. Since Ganganelli had been associated very closely with the Society in his younger days, when he had been a teacher of theology at Bologna and Milan, and since he owed much of his advancement to Jesuit support, there were those who believed that in securing his election they had saved the Jesuits. There were more however who were satisfied that the cold shoulder which the Franciscan had turned towards his former friends in the time of their troubles foreshadowed unfriendly conduct towards them if he became Pope, and it is certain that the Bourbon powers, though there were other anti-Jesuit cardinals whose election they would have preferred, believed that in securing the election of Ganganelli they had secured what they wanted.

Besides being a sound theologian the new Pope was a kindly man, and of a strict simplicity and purity of life. He had easy manners, charm, and tact, and he understood well how to conceal his feelings. But he had lived in academic, though not in cloistered seclusion, he had never been outside Italy, and he had no acquaintance with political diplomacy. He was timid, hating to give offence, and he would certainly not seek to force a major issue by any trial of strength. His whole career suggested that, while he was quite without greed, or nepotism, or the human failings often associated with the Borgia popes, he was equally without that zeal which had animated the great pontiffs of the Catholic reformation, who had purged the Church, defined the faith, and seen the Cross carried to the Americas, to the Indies, and to China.

Yet Clement XIV, if he were to succeed, would need unusual qualities, for the storm was assuredly rising. Neither the brave stand of his predecessor, Clement XIII (1758–69), who in 1765 had cast a defiant brief, extolling the virtues of the Jesuits, in the very teeth of the governments which were expelling them, nor the urbane wisdom and generosity of spirit of the popular previous Pope, Benedict XIV (1740–58), had proved sufficient to meet the needs of the times. Neither a policy of concessions nor a policy of intransigence had been adequate. Spiritually, politically, and economically the Church had continued to lose ground, and in the persons of the Jesuits she was being insulted every day. Possibly it was a situation which only time could have cured, and which no occupant of the Chair of Peter would have been able to save. All that can be said with certainty is that it was one which called for powers greater than those at the command of Clement XIV.

When allowance has been made for eighteenth-century conventions concerning the role of the State in spiritual affairs, when the traditional view that a Pope should be personally acceptable to the leading powers has been kept in mind, and when the case for having political ambassadors 'in the wings' at the time of a Conclave has been acknowledged, it is still difficult to read of the political pressures which were brought to bear on the Conclave of 1769, or on the new Pope after his election, without feeling that, by yielding to such pressures, cardinals and Pope alike involved themselves in a moral defeat. Well might Pius XI later refer to these events as 'a painful page in our history'.[1]

The most consequential figure behind the scenes, when the cardinals assembled, was the Spanish foreign minister, the Marchese Grimaldi. For the benefit of the Bourbon courts, and for the use of the Spanish ambassador at Rome, Grimaldi had classified the cardinals as 'very good', 'good', 'doubtful', 'indifferent', 'bad', and 'very bad'. The election of any of the very bad was to be prevented by the use of the 'Exclusive', that is of the veto which tradition allowed a cardinal representing the Emperor, the King of France, or the King of Spain to present at a Conclave. The bad were likewise if possible to be excluded, but only by the normal means of argument and persuasion. There was only one very good

[1] Ranke (*History of the Popes*, Colonial Press, 1901, Vol. 3, p. 147) wrote that 'the election of Ganganelli was effected principally by the influence of the Bourbons and at the immediate suggestion of the French and Spanish cardinals'. His view must be preferred to that of Augustin Theiner, the historian of the pontificate of Clement XIV, that 'the election of Clement XIV was solely effected by the immediate inspiration of the Holy Spirit, and not only without their (the Bourbons') co-operation but against their will.' (*Histoire du pontificat de Clément XIV*, Brussels, 1853, Vol. I, p. 254.)

Clement XIV. From the portrait at Stonyhurst, originally disguised by
over-painting to suggest an Anglican divine.

cardinal on Grimaldi's list, namely the Neapolitan Sersale – this meant that Sersale was an open and determined opponent of the Jesuits. There were eleven in his good category, including Ganganelli. But the powerful Neapolitan minister Tanucci who, with Pombal, was the soul of the anti-Jesuit movement, disagreed with the Spanish minister about three of those classed as good, and one of those about whom he disagreed was Ganganelli, whom he described as a 'Jesuit'. Tanucci had to be respected, for he had at last secured the expulsion of the Jesuits from Naples only eighteen months before the Conclave assembled; their banishment, he had explained to the protesting Clement XIII, was 'as necessary for the peace and security of princes and peoples as expectoration for the human body'.[1] Grimaldi thought it prudent to send him some blank Spanish Exclusive forms on which he could put any names which he felt needed adding to the list of very bads.

The government of Louis XV of France, which had been less enthusiastic than that of Madrid about expelling the Jesuits, was likewise less violently obsessed with the idea that it was necessary to secure the election of a Pope who would suppress the Society altogether. But it was the policy of the French minister, Choiseul, to strengthen the Family Compact with Spain, in face of their common enemy England; so the French ambassador at Rome, the Marquis d'Aubeterre, and the influential Cardinal de Bernis, who carried his sovereign's Exclusive, were given instructions to lend general support to the Spaniards, while avoiding taking the initiative. Presented with the classification of cardinals which Grimaldi had drawn up, Choiseul protested that the number of cardinals regarded as eligible for election was too small, and pointed out that three of those classed as good were too elderly, being in fact over eighty. He further angered Tanucci by insisting that Cardinal Ganganelli, so far from being written off as bad, should be promoted to the select category of the very good, hitherto only occupied by Sersale.

By the time the ambassadors and the court cardinals representing the Bourbon rulers had finished arguing together, which was not before the end of April 1769 (the Conclave had opened in mid-

[1] Tanucci to Orsini, December 15, 1767 (Pastor, *op. cit.*, Vol. XXXVI, p. 245).

February), they had ruled out exactly half the college of cardinals (23 out of 46) on the grounds that they were known to be favourable to the Jesuits. And the Spanish ambassador, Azpuru, was in favour of excluding yet more, and of a withdrawal of the ambassadors from Rome unless one of the handful they favoured were elected. And further, Charles III of Spain and the Neapolitan and Portuguese governments were insisting that a written promise, or failing that an oral promise in front of witnesses, to suppress the Society, should be exacted from the cardinal elected before he was named Pope. To the credit of Bernis and of the other French cardinals they insisted that this was impossible; it would be simony. Nor was it possible that the question of the Jesuits should be discussed within a Conclave, which was solely concerned with an election. There was also a gratifying show of spirit by the whole body of the cardinals in regard to Sersale, whose candidature was being pressed quite shamelessly by all the governments; they resolutely refused to have anything to do with electing one whose only titles to consideration appeared to be his hatred of the Jesuits and his friendship with the courts. The Cardinal Archbishop of Milan, Pozzobonelli, who 'represented' the Emperor, seemed likely, for a time, to be elected, since he was held to hate the Jesuits sufficiently; but even that merit was insufficient to overcome the liability, from the point of view of the Bourbon camp, of his friendship with the Hapsburgs.

So it came about that Ganganelli gradually emerged as the strongest candidate. His simplicity of life and his good record of work could not be denied, he had persuaded the Bourbon party that he was an ardent anti-Jesuit, and yet he had contrived to leave some of the cardinals under the impression that he was still the friend of the Society that he had been in his youth. This was, indeed, remarkable, since he had become the favourite of the Spanish party after they had found that they could not gain the election of Sersale. It looks as though Ganganelli played a double game, making statements to some which seemed to show that he was favourable to the suppression and to others which seemed to show that he was not.[1] Yet it would be wrong to picture him

---

[1] See the evidence in Pastor, Vol. XXXVIII, p. 81.

as a coldly calculating liar. His character was rather that of a weak man, ready to agree with the views of the latest speaker, and of an ambitious man who made a point of not giving offence. He must also be acquitted of the charge, made by Tanucci, that he gave a precise undertaking to suppress the Society. There was no simoniacal bargain struck at the Conclave, though Ganganelli does seem to have committed to writing the statement that, if the canonical regulations were observed, the suppression would be possible and even profitable.[1]

Clement XIV began his pontificate with the kind of acts of appeasement which his character had led his critics to expect. Side-stepping, for the moment, the dangerous issue of the Jesuits, on the plausible grounds that, if he suppressed them at once, it would suggest that a bargain had been struck at the Conclave, he proceeded to try to gain the goodwill of the Powers by what, unfortunately, was really a series of surrenders. Thus, without attempting to secure an abrogation of any of the anti-clerical acts of the Portuguese government, since its suppression of the Jesuits, he restored diplomatic relations with Portugal, sent a Nuncio to Lisbon of Pombal's own choice, conferred the red hat on Pombal's brother, and when he died conferred one on the brother of the Portuguese Foreign Minister. The Bishop of Coimbra, who had been imprisoned by Pombal for condemning the works of Febronius, Voltaire, and Rousseau, he invited to resign his See 'for the sake of peace'. When, in return for so many signs of goodwill, Pombal agreed to the reopening of the nunciature at Lisbon, and allowed the Portuguese once more to be in contact with the Curia, the Pope's heart was so rejoiced that he had a medal struck with the words *Sol refulsit*. But the Roman wits soon added *et nos in tenebris ambulamus*.

He appointed as his Secretary of State Cardinal Pallavicini, who

[1] The evidence is discussed in Pastor, Vol. XXXVIII, pp. 77–82. Even the most bitter of Clement XIV's critics, Crétineau-Joly, discounts the idea of Ganganelli's giving a written undertaking to suppress the Society (cf. his *Histoire Religieuse, Politique et Littéraire de la Compagnie de Jésus*, Vol. 5, p. 334). The first written undertaking on the matter seems to be that contained in Clement XIV's letter to King Louis XV of September 30, 1769 (cf. Theiner, *op. cit.*, Vol. 1, p. 258).

had been Nuncio at Madrid and was deeply devoted to King Charles III. He wrote in his own hand to the different sovereigns, announcing his election, instead of using the customary form. He refused to read aloud, as was customary on Maundy Thursday, the unpopular bull, *In Coena Domini* (which listed the current Papal censures and in which Clement XIII, as recently as the year 1768, had excommunicated the Bourbon Duke of Parma for his attacks on the Church), taking the line that it was unsuitable to read such harsh censures on an occasion which should be one of reconciliation of the faithful with God. Soon the Austrian Chancellor Kaunitz was observing that the new Pope was willing to go to great lengths to please the princes, his guiding principle being to agree to everything which was at all possible.

So this amiable Franciscan friar, whose favourite occupation was riding (until his constant falls made him take to a carriage) and who loved practical jokes and horse-play with his fellow Franciscan and confessor Bontempi (though they were described as unsuitable for any sexagenarian, let alone for a Pope), continued to hope that he could restore peace to the Church and to the world by irradiating cheerfulness and trying to remove the sources of friction. Amongst these sources were certainly the Jesuits and, on the whole, the college of cardinals. It was said that he would gladly dispense with both if the operation would not be too dangerous and unpleasant.

The ambassadors were patient at first, being confident that he would honour the 'understanding' on which he had been elected, and accepting his argument that it would be indecent for him to act too soon. But as they began to suspect that, in his anxiety to avoid the odium of suppressing the Society, he did not intend to act at all, their attitude changed. For the government of Madrid was absolutely unwavering in its determination to secure the suppression, and the government of Paris was unswerving in its determination, for political reasons, to keep in step with the government of Madrid.

The implacable attitude of the Spanish government was made very clear by the interest which she maintained in her own Jesuits after they had left her shores. She paid them a tiny pension, as a small compensation for her seizure of their property, but she discontinued payment of it to any of them who attempted to make any contact with relatives in Spain or who took any action of which her agents, who were vigilant in Italy, disapproved. The Papal States, having absorbed the Portuguese Jesuits, were hardly in a position to absorb any more, so most of the Spaniards were landed in Corsica. Few had with them any possessions other than their breviaries and rosaries so that their plight on their arrival on that island, then engaged in a civil war, was a hard one. Corsica could hardly have absorbed the full four thousand, but it is estimated that about a thousand of those who came from Central and South America, from Africa, or from farther east had died from the hardships of the voyage, while as many as were able escaped from Corsica into Italy.

In the diplomatic field the resolute attitude of Spain was made clear by her representations in Paris that she was ready to renounce the Family Compact with France if Choiseul did not show a greater determination to compel Rome to proceed to the suppression. This so perturbed Choiseul that, in August 1769, he told Cardinal de Bernis (now French ambassador at Rome) to threaten to break off French relations with Rome unless the Jesuits were suppressed within two months. In a confidential covering note Choiseul told the Cardinal he expected the Pope was afraid of being poisoned by the Jesuits if he took any action. He did not trust the Pope at all. 'It is difficult for a friar not to be always a friar, and more difficult still for an Italian friar to handle matters openly and honestly.'[1] As for the Jesuits, he protested in another letter that they were nothing to him personally, but went on: 'they have become so much the bugbear of governments that the people at Madrid forget England, Pitt, and the most vital questions, thinking only of Loyola's disciples and of pestering me. The devil take the Jesuits, and the Pope too, if he doesn't rid me of them.'[2]

However, Choiseul fell from power at the end of the year 1770 and Bernis, rightly recognizing that Clement was justified in asking for time, fell back upon a policy of prodding. He also held out the bait of the restoration of the Papal city of Avignon, which had been seized by France from Clement XIII. It was a tempting bait,

[1] Theiner, Vol. I, p. 376. [2] Pastor, Vol. XXXVIII, p. 153.

especially as Naples would then be obliged to restore the similarly
situated Papal *enclave* of Benevento, in the kingdom of Naples,
which Tanucci had seized. But, as always with such bargains, there
was the difficult practical problem of which party should move
first, and the French mistrusted Clement XIV sufficiently to refuse
his repeated suggestions that the restoration should precede the
suppression.

By the beginning of the year 1772 it was beginning to look as
though, against the odds, Clement's policy of procrastination
might possibly save him from ever having to take the drastic step
which he feared, but which he did not repudiate on principle.[1] But
in July of that year there arrived in Rome a man whose firm
determination it was to succeed, and quickly; this was the new
Spanish ambassador, Jose Moñino. Moñino was not to be put off
by the little gestures, characteristic of eighteenth-century diplomacy, with which Clement strove to suggest that he was hostile
to the Jesuits and friendly to the King of Spain. He remained
obstinately unimpressed when the Pope withheld from the Jesuits
of the *Gesù* the loan of the sun-shades belonging to Saint Peter's,
which they were normally allowed to carry in their processions;
nor was he softened by Clement's solemn undertaking that he
would shortly bless the consecrated swaddling clothes which he
was sending for the use of the new-born Spanish prince. Moñino
meant to coerce the Pope. There was to be no more bargaining
about Avignon and Benevento. The Pope was to draw up a Brief
of Suppression. If he failed to do so all the Religious Orders in Spain
would be suppressed. In September he produced at an audience a
document containing eighteen articles, upon which he and Bernis
had agreed, and which he bullied the Pope into accepting in
principle. This document covered all the main points and used
many of the phrases which Clement later employed in his Brief of
Suppression; when he accepted it the Pope had surrendered to the
Powers.

Throughout the following winter the Pope would still not

---

[1] Theiner insists (*op. cit.*, Vol. 1, p. 258) that Clement XIV was 'convinced that
the Society of Jesus had served its purpose and that its conservation was thenceforth
impossible.'

commit himself to a date for the publication of a brief. Moñino strengthened his hand by securing the whole-hearted support of the Augustinian General, F. X. Vasquez – who needed little persuading – and he bribed the Pope's Franciscan confessor, Bontempi, so handsomely that this closest friend of Clement XIV became the tool of the Spanish ambassador. But what caused the last defences of the Jesuits to crumble, and then to collapse in ruin, was the acquiescence of the Empress Maria Theresa in their sup-pression. In April 1773, being pressed by Charles III of Spain, she replied that, although she had always held the Society in high esteem, as its zeal merited, she would not wish to oppose its sup-pression if the Pope considered it expedient for the well-being and unity of religion.[1] This was something less than Kaunitz would have liked her to say, but it was something more than suited her own conscience. She had, however, her children to consider. Good relations with the Bourbons had never been more important to her for she was engaged in marrying off her daughter, Marie Antoinette, to the Dauphin. Nor was she likely to be given spiritual advice against ruining the Society in this way, for her confessor was an Augustinian. All the same, there were sympathisers with the Jesuits who, some twenty years later, when Marie Antoinette went to the scaffold, drew their own conclusions about the verdict of Heaven upon the Empress's letter.

Maria Theresa's attitude was decisive not only because she spoke for the wide dominions of the Austrian Empire, which at this time included the Netherlands, Galicia and Lombardy, but because most of the German states would be sure to follow her lead. And since her son Leopold was Grand Duke of Tuscany there was no need to expect opposition in northern Italy. She made, however, one reservation. She would not admit the right of the Pope to dis-pose of either the houses or the persons of the suppressed Society. She knew very well that a real problem would arise over education and she firmly intended that the ex-Jesuits, though they might be secularized, should continue to teach.

The Brief suppressing the Society of Jesus was drawn up in the

[1] Pastor, Vol. XXXVIII, pp. 259, 260.

utmost secrecy and signed by Clement XIV in the middle of June 1773. He then handed it over to Moñino for printing, since he could not trust the discretion of his own press. The printed copies were dated July 21, and were despatched to the European capitals, but the governments waited to publish them until Rome had done so. It was not until August 16 that Cardinal Macedonio, secretary to the newly formed Congregation for the Suppression, drove to the Gesù, accompanied by soldiers and police, and read out to the General of the Society, Lorenzo Ricci, the brief by which it was dissolved.

As the General listened to the words of *Dominus ac Redemptor Noster* he learnt that, although to the Religious Orders belonged the first place in securing the welfare and happiness of the Catholic commonwealth, yet when they had become a 'cause of prejudice and disturbance' Popes had not hesitated to 'impose new laws on them, recall them to their original strictness of life, or disperse them and uproot them from the land'. Thus had he dealt with the Templars, in the year 1312, and with a number of other Orders. Even from its inception the Society of Jesus had shown jealousy towards the other Orders, towards the secular priesthood, towards universities and schools, and even towards the princes of states. 'Now, therefore, having perceived that the said Society of Jesus could no longer produce the abundant fruits and advantages for which it was instituted . . . but, on the contrary, that if it continued to exist it was almost impossible that the Church should have true and permanent peace . . .' and for other reasons 'which We retain concealed in Our breast . . . after mature deliberation, with certain knowledge, and in the fulness of Our apostolic power, We dissolve, suppress, extinguish, and abolish the said Society. We take from it and abrogate each and all of its offices, ministries, administrations, houses, schools, and habitations in all provinces, kingdoms, and states whatsoever . . . we suppress all its statutes, customs, decrees, and constitutions, even when fortified by oath, apostolic confirmation, or otherwise. . . . We declare, therefore, that it is perpetually broken up and dissolved, alike to the spiritual as to the temporal. . . .'

The General was, however, to be reassured that the Pope was

seeking not only 'the advantage of the Church and the tranquillity of nations' but 'to bring aid and consolation to each of the members of the Society of Jesus' who are to be 'delivered from all the pains which have tormented them, and from so many discords and contentions, that they may more fruitfully cultivate the vineyard of the Lord and more abundantly work for the salvation of souls'. This might seem reassuring, but for General Ricci and some thirteen other leading Jesuits at Rome opportunity for working in the vineyard of the Lord would be restricted by the fact that they were shut up in the Sant' Angelo and left there to die. Essentially a mild man, indeed rather naïve, Ricci had never believed, up to the last, that the Pope would really suppress the Society. When it was done he made no resistance and, during the close and harsh confinement to which he and his companions were subjected in strict separation from each other, he only asked that the cause of his imprisonment be made known to him. But although the papers of the Jesuit houses were examined in detail by the Congregation for the Suppression, and although a lengthy interrogation of the prisoners was held at the Sant' Angelo, nothing was ever proved against them and no verdict was ever pronounced. Ricci remained in prison on the grounds that he was trying to rally the scattered Society, which he denied, and which, indeed, he was not in a position to do. He petitioned the Pope for his release, but Moñino insisted he should remain in confinement. Clement XIV died in September 1774, and eleven months later Ricci appealed to the new Pope, Pius VI, pointing out that for fifteen years he had directed the Society of Jesus without complaint being made against him, yet he had now been kept in custody for two years without cause shown. The new Pope allowed him to move more freely in the castle, but Moñino firmly opposed his release, and in November 1775 he died there. He was, however, allowed burial in the Gesù (now served by Franciscans) whereas his faithful secretary, Gabriello Comolli, who had died the year before, had been buried secretly, and without the proper benefits of religion.

There had, unexpectedly, been little commotion over the Suppression in Rome or elsewhere in Italy. This was partly because, though the people (to judge from the crowds at the Jesuit churches in the summer of 1773) were generally on the side of the Society, the occupation of its houses was well organized, to avoid demonstrations, so that even the secular clothes, to be worn in future by its members, had been made ready, to enable them to emerge inconspicuously into the street. The houses themselves were generally handed over to other Religious Orders.

And the rest of the proceedings went according to plan. Avignon and Benevento were restored to the papacy in the spring of 1774, the Pope's confessor, Bontempi, received his promised pension of 1,500 *scudi*, and the services of the other leading actors in the drama were suitably recognized. A solemn Te Deum was sung in all the churches of Portugal, the Papal Nuncio attending in person at Lisbon. The Heads of the Catholic states wrote to congratulate the Pope.

So for forty-one years the Society of Jesus, which Clement XIV had 'perpetually broken up and dissolved', remained suppressed. Yet even during that relatively brief period it survived for a time in Prussia and continuously in Russia, where the rulers refused to implement the brief, while in Germany and Austria generally the Jesuits continued not only to teach (which Rome allowed them to do everywhere, if they were secularized, and if they worked only at the request of their bishops) but also very generally to live in community, which Rome did not allow.

Yet the blow was a shattering one, chiefly because it was impossible for the Society to recruit novices, save for a handful in Russia. And when it was restored in the year 1814 the entire body of its theologians and professors had died. The great tree which had sustained the far-flung missions of four continents and had carried so large a share of the higher education of Europe had been uprooted. It was necessary, in the nineteenth century, to start afresh with new seed.

What verdict should be passed on the Pope's action?

Constitutionally speaking he had the right to do what he did. All Religious Orders exist by permission of the Pope, and he can withdraw his approval at will; he is not dependent upon the findings of a court. But obviously he has a grave moral responsibility to preserve those branches of the Church which have been continuously approved and which have borne rich fruit. Unless they have become corrupt (which Clement did not claim) a Pope is clearly betraying his trust if he sacrifices them. No doubt it may at times be part of his duty to make concessions to public or political demand when the wider interests of the Church and the continuance of her work for souls demand it; but in that case the grounds for such drastic action should surely be fully and fairly stated, whereas *Dominus ac Redemptor Noster* said no more than that the Society was unpopular and had sometimes deserved to be. The real grounds, 'hidden in Our Heart', and not expressed, seem to have been political pressure from Spain. Moreover, even supposing it had been right for Clement to do what he did, there was much that was objectionable about the way in which he did it. The fact that his predecessor had issued a Bull warmly commending the Society as recently as four years before his own election made it inopportune for him to say in his Brief that legitimate complaints against the Jesuits were of long standing. Intentionally or unintentionally he had misled many of the cardinals both at the time of the Conclave and after. He showed a want of humanity in the way in which he carried out the suppression. And his attempts to treat defeat as though it were victory, on this occasion as on others, were naïve and flippant.

For a defeat it was, the most serious the Church had suffered since Luther's revolt. The Pope had been persuaded to suppress the Jesuits not because, as was claimed against the Templars, they had lost their virtue and become corrupt—there is no suggestion of this in the Brief—but because certain of the governments demanded he should do so since they found the Society inconvenient. He was simply yielding to pressure. It may be possible to dignify this pressure by calling it the pressure of the Enlightenment, and some eminent historians – even von Ranke himself – have written of the 'serene wisdom' of this 'enlightened Pope' which persuaded him to sacrifice his 'Janissaries' for the higher interests of the Church. But that view is only tenable on the assumption that the higher interests of the Church were those of the Febronians, the Jansenists, the *parlements,* or the governments. It is not tenable from a Roman standpoint, which was the standpoint of Clement XIV. By no casuistry could it be argued that Clement was dismissing his supporters in order to strengthen the Holy See in protecting the Church against the growing infidelity. His act was an act of appeasement, and in due course his successor would suffer in full measure for it. Ranke himself recognized what was involved – nothing less than the entire structure of faith and order: 'Since the outworks had been taken, a more vigorous assault of the victorious opinions on the central stronghold would inevitably follow. The commotion increased from day to day, the defection of men's minds took a constantly widening range. . . .'[1]

[1] *Op. cit.,* Vol. III, p. 150.

CHAPTER TWO

Pius VI and the Enlightened Despots

When the death of Clement XIV came in September 1774 it was still little more than a year since he had suppressed the Society of Jesus. And since it was rather a macabre death there were those who were ready to link the two events together. During the last years of his life the Pope was suffering increasingly from some skin disease and to remedy this he took, as was the custom of the time, increasing quantities of mercury in the medicines with which his physicians tried to cure him. In the end his whole body became poisoned, and though he bravely went on trying to fulfil public engagements in Rome, on September 8, 1774, he collapsed unconscious outside the Quirinal on his return from one of them, and by the 24th of the month he was dead. His body immediately assumed a black and blue colour, and when it was exhibited in Saint Peter's it was necessary to cover the face with a mask.

Clearly Rome would not have been Rome had there not been many who were willing to interpret these significant signs according to their tastes. The most popular view was that the Pope had been poisoned by the Jesuits. Another was that he had been visited, after the suppression, by the wrath of God, Who did not intend to allow him to preside over the Holy Year ceremonies which were to follow in 1775. It would be improper for the historian to comment on the latter proposition; of the former it may be said that the considered opinion of friend and foe alike, both at the time and since, is against it.[1] Even Tanucci, whose fear and hatred of the Jesuits were unsurpassed, was satisfied by the assurances of his

[1] Oddly enough, Cardinal Bernis and Pope Pius VI both seem to have believed it (cf. A. de Saint-Priest, *Histoire de la Chute des Jésuites*, 1844, pp. 168–70). Yet, as Crétineau-Joly pointed out (*op. cit.*, Vol. 5, p. 392), from the Jesuit point of view there had ceased to be much point in poisoning the Pope *after* the issue of the Brief of Suppression.

friends in Rome that there was no truth in the rumours. Since, however, it was important that in some way the Pope's death should be turned to the discredit of the Society, Tanucci put it about that the story was being spread by the Jesuits themselves, as a warning to princes generally and the Bourbons in particular. The Jesuits, he said, liked to 'display their power, just as women are not displeased to be thought of easy virtue, for this shows that men like them, and it entices them to compete for their favours.'[1] The only sense in which Clement XIV was killed by the Jesuits was by his fear of them. Of this fear there were numerous witnesses; he began to take elaborate precautions about his food, and about his guards, especially when he was on holiday at Castel Gandolfo.

The unpopularity of Clement XIV's pontificate, in Rome and the Papal States, was due to other causes as well as to the suppression. The bad harvests and the rise in the price of bread, which had been a feature of his predecessor's pontificate, had caused riots which became more serious in his own reign and which were increasingly directed against the Pope. This was partly because he was known to have been the one cardinal who, in the previous reign, had opposed the use of the famous 'treasure of Sixtus V' to buy corn and alleviate the distress, and partly because, the state of the Papal finances being what it was, there was resentment against the Pope's spending money on buying works of classical art and founding the *Museo Clementino* at the Vatican. The latter complaint was hardly a fair one; the sums spent on purchases for the new museum were small, and every Pope was supposed to add in some way to the adornment of Rome. But that it was made, and insistently, was an indication of the Pope's unpopularity. The most material grievance against him was the well-founded suspicion about the honesty of one Niccolò Bischi, who had control of the provisioning of Rome. When the Pope died Bischi had to leave the country quickly. His friend and patron had been the Pope's confessor Bontempi, and Bontempi was another who had to make good his escape.

[1] Tanucci to Nefetti, August 8, 1775, in Pastor, Vol. XXXVIII, p. 538.

While Rome was arguing about the circumstances of Clement XIV's death, and was hounding his friends, the Conclave to elect his successor was hanging fire. In this period of political pressure on the papacy, when the courts of Europe were acting together to ensure that they secured a Pope who would not be a nuisance to them, in an ultramontane sense, there were liable to be long delays before conclaves got down to their work because it was considered important that serious voting should not take place until a full muster of cardinals had collected from the continent as a whole. If the Italian cardinals, and especially those resident in Rome, were in a large majority, as they were likely to be in the early days of a Conclave, they would tend to elect a *zelante*, by which was meant one who would press the rights of Rome against the governments. But if the more distant cardinals were awaited, especially those bearing the royal Exclusives, then matters would be different. It is not without significance that Clement XIII, the ultramontane and friend of the Jesuits, had been elected after a mere seven weeks, and in the absence of several of the more distant cardinals, whereas the election of Clement XIV had taken more than three months, because the ambassadors had insisted that voting should await the arrival of the cardinals from Spain. The Conclave which elected Cardinal Braschi, as Clement XIV's successor, in 1775, lasted for nearly five months while governments contended not only with the Roman or curialist party but also with each other. In the end the cardinals elected a man who had been Clement XIV's treasurer, but not before they had satisfied themselves that he was of the opinion that it was out of the question to consider restoring the Jesuits.

Giovanni Angelo Braschi, who thus became Pope Pius VI, came from a noble but not a wealthy family of Cesena, in the northern part of the Papal States. He was a cultured man, very interested in classical antiquity; his had been the responsibility for selecting those sculptures for the *Museo Clementino* which had been made into a cause for offence against his predecessor. As Pope he was able to improve the collection, adding some Greek sculpture from the recent excavations at Tivoli (being careful to label each piece *ex munificentia Pii VI*), enlarging the museum, and panelling it with a very rich marble. He was criticized for extravagance, but praised for throwing open his collection, and also the Vatican Library, to scholars from all nations. Less useful, more expensive, and of debatable artistic merit, was the vast new sacristy which he built for Saint Peter's, though the need for a sacristy worthy of the greatest cathedral in the world was not to be denied. The most aesthetically satisfying of the new Pope's undertakings for the glory of the city of Rome was the re-erection of three Egyptian obelisks brought there by the Caesars. By siting them with skill, one on the Quirinal, one opposite the *Santa Trinità dei Monti*, and one on *Monte Citorio*, he was following in the footsteps of Sixtus V (1585–90) in lending this distinctive quality to the vistas of Rome which was congruous with her imperial history.

Not for nothing, then, was Pius VI regarded with favour by the cultured Europe of his day; Rome attracted once more a steady stream of scholars and writers, of whom the greatest was Goethe, and she set once more, with Antonio Canova, the artistic fashion in sculpture, and with Jacques Louis David the coming fashion in classical painting. Classical antiquity was the rage, and Rome was the natural centre for its study. But ruins, too, were becoming romantic about this time, and Rome was the city of ruins. Their attractions were reflected in the engravings of Giambattista Piranesi which have preserved for English posterity, in many a corridor and common room, the Rome of Pius VI.

The Pope was not only artist and antiquarian, he shared the enthusiasm of his time for useful undertakings. This was the age of the cutting of canals, of the wider application of water power and machinery, of the draining of marshes, of the more scientific planning of agriculture. If it was fitting that the capital of the Head of the Church should set artistic and cultural standards it was also fitting, in the view of Pius VI, that his states should be notable for endeavours of economic engineering. He undertook a vast project for draining the Pontine marshes, between Cisterna and Terracina, with the intention of reducing the scourge of malaria and extending the area of cultivable land. In the first purpose he was unsuccessful; indeed the removal of the trees was said to make the gaseous exhalations from the marshes even worse. But by the diversion of the mountain water down a new canal (the *Linea*

Pius VI. From the portrait at Versailles. (*Giraudon photograph.*)

Pia) some land, certainly, was reclaimed, though the main task still remained and was not seriously tackled till the days of Mussolini. A useful part of the scheme was the building of a new road from Velletri to Terracina, which shortened the distance from Rome to Naples.

Every spring, except when he was ill, or away on his visit to Vienna, Pius went down to Terracina to see how the work was getting on; his personal interest in every aspect of it was very much in the fashion of the enlightened despots of his day of whom, in some ways, he was typical. The work was financed by a joint-stock company and involved no increased taxation, but it did not escape notice that the Pope's nephew, Luigi Onesti-Braschi, was granted concessions on the reclaimed land; nor were these the only benefits enjoyed by Luigi. At his wedding the Pope gave him a casket containing 10,000 gold doubloons, he was enabled, for a small rent, to acquire the Jesuit lands at Tivoli, and he was allowed to buy the duchy of Nemi. As Duke of Nemi he granted formal audiences to cardinals; the Emperor made him a Prince of the Empire; the King of Spain made him a Grandee; his younger brother was made a Cardinal. This sort of thing was rather reminiscent of renaissance nepotism at Rome, though it was the common form in the European courts of the eighteenth century and passed without comment there. Much more serious was the mistake the Pope made in allowing himself to be named the heir, for the benefit of his nephew, of a certain Amanzio Lepri, who wanted to make amends for the extortions of his father, who had been a tax-collector. Unfortunately Lepri's niece laid a counter-claim to her uncle's estate and the Congregation of the Rota found in her favour against the Pope – a verdict which reflected creditably on Roman justice but which was very embarrassing for Pius VI.

Though subject, from time to time, to rather prolonged periods of illness, the Pope was one of those thick-set, energetic men, with a commanding eye, who like to see things for themselves. This, rather than any exaggerated deference towards the courts, accounts for his retaining as Secretary of State the obedient Cardinal Pallavicini who had served those courts better than he had served

D

his master. At his death in 1785 he was replaced by Cardinal Boncompagni, whom the Pope could equally easily ignore.

Pius VI's relations with the powers were complicated by his finding himself in one of the most curious cleft sticks ever to be occupied by a Pope. On the one hand the papacy was committed to keeping the Society of Jesus suppressed; no language could be clearer than that of the Brief of Suppression, which Pius VI confirmed: the Society had been 'dissolved' and 'broken up' 'perpetually'. On the other hand Frederick II of Prussia and Catherine of Russia refused to accept or to implement the brief because of the consequences it implied for education in their states, where they deemed the Jesuits to be irreplaceable. The Pope was therefore put into the position of being compelled to try to persuade those rulers to enforce what would amount to the elimination of Catholic higher education in their states; and the Head of the Church found himself in the Gilbertian position of rebuking Protestant and schismatic rulers for failing to deprive their Catholic subjects of their confessors and spiritual guides. When he showed some natural disinclination to pursue this unpalatable policy with much vigour he was compelled thereto by His Most Christian Majesty of France and by the Catholic King of Spain. The Pope and the Catholic rulers were now, officially speaking, in alliance against the heretic and schismatic rulers, not with a view to furthering the cause of the faith, but with a view to the suppression of those who, often alone, bore the heat and burden of the day in the central and eastern territories of the continent.

It has often been observed that God moves in a mysterious way in safeguarding the life of His Church, but seldom has He moved more mysteriously than in choosing Catherine the Great or Frederick the Great as His agents against the Pope. Of the two Catherine was the more effective. Frederick, friend of Voltaire, sceptic, cynic, and realist, was wont wittily to protest that it was really not for him, the heretic, to espouse the cause of the Jesuits at Rome, as some members of the Society tried to persuade him to. He agreed with d'Alembert, who wrote to him that it would be 'singulier, Sire, que tandis que leurs Majestés Très-Chrétienne, très Catholique, très Apostolique, et très-Fidèle détruisent les grenadiers du Saint-Siège, votre très-hérétique Majesté soit la seule qui les conserve.' He saw no reason why he should embroil himself with the Catholic monarchs by standing out as the champion of the Jesuits; on the other hand he took the line that within his own kingdom he was master. If he wanted the Jesuits to stay in Prussia (especially in Silesia which he had seized from Austria) they should stay. Pius was willing that the Jesuits of Silesia should continue to teach, but only if they were secularized, if they were put under the Bishop of Breslau, and if they abandoned their distinctive dress and all distinctive organization as a corporate body. To these terms Frederick eventually agreed; they had the advantage of giving him control over the Society's property, and better opportunities for interfering in the curriculum of the schools.

So Frederick, though he persisted in his refusal to publish the Brief of Suppression, ended by adopting very much the same policies towards the ex-Jesuits as were adopted by the Emperor Joseph II of Austria and most other rulers. Only in Catherine's dominions did the Society continue to live as before, retaining its corporate existence, under its own Provincial, and with a noviciate to train new members.

What made this paradox of history so peculiar was that Catherine was very much a child of the Enlightenment, and had told Voltaire that she was prepared to tolerate all religious groups except the Jesuits. When the Bourbons were expelling them from western Europe she was still full of suspicion against them, supposing that they were a danger to states. But in the year 1772, one year before the Suppression, occurred the first of the partitions of Poland, which brought the Polish territories on the banks of the Dvina and Dnieper (now called White Russia) into the Tsarina's empire. These newly incorporated territories were of course Catholic and, encouraged by the Bishop of Vilna, some of the clergy exercised the option, allowed to them by Catherine, of emigrating to those parts of Poland remaining under Warsaw. The Jesuits however, who were established at Polotsk on the Dvina, in the incorporated territories, placed their duty to their parishes and schools above their patriotic sentiment and remained where they were, becoming subjects of a new sovereign. This was naturally pleasing to

Catherine, who sent for Father Stanislaus Czerniewicz, the Rector of the Jesuit college at Polotsk, appreciated his abilities, and was favourably impressed by the companions he brought with him. So when in the following year Clement published his brief, Catherine refused to receive it in her dominions; moreover she saw that the college at Polotsk might attract some of the gifted members of the Society expelled from other countries and so add lustre to the intellectual achievements of her own dominions. Thus there developed a curious contest, in which Pius VI's Nuncios at Warsaw struggled to secure from Catherine the suppression of the Society at Polotsk, and the Jesuit Rector himself, in obedience to Rome, petitioned the Tsarina to suppress his own college and dissolve his own community while on her side Catherine resolutely refused to do anything of the kind.

Matters were brought to a head by the need for a noviciate for Czerniewicz's community. They had to have a source of recruitment and Catherine had no hesitation about allowing them to build a noviciate; when Czerniewicz explained to her that this was no use without the permission of Rome she opened negotiations with the Nuncio at Warsaw. These having proved abortive she secured that the Catholic Bishop of Mohilev, Stanislaus Siestrzencewicz, be appointed by Rome as Apostolic Delegate, with full powers over religious congregations in White Russia. The new Legate then did what the Tsarina wanted; once the Polotsk Jesuits were under his control he allowed them their noviciate and everything else they required. In doing so he was certainly being disobedient to Rome, but in view of the favourable conditions allowed to Catholics throughout her dominions by Catherine, and her threats of very different treatment if the noviciate or other affairs of the Jesuits were interfered with, there can be no doubt that at this juncture the Bishop served the cause of the Church better than did the Pope.

Not the least remarkable feature of this odd affair of the Jesuits at Polotsk was the dimensions which it assumed on the diplomatic stage of Europe. The Bourbon courts protested strongly to Rome about the opening of the noviciate, and about the Pope's failure to secure the publication of the Brief of Suppression in Russia. This only confirmed Catherine in her determination to support the Society. In 1779 she rejected the Spanish offer of a favourable trade treaty if she would suppress it. In 1780, when she went to meet the Emperor Joseph II at Mohilev, she paid a special visit to Polotsk to inspect the building which was being put up there for the Jesuit novices. Here was a diplomatic gesture too marked to be ignored, and Joseph decided to forget about his mother Maria Theresa's instructions that he should avoid the Jesuit churches and instead attended Mass at them and congratulated Czerniewicz and Siestrzencewicz on their achievement. From the small centre at Polotsk the Society was nourished and enlarged in Russia, receiving immigrants from some of the houses closed elsewhere; soon it was undertaking missions to the region of the Volga, and even to China. In 1801 the new Pope, Pius VII, formally confirmed the continuance of the Society in Russia; but by that year the French Revolution had removed the pressure of the Bourbons on Rome, and Napoleon had removed the pressure of the revolution.

Pius VI said enough, from time to time, to show how widely his personal feelings differed from his official policy in this matter of the continued activity of the Jesuits in Russia. Yet he wrote letters to the Bourbon rulers saying that what was going on in Russia was 'null and void', and assuring them that he had no intention of cancelling his predecessor's brief or of allowing the Society to be restored anywhere else. This was humiliating, and if Catherine gained prestige by her defiant support of the Jesuits the Pope lost prestige, for the whole affair only served to underline his subservience to the Bourbons; it was freely said and generally supposed that the Papal Secretary of State, Cardinal Pallavicini, was in the pay of the Spanish ambassador.[1]

Yet despite papal disavowals of what was going on in White Russia the Jesuits there were not schismatic, nor would Czerniewicz, who was a good Jesuit, have allowed himself to get into such a position. He was protected by the fact that the brief was not published in Russia (which was needed to make it operative there) and by Bishop Siestrzencewicz's powers as Apostolic Delegate.

[1] An opinion accepted by Pastor, Vol. XXXIX, p. 265, though he does not give his evidence.

Had the Pope formally disavowed Siestrzencewicz and suspended
Czerniewicz that would have been an end of the matter; but he
did not go so far as that because Catherine's reaction would have
been such as to spell disaster for the Catholics in Russia.

Bullied by the Bourbons into suppressing the Jesuits, the papacy
had given way to the 'kingdoms of the north' in allowing the
Society to continue. In both processes it had lost prestige. And now
new humiliations were at hand, coming this time from His
Catholic Majesty the Emperor of Austria.

For four centuries the Hapsburgs had provided the surest
support for papacy and Church, and in the nineteenth century they
would do so again. But with the death of Maria Theresa in 1780, her
son Joseph, whom she had done her best to bring up in the ways of
filial respect for Rome, began to fulfil her worst fears by pushing to
their logical conclusion the principles of state religion taught by
Febronius. By the time of Joseph's accession these principles had
not only spread into many parts of Germany but had penetrated
far into enlightened Vienna, and especially into the faculty of
theology at the university. They found their focus in the claim that
the spiritual authority of the Church, represented by the Pope,
extended only to matters of faith; matters of order or discipline,
though they might regulate the lives and even the training of the
secular clergy and of the Religious Orders, belonged to the State.
This was an advanced secularist position, ahead of that adopted by
the State or by the Gallican clergy in France, and if fully adopted
it was likely to lead the State into controlling matters which were
evidently spiritual in character.

When the Emperor insisted that all papal briefs or bulls required
his *placet* before they could be published in his dominions, he was
only insisting on something which, unpalatable as it was to Rome,
had often been insisted on by other rulers. When he extended
equal opportunities for state employment to Lutherans and
Orthodox, alongside Catholics, or insisted on his right to nominate
to bishoprics both in his hereditary territories and in the Duchy of
Milan (where the Pope had hitherto nominated) he could likewise
point to precedents where the Pope had approved similar arrange-

ments. But when he said that priests must no longer be trained in
episcopal seminaries but in general seminaries run by the State,
when he said that the Religious Orders must not owe allegiance to
any foreign Heads, or purchase books abroad, when he suppressed
many of the Orders altogether, along with the 116 confraternities
of Vienna (which he amalgamated into one confraternity of his
own liking, pursuing pious works of which he approved), when
he rearranged all the dioceses and parishes without the approval of
Rome, when he fixed the number of Masses which might be said in
the different churches of Vienna, when he made marriage a civil
contract, and above all when he subjected the whole behaviour of
the clergy and the whole administration of Church property to a
State Court of Ecclesiastical Commission – then he was carrying
to its logical conclusion the Febronian principle that, whatever it
might believe, how the Church acted and administered itself in this
world was the affair of the State.

In the face of what Joseph II was doing Pius VI's decision to go
himself to Vienna, in the spring of the year 1782, to discuss their
differences, is not surprising; but it was strongly opposed at Rome
and may well have been unwise. Cardinal Bernis, the French
ambassador, had his own political reasons for disliking the proposed
visit, but he may all the same have been justified in attributing it to
'too much pride and presumption' and 'the most crass ignorance
of the world and of courts'. 'God is not obliged', he warned, 'to
repair by miracles the imprudences of His Vicars'.[1]

The idea, however, was attractive to Pius VI. He liked to handle
all important matters personally, and directly, having considerable
confidence in his own presence and address. He had already met
Joseph when the future Emperor of Austria had been at Rome at
the time of the Conclave of 1769. He believed that the Emperor,
though wrong-headed, was essentially reasonable, and even well
intentioned, and that he himself was the person who should explain
to him the true state of affairs in matters ecclesiastical. Nor was it
far from his mind that the journey would give him an opportunity
of gaining a first-hand acquaintance with the eastern and northern
regions of his own states, of making personal contact with the

[1] Bernis to Vergennes, February 13, 1782 (Pastor, Vol. XXXIX, p. 449).

Republic of Venice, perhaps even of exerting some influence in the Grand Duchy of Tuscany, where Joseph's younger brother Leopold was openly patronizing the Jansenists. He had begun seriously to contemplate the journey when the Emperor started interfering with the Religious Orders; but his mind became made up when Joseph claimed the right to institute the bishops of Milan and Mantua, a patronage which had always been the prerogative of the Pope.

Leaving Rome on February 27, 1782, Pius travelled simply, at his leisure, calling on all his relatives when he reached his home-town, Cesena, taking almost a month on his journey, receiving ovations as he went. The Emperor met him at Neunkirchen, near Wiener-Neustadt, and rode with him to the capital, where he lodged him in the palace of the Hofburg. There was much talk about the 'Two Heads of Christendom'; there were receptions, and presents, and enthusiastic crowds, besides long and friendly conversations about all the topics in dispute. More than ever convinced of the value of his initiative, the Pope accepted the invitation of the Elector Karl Theodor of Bavaria to Munich, whither his progress was another triumphal procession. From there he went on to Augsburg, so illustrious in Protestant history, where those outside the Church received him as well as did those within. On his way back to Italy he passed through Trent, spent several days at Venice, and inspected the new works in the harbour at Ancona. Not until June 12 was he back at Rome.

Whatever feelings of personal friendliness he may have left behind him north of the Po did not show themselves in the Emperor's subsequent actions. The course of Josephist reform remained unchanged, indeed many of its worst features, including the establishment of the state seminaries and the institution of the Court of Ecclesiastical Commission, belonged to the summer immediately after the Pope's departure. And in September of the following year (1783) he proceeded to publish the names of the incumbents he proposed for his new episcopal Sees (which had not been approved by the Pope) and to nominate a new archbishop for Milan (traditionally a papal nomination). Pius VI had not properly grasped the fact that Joseph II was a seriously and even a religiously minded man who was acting on a principle – a Febronian principle – in which he believed; it was not – as Pius supposed – that he was ignorant of Roman tradition, or in need of having the canon law explained to him by the Pope; he knew about these things, but he was an amateur *philosophe* and he had his own ideas. His mother, whom he had loved and respected, and whom he had deeply distressed by his attitude towards religion, had been quite unable to change his viewpoint. Cardinal Herzan, the Emperor's ambassador at Rome, understood his master's mind in these matters, and the Pope would have done well to have paid greater attention to his warnings. But Pius paid little attention to any of the cardinals, and Herzan particularly annoyed him by showing, in too marked a degree, the tendency of cardinal-ambassadors to place their loyalty to their rulers above their loyalty to the Church.

Besides being a political philosopher the Emperor was an eccentric; he had a childish love of springing surprises. In November 1783 he returned to its sender the Pope's brief protesting against his having appointed an Archbishop of Milan with the observation that the Pope could not have meant it to be taken seriously. But within a few days he had set out for Italy, and from his brother Leopold's palace at Florence he wrote on December 20 to Cardinal Herzan at Rome saying: 'I propose to alight at your residence, change my clothes, go with you straight to the Pope without warning, and confront him in his room, which I shall reach by a back staircase'.[1] By the 23rd he had arrived in the city and paid his call on the astonished pontiff. On Christmas morning he was at the foot of the Papal altar in Saint Peter's for High Mass. Four days later he was off to Naples where Tanucci was now dead, but where his successors were continuing his anti-clerical and anti-Roman policies. These Neapolitans now received the encouragement of a visit from the Temporal Head of Christendom who had given so clear a lead as to the way in which the rights of the Spiritual Head might be ignored. By January 18 the Emperor was back in Rome and before he left, on the 21st, Pius had signed an agreement transferring to Joseph, as Duke of Milan, the right of nomination to the bishoprics, abbeys, and other religious institutions in the

[1] Pastor, Vol. XXXIX, p. 471, Note.

duchies of Milan and Mantua. It is true that Pius preserved the principle that in these lands the nomination did not belong of right to the temporal ruler – he made a free present of it to Joseph. But the substance of victory remained with the Emperor.

Inspired by his older brother, Leopold of Tuscany now made a spirited attempt to become effective Head of the Church in his own Grand Duchy. His principal agent was one Scipione de Ricci who, oddly enough, was a great-nephew of that Lorenzo Ricci, last General of the Jesuits, who died in the Sant' Angelo. This nephew was not only hostile to the Society, he was an ardent Jansenist, closely in touch with the Jansenists at Utrecht, and also with those at Rome like the Cardinal Corsini (to whom he owed his advancement) who were sympathetic with the Jansenist cause. Leopold made him Bishop of Pistoia and gave him a free hand to apply his Jansenist principles. The results were remarkable. Relics were burned and side-altars abolished. The Mass was said in Italian. Veneration of the Sacred Heart of Jesus (associated with the Jesuits) was denounced as 'cardiolatry'; Rome was denounced as 'Babylon'. On his walls he hung portraits of the Jansenist writers who had been denounced in the Bull *Unigenitus*, together with a picture of Joseph II tearing up a painting of the Sacred Heart. He founded a Jansenist periodical, *Annali ecclesiastici*, in imitation of the *Nouvelles Ecclésiastiques* at Paris, and he published pamphlets in support of the heretical Jansenist teaching on Grace.

With these religious principles of the Bishop of Pistoia Leopold was in personal sympathy. In support of them he was prepared to prevent the Florentines from singing their hymns at the street shrines of the Blessed Virgin and even to limit the number of candles they might use in the churches. But he was much more interested in constitutional questions of Church government; he was more a Febronian than a Jansenist, believing that the first necessity was to secure State control over the Church, but hoping and expecting that this would lead on to greater purity and austerity in religion. Idolatry and moral laxity, which could no longer be attributed to the Jesuits, had now to be attributed to the papacy alone; by checking the 'encroachments' of Rome, by 'restoring' the control of the State, and under the State of the bishops, abuses would be weeded out and the purity of the Church of the first six centuries recovered.

Leopold wanted to hold at Florence a Synod of the whole of Tuscany, at which decisions would be taken which would amount to a veritable Reformation in the Grand Duchy. But apart from Ricci and the occupants of two of the smaller Sees, he could obtain no support from his bishops. Florence, San Miniato, Pisa, Siena – they were all against him. Even so, he encouraged Ricci to go ahead and hold a Synod at Pistoia, in 1786, which was attended by some 234 clergy, many of whom came from outside his own diocese, having been invited specially on account of their known Jansenist sympathies. This Synod endorsed all the distinctive tenets of Jansenism, together with the famous Gallican articles of 1682. It recommended the introduction of French Jansenist catechisms, together with the study of Quesnel's *Réfléxions Morales*. It called for the abolition of all Religious Orders founded since the days of Saint Benedict and the end of perpetual monastic vows. It demanded that no town should have more than one monastery, which was to be situated in the 'loneliest and most remote place'.

Though it was held under the patronage and protection of the Grand Duke, the Synod of Pistoia made little impression in Florence or in the rest of Tuscany, and even Leopold saw that it was no use trying to hold a more representative synod along the same lines. For the quick-tempered Tuscans had had enough. Up in the hills, at Prato, they had heard that their most highly prized treasure, the girdle supposed to have been worn by the Blessed Virgin, was to be taken from its chapel in the cathedral, and that the altar itself was to be removed. One Sunday evening in May 1787 they sounded their bells, poured into the cathedral, wrecked Ricci's episcopal throne, burnt his new-fangled missals, breviaries and prayer-books, and then destroyed his palace. It was the end. Leopold, still sure he was right, was powerless. At first it seemed that he would have his chance to pursue his policies in a wider sphere, for in 1790 he left Florence to become Austrian Emperor in succession to his brother. But in 1792 he died. In 1794 the Papal

Bull *Auctorem Fidei* formally condemned the resolutions of the Synod of Pistoia and though Leopold's successor, the Grand-Duke Ferdinand III, in common with many governments, refused to publish the Bull, Ricci himself submitted in the year 1805.

The check to Leopold's plans for Church reform in Tuscany in the year 1787 was important because it was suffered by a ruler with the exceptional abilities and prospects of this younger brother of Joseph II. It also came at a time when the broad plan of Josephist reform was beginning to break down on several other fronts. The weakness from which it was suffering was that it only had the support of enlightened reformers, such as university professors, together with those holding minor positions in the Church who stood to gain by it. It had no solid backing either amongst the higher ranks of the hierarchy or amongst the populace. The latter, conservative as ever, resented the destruction of what they had been brought up to revere, while the bishops were by no means always persuaded of the advantages of being controlled by the secular government on their doorstep rather than by the spiritual government operating from a convenient distance. They were interested in their independence, and especially in their jurisdiction; if the secular rulers could help them to protect this against papal encroachment well and good, but if those rulers really wanted to appropriate jurisdiction to themselves that was another matter. Attacks on their traditional rivals, the Religious Orders, and especially the Jesuits, they would endure with equanimity; the Religious Orders had few friends except the papacy. But State seminaries, State marriage, or State-sponsored synods, at which the lower clergy were invited to suggest reforms in Church government, were all very far from their liking.

The mixed feelings of Church leaders in Germany were brought into the open by the affair of the Punctuation of Ems. Four powerful Metropolitans of the Empire, the Elector-Archbishops of Mainz, Treves, and Cologne, and the Archbishop of Salzburg, banded together with a view to 'reasserting' their 'traditional rights' against 'Roman encroachment'. The immediate cause of their concern was the establishment by Pius VI of a new papal nunciature at Munich. There had for long been a nuncio at Vienna, and another at Cologne, but neither was well placed for dealing with affairs in central or southern Germany; moreover the Elector of Bavaria, Karl Theodor, who had entertained the Pope on the occasion of his visit, was set upon having his own nuncio, and he was hard to refuse.

The episcopal objection to nuncios was that they took under their wing a wide range of jurisdiction, particularly in the field of dispensations and appeals, to which the Pope laid claim, but which, where there were no nuncios, would normally fall to the local Ordinary. Bishops, therefore, did not generally like nuncios; whether rulers liked or disliked them depended upon whether they were trying to curb the power of the papacy in their dominions or whether they were trying to curb the power of their own archbishops. Joseph II was still bent on curbing the papacy, so he supported the anti-nuncio movement, insisting that he did not recognize any jurisdictional rights as pertaining to nuncios. Karl Theodor of Bavaria, on the other hand, wanted a nuncio at Munich so as to humble his local enemy the Archbishop of Salzburg.[1]

To the Emperor the row about the nuncios seemed to provide an opportunity for him to push further his plans for bringing the Church in Germany as a whole under imperial control. So he advised the metropolitans to summon a congress which would consider the entire field of Roman encroachments and of Church reform, and this duly met in July 1786 at Ems. It was not attended by the metropolitans themselves but by their suffragan bishops or other representatives. It bore some analogy to the Synod of Pistoia of the same year, at least in its agenda; indeed one of the documents it considered was Leopold's letter to the bishops of Tuscany which had provided much of the agenda at Pistoia. The

---

[1] The papal case for nunciatures in Germany was most vigorously put by Mgr Bartolomeo Pacca (the later Cardinal pro-Secretary of State of Pius VII) who was sent as nuncio to Cologne in 1786, and in 1832 published his *Memorie storiche di Mgr Bartolomeo Pacca . . . sul di lui soggiorno in Germania dall' anno MDCCLXXXVI al MDCCXCIV*, the first part of which deals with the nunciature question. A documented account of the controversy and of the Conference of Ems is in Pastor, Vol. XL, pp. 29–61.

two brothers were, in fact, with these synods and congresses, pursuing common objectives, which they discussed together.

The Punctuation of Ems, of September 1786, was the upshot of the congress. It set forth a series of proposals for limiting the power of the papacy in Germany. The judicial powers of nuncios, the traditional papal provision to certain benefices, and the papal jurisdiction over the Religious Orders were all denounced; papal briefs and the resolutions of Roman congregations were to be regarded as invalid unless endorsed by the bishops; the entire system of Roman taxation was to be reconsidered by the German Diet.

These resolutions were accepted by the metropolitans. But suddenly the Emperor saw the red light – when his Chancellor, Kaunitz, pointed it out to him. What if these German metropolitans were about to claim just those powers which the Emperor was claiming for himself? The right to stop the entry of papal briefs, the right to regulate the Religious Orders, as well as other rights implicit in the Punctuation of Ems, belonged, in the view of the Febronian reformers at Vienna, to the Emperor or to the Diet; they had not been given by God to the bishops. The Emperor's comments on the Punctuation were therefore chilly; he recommended that the metropolitans should obtain the views of all the German bishops on it and also those of the competent secular authorities. Considerable divergencies of view soon arose amongst the bishops and amongst the lower clergy. When the Emperor insisted that the matter be referred to the Diet that only added to the delay and the confusion. Opposition to the metropolitans from the King of Prussia as well as from the Elector of Bavaria made any move to increase their authority in Germany as a whole more and more unlikely.

Seeing that they were only falling from the Pope's frying pan into the Emperor's fire the metropolitans of the Rhineland made their separate peace with Rome and Salzburg had to follow suit, the whole affair being wound up by a lengthy brief and memorandum sent by Pius VI in November 1789 which defended the traditional rights of the nunciatures and yielded nothing on the many matters in dispute. Rome had won, as she had won in

Tuscany. When it came to the point the great archbishop-electors
of the Rhineland had shown that, much as they would have liked
to absorb all the authority, spiritual as well as temporal, into their
own hands, they would prefer to see some of the spiritual authority
remain in the hands of the Pope rather than see it pass into those of
the Emperor.

And on the Emperor's side there were special considerations in
Germany, which did not apply in France, and which made the
Hapsburgs much more reluctant to support an anti-Roman attitude
on the part of the bigger German bishops than the Bourbons were
in supporting the French bishops. The heart of the difference lay
in the fact that France was a unified kingdom in which the political
power of the King was supreme whereas the Holy Roman Empire
was only a loose confederation in which the Emperor was *primus
inter pares*. The metropolitans of the Rhineland, who were taking
the lead in limiting the authority of Rome, were also political
princes concerned to limit the authority of Vienna. Maximilian
Franz Joseph, Elector-Archbishop of Cologne, was the younger
brother of the Emperor; Klemens Wenzeslaus of Treves was also
a Hapsburg; Friedrich Karl Joseph von Erthal, of Mainz, was in
friendly alliance with the King of Prussia. Each of these archbishops
was the temporal ruler of a small state and an Elector of the Holy
Roman Empire. When Hontheim, whom they befriended, argued
in his *Febronius* for State control over the Church he was arguing
for something which was already a fact in their electorates owing
to their own dual character. But this did not endear them to the
Emperor, although he shared their philosophy. He might like
Febronian principles, but he did not want to see them practised by
those whom he regarded as his subjects. From his point of view the
pretensions of these archbishops were simply particularism, both
political and ecclesiastical. They were a menace alike to the
temporal and to the spiritual unification of the Empire under himself. They were an anti-imperial move in the centuries-old contest
between the Emperor and the princes. Whereas Louis XIV or
Louis XV could often ally with the French bishops against Rome,
on the agreed understanding that the bishops enjoyed the plenitude
of the spiritual jurisdiction and the king the plenitude of the

temporal power, the Emperor could find no such basis for understanding with his own powerful metropolitans for they claimed to represent both powers – and so did he.

In one part of his dominions Joseph II's religious policies brought about rebellion and ended in revolution. The students in the seminaries of the Netherlands were not prepared to accept the Emperor's suppression of those episcopal institutions and their replacement by two which would be run by the State. At the end of the year 1786 they came out in revolt at the nationalized seminary of Louvain, and after serious disturbances the majority of them were either sent home or locked up. The Nuncio, accused of inciting the students, was expelled, and the Cardinal Archbishop of Malines was summoned to Vienna to explain his opposition to the government's measures. But what had been merely a students' revolt became, during the year 1788, a general movement against the Emperor's centralizing reforms, and by August 1789 the government gave in on the issue of the seminaries in the hope of appeasing the wider hostility. It was too late; by the end of the year the rebels were everywhere victorious, government troops were deserting, and the Austrian commander, General Trautmansdorff, was forced to flee.

In this crisis the Austrian Chancellor Kaunitz had to ask Pius VI to persuade the Belgian bishops to support the imperial government in the Netherlands promising that, if he would do so, all the anti-clerical legislation in the province should be revoked, and even holding out the hope that the same should be done elsewhere in the Hapsburg dominions. But again the surrender came too late; for although Pius duly sent a brief, on January 23, 1790, to the hierarchy of the Netherlands, congratulating them on their stand, telling them of the Emperor's promises, and urging them, now that the danger to the Church had been averted, to rally in support of the legitimate government, the Archbishop of Malines, as President of the Estates of Belgium, had already proclaimed the independence of the country. Led by the Church, the revolution against the Emperor had succeeded.

But a greater danger to the independence of the Belgian Church and to the new 'Estates of Belgium' now threatened. The French Revolution was about to enter its messianic phase. In May 1791 the frightened Estates, feeling exposed without a powerful protector, made Joseph's successor Leopold their ruler as Duke of Brabant, and with Leopold's death in the following year Francis II inherited the position. But neither he nor those who supported him in the Netherlands proved capable of withstanding the tremendous tide which was to flow east from France, sweeping away all independent authorities, not only in the Netherlands but likewise in the Rhineland. All the old landmarks were submerged beneath the new flood, archbishop and nuncio alike in the Netherlands, archbishop and nuncio alike in the Rhenish Electorates lost their lands and jurisdictions, as did the agents of the imperial power. The whole of the left bank of the Rhine became annexed to France, while on the right bank the territories of the ecclesiastical princes provided much of the compensation paid to Prussia and other states which lost territory on the left. That characteristic German phenomenon, the ecclesiastical prince who was also a temporal ruler, disappeared for ever, and with his disappearance went the religious protection of many Catholic populations, now handed over to Protestant German régimes. But, from the Church's standpoint, in the long run there proved to be gain, as well as loss, in the change. For with the end of the ecclesiastical electorates, and of the twenty-two prince-bishops, a dangerous identification of Church and State, natural nursery for Febronian principles, disappeared from the scene in Germany, leaving the way open for the development, during the coming century, of a clearer and healthier distinction between the spiritual and temporal power.[1]

When the Emperor Joseph II died in 1790, admitting the failure of his religious reforms, it was beginning to look as though Rome, weak as she was in the days of Pius VI, had successfully met the latest attempt to secure State control over religion. The Febronian

---

[1] Cardinal Pacca, after his experience as Nuncio at Cologne, wrote: 'It cannot indeed be denied that various prince-bishops, at the time of my stay in Germany, occupied themselves more in secular affairs of temporal government than in the regulation of the Church which had been entrusted to them' (Pacca, *op. cit.*, p. 181).

E

tide had begun to turn in Tuscany, in the Rhineland, in the Netherlands, even in Austria. Yet in fact, in the very year in which the
Emperor died, some of the principles for which he stood, in matters
ecclesiastical, were given new and striking expression in France in
the Civil Constitution of the Clergy. At the age of seventy-three
Pius VI, who had now reigned for fifteen years, was called upon to
confront a new political assault, this time from men whose
manners and methods would cause those of the Austrian Emperor,
now dead, to be remembered as a model of courtesy and consideration.

CHAPTER THREE

Pius VI and the French Revolution

The Bourbons had tried to destroy the Jesuits. The Hapsburgs had tried to gain administrative control over the Church. The French Revolution now tried first to run and later to ruin the Church. What each had in common was that each was trying to 'renew' the Church, to restore her to her 'primitive simplicity', to rid her of 'accretions and superstitions', to free her from the 'incubus of the Papacy'.

Ironically, it proved in the end to be the papacy, in the person of the obstinate, simple, and saintly Pius VII, that renewed her life, by means of his own dedication in adversity. Her would-be reformers and patrons, Charles III of Spain, Joseph II of Austria, and the enlightened men of the French National Assembly, alike proved incapable of achieving it, though not for want of high philosophy nor, indeed, of good will very often towards Christianity.

The Bourbon, Hapsburg, and French revolutionary offensives had in common the aim of reviving the Church through the agency of the State. They did not seek to destroy her – only the later phase of the French Revolution sought to do that – they sought to improve her, to bring her up to date and into harmony with their own enlightened principles, and to ensure that she ceased to be an obstacle to their own plans or a rival to their own authority. What they were denying was the need for the centuries-old dualism, at least in the sphere of discipline, represented by distinct spiritual and temporal powers. Just as their philosophy had sometimes weakened their sense of the conflict within man's own nature so their political theory, which envisaged an immensely extended and beneficent role to be played by an enlightened state, ruled by themselves, left no room for a rival power at the elbow of the secular ruler – for instance a nuncio insisting that he was over-stepping the limits assigned to secular government.

The Roman claim was that there were, and always had been in western Christendom, two powers, and that this situation would remain unchanged whatever form secular government might take. And up to a point the opposition agreed, allowing the Pope his supremacy in matters of faith, but not in matters of discipline or devotion. This last distinction proved, however, to be unreal and incapable of administration. It was not possible to distinguish between faith and its organization and practice. Thus Joseph II and his brother Leopold objected to devotion to the Sacred Heart, to much of the invocation of the saints, and to various of the rules followed by Religious Orders, for which they wished to substitute uniformly their own version of the Rule of Saint Benedict. These practices, they claimed, were merely matters of devotion or discipline. But actually they all rested on principles of faith: for instance, it was because of the place occupied by the saints in the Catholic scheme of Heaven and Earth – which was a matter of faith – that it became natural and desirable for the faithful to invoke their intercession. Every article of faith was liable, in some respect, to affect the external practices of the Church.

Pius VI, driven right onto the defensive, clung to the traditional positions of the Church. No aspect of its religious life, he claimed, could lie within the jurisdiction of the State. So far as the Religious Orders were concerned all aspects of their life lay wholly within the jurisdiction of Rome. So far as the secular clergy were concerned, authority over them, in matters touching religion, rested with the bishops. The bishops might claim that their authority came to them directly from God, though the Pope claimed (and the Vatican Council later ruled) that it came to them through Rome. Both were agreed, however, that in matters of faith and morals the last word rested with the Pope, even if some (e.g. those who supported Bishop Hontheim) would allow that the State had rights in the sphere of discipline and devotion. In the sphere of jurisdiction the papacy had never given up its claim to entertain appeals from any ecclesiastical court, hotly as this claim was contested both by bishops and by secular rulers. But more usually the Pope found his authority invoked in support of that of the bishops against rulers trespassing into the spiritual sphere. Such had been the position in the Netherlands when Joseph II had been trying to set up State seminaries there, claiming that the education of the clergy was merely a matter of discipline and order, and his own concern. But the bishops – even those who were prepared to allow to the secular ruler rights in the sphere of discipline and order – had appreciated as keenly as did the Pope that faith was intimately involved in the ordering of the training of priests.

In practice, the powers of the papacy, in eighteenth-century Europe, varied very greatly in the different countries. Sometimes they were only a matter of precedent, sometimes they were embodied in a Concordat. In France, as we saw earlier, the King had acquired, by the Concordat of 1515, the right to nominate all bishops, the Pope investing them with their spiritual powers and receiving their first year's revenues in the form of annates; the Pope still claimed the right to entertain appeals at Rome, and to send nuncios to represent him at Paris, and to have his briefs published there, but all these rights were contested both by the King and by the Gallican clergy. The Spanish monarchy and hierarchy were even more independent of Rome than were those of France; those of the Holy Roman Empire were less so. In some places, e.g. in the Duchy of Milan, the Pope enjoyed a right of nominating as well as investing the bishops, but he did not normally enjoy these rights outside Italy. Amongst the points on which he insisted universally, as matters of fundamental principle which could not be surrendered, were his investiture of bishops, his exclusive control over the Religious Orders, his concern with the education of the clergy and the discipline under which they lived (e.g. their celibacy), his authority in faith and morals and over the forms in which they were expressed (e.g. the Liturgy and the Breviary) and over the catechisms in which they were taught to the young.

All these powers were now to be denied by the French Revolution.

Those who had experimented with the inviting but dangerous idea of reforming the Church by the agency of the State in the relative tranquillity of the Rhine, the Danube, or the Arno, were now to see and soon to be shocked by the same idea being put into practice in Paris, with a truly Gallic logic and relentlessness, and what they saw there provided one reason why they halted in their own path.

There had been little to suggest that a storm of such violence was approaching. The French Estates General, which met at Versailles on May 5, 1789, was not an anti-Catholic or even an anti-clerical body. A quarter of its members – about 300 out of about 1,200 – were priests. On the day before the first formal session the deputies met at the Church of Notre Dame and went in procession, carrying the Sacred Host, to the Church of Saint Louis, to attend Mass, a Te Deum, and a sermon which lasted for two hours; the reform of France, it was supposed, was to be carried out beneath the banner of the Catholic Church. Moreover the most decisive step taken during those early days of the Revolution was taken by the priests, for on June 22 a majority of them voted to abandon their seats amongst the First Estate and join the Third Estate, for the procedure of the 'verification of powers'. In this way they weakened the division into three estates and were directly responsible for helping to form that Constituent National Assembly which carried through the first French Revolution.[1]

Initially, then, there seemed to be no necessary antagonism between the Church and the movement for reform. Not only did the clergy come to take their place with the Third Estate, but the bishops joined the nobility in renouncing their privileges at that emotional night session of the Assembly on August 4 when they gave up not only their feudal dues but the tithes which were the Church's chief source of revenue. And further, the Church had already indicated that she regarded herself, like everything else in France, as being ripe for reform; her clergy had said as much in the pamphlets they had put out before the meeting of the Estates General. Most of these plans were put forward by the lower clergy and were Jansenist – or more accurately Richerist[2] – in their

[1] M. G. Hutt, however, in an article in the Journal of Ecclesiastical History, Vol. VI, No. 2, *The Rôle of the Curés in the Estates General of 1789*, draws attention (cf. pp. 194 and 218) to the fact that 35 per cent. of the curés did not vote to join the Third Estate for the purpose of the verification of powers and that a still larger proportion were opposed to losing their identity as a separate Estate.

[2] See Appendix I, p. 296.

inspiration. It would be wrong to identify them as the work of a particular organized party, but they did bear a strong analogy to those put forward at the Synods of Utrecht and Pistoia, and they belonged to the same clearly marked current of opinion which had been expressed for long in the *Nouvelles Ecclésiastiques*. They favoured improvements in the position of the lesser clergy, as against the bishops, and of the secular clergy as against the Religious Orders; and they asked for administrative independence of the Church in France from Rome. They show the more vocal French curés to have been a body of clergy rather narrowly French in outlook, with little sense of the universality of the Church, and also rather strongly class-conscious. They enjoy using the argument that the lower clergy are descended from the seventy-two sent out by Our Lord. But they also have the prejudices of their superiors: they are pained and surprised by the increased toleration recently extended by the Crown to Protestants, Jews, and agnostics, and they are bitter in their comments on the Religious Orders. Let the monasteries, we read again and again, 'be reformed' and the monks be made to do 'useful work'; they should not be allowed merely to devote themselves to prayer and contemplation.

The curés had been so successful in projecting their point of view, and their more favoured rivals, the Religious Orders and the cathedral clergy, had been so ill organized and so unpopular politically that it is not surprising to find that the arrangements for the election of the Estates General put the parish priests into a strong position. It had been decreed that, whereas only one out of every ten canons, only one out of every twenty cathedral clergy, and only one from each monastic house could vote in each constituency for a member to go to Versailles, every curé could do so if he could find his way to the voting station – not always a very easy matter. The result was that, when the First Estate assembled at Versailles, it was found to include some 203 curés, out of a total of perhaps 295 clergy of all kinds. There were only seven monks. The reform of the ancient Gallican Church, in so far as it rested with her own hierarchy, would rest with her parish priests. Nor should it be forgotten how large a share those priests had often had in selecting the representatives of the Third Estate.

To those interested in the Church and her reform, rather than in secular government, the Estates General, assembled at Versailles, looked significantly like the Great Synod, or National Council invoked by the Jansenists, or by Hontheim. It seemed like the Synod of Utrecht or the Synod of Pistoia writ large, presenting Louis XVI with a wonderful opportunity of achieving all that Joseph II or Leopold had dreamed about but had never been able to accomplish. Such views were not absent, too, from the minds of more exalted members of the French hierarchy, some of whom were by no means impervious to the reforming ideas or hostile to the notion of allowing the laity some share in decisions which would affect Church discipline. When the majority of the curés decided to throw in their lot with the Third Estate, and the First Order ceased to be a separate Order, those who moved across were led by two archbishops – Vienne and Bordeaux. But the dream of the Gallican Church peacefully undertaking its own reform, under the guidance of its bishops and lower clergy in assembly united, and in association with the secular power, represented by the rest of the Assembly and the King – remained a dream. It remained a dream partly because most of the French bishops expected a larger say than that in what was to be done, and partly because Pius VI also saw the analogy between Utrecht, Pistoia, and Versailles. Joseph II and Leopold were still alive and unrepentant, and the Pope was hardly likely to abandon control over order, discipline or devotion in the Gallican Church to any mixed assembly, or to the monarchy, or indeed to anybody other than her bishops and himself.

Even so, the Pope might have been overborne in his opposition if the King had taken his stand firmly with the Assembly. Had Louis XVI shared the attitude on Church matters made fashionable by his brother monarchs of Austria and Spain, it is hard to see what could have prevented the Assembly from carrying through successfully, and without schism, a major reorganization of the French Church which would have made it much more closely dependent on the State. Many of the bishops would have disliked it, and opposed it, but their royalism (so much stronger than their link with Rome) would have left them little choice. By rather an odd chance, however, the King did not share the fashionable Febronian outlook of his times. It did not seem to him natural that a complete reshaping of the discipline and order of the Church should be carried out in France without the co-operation of Rome. Moreover he was religious, and filial, and believed (most unfashionably) that it was his duty to observe his coronation oath to protect the Church, and that this meant protecting the rights of her Head as well as of her members. So when the great new scheme for reform began to emerge in the Assembly in the shape of the Civil Constitution of the Clergy, Louis, knowing the views of Rome, and of most of his bishops, did his best to delay its formulation, and only approved it reluctantly on July 22, 1790, excusing himself by saying that he had had no official advice from Rome – which, indeed, was true; it arrived the next day. And when the Pope finally condemned the Civil Constitution, root and branch, on March 10, 1791, the King's mind began to move rapidly towards that break with the Revolution to which he soon strove to give effect in his flight to Varennes. When the Revolution estranged the Church it also estranged the King.

As it finally emerged from months of debate the Civil Constitution was a much more radical measure than most of the parish priests and almost all the bishops had envisaged. Although it found some support amongst the curés, and with a very few of the more Gallican bishops, most of the clergy regarded it as too evidently an act of hostility towards the papal authority, and also towards the Church; and it was not the first. That Assembly which had seemed in the early weeks of its life to be Catholic in temper, and to which the hierarchy had yielded both its feudal privileges and also (when it renounced the tithe) its main source of revenue, had become, as month succeeded month, more and more hostile to the traditional position of the Church. When, on April 13, 1790, it rejected Dom. Gerle's motion that Catholicism be declared the religion of the State many of the curés took alarm.

Why had this hostility developed?

At bottom because the largest lay element in the Assembly, the lawyers, belonged to a class which had been deeply involved in the work of the *Parlements* and so, for nearly a century, had been in opposition to Rome, to the Jesuits, and usually to the bishops, having taken its stand with the Jansenist opposition. Sometimes these lawyers sincerely believed in Jansenist principles, but very often they were Voltairean and sceptical; in either case their traditions were opposed both to Rome and to the Gallican episcopacy. These were the men who, confronted by the bankruptcy of the State, saw expediency and principle happily married in the movement to nationalize the property of the Church, which was decreed on November 2, 1789, and which was the natural prelude to the issue of the paper money, the *assignats*, in April 1790.

This nationalization was also the natural prelude to the entire scheme of Church reform undertaken by the Assembly. For now that its property had been taken away from it the Church would have to be paid for by the State, so the Ecclesiastical Committee of fifteen (which contained only five clergy) conceived it to be its duty to reorganize the administration of religion to the best advantage of the tax-payer, who would now have to foot the bill, and who would need to be assured that he was getting value for his money. Naturally the first casualties were the Religious Orders. Once their property had been nationalized they were bound to disappear because nobody was interested in paying for their maintenance. How could it be demonstrated that it was to the advantage of the tax-payer that men should devote themselves to prayer and contemplation? No state system could possibly provide for contemplatives; even the secular clergy were largely against them. The spiritual élite of the Church (alongside some who were merely lazy, or even fraudulent) could only exist, as they always had existed, by the protection of Rome. The only Religious Orders which could be allowed were those of nuns engaged in educational, nursing, or other charitable work. The men's Orders were accordingly dissolved, as well as many of the women's, in February 1790; religious vows, which had already been declared to have no legal validity, were now prohibited altogether.

The French Religious Orders having thus followed in the wake of the expelled Jesuits it was time to consider the position of the secular clergy in a reformed Gallican Church. The majority of the Assembly was prepared to recognize that they had a useful function to perform. But their numbers could be reduced; it was considered unnecessary to have more than one parish priest for every 6,000 souls; and it would be convenient as well as economical to reduce the number of bishoprics and make them co-terminous with the new secular departments. Bishops could then be elected, in the same way as other departmental officials, and the lesser clergy be chosen in the same way as the lesser officers of State. Bishops were to be paid according to the size and importance of their Sees (from 12,000 to 20,000 *livres*) and curés according to the extent of their parish responsibilities (from 1,200 to 4,000 *livres*, which guaranteed a minimum of about twice what it had been customary to pay before). If any clergy were absent for more than a fortnight, or took on work which might interfere with their professional duties, the civil authorities could dispossess them. The Pope, on the other hand, lost all authority over them. He was no longer to invest the bishops with their spiritual powers; in future he must rest content with a letter from the new incumbent informing him that he remained in communion with Rome.

So, by this Civil Constitution of the Clergy of July 1790, was set up a national and elective structure for the Church in France. At every stage it had been contested, not only by the bishops but by most of the clergy in the Assembly, as had the nationalization of the Church property. Its chief architects were the Jansenistic lawyer Armand-Gaston Camus, who believed in the absolute right of the Assembly to reorder the religion of the country, and the free-thinker Jean-Baptiste Treilhard. Their favourite argument, to justify what they were doing, was the need to restore the Church to her 'primitive simplicity', when she had possessed no endowment, and when her bishops had been elected. And they insisted that they were only concerned with temporalities and organization; they had not touched faith or morals. The 'outward fabric' of the Church in France, they claimed, was the affair of the general public.

The clerical deputies and their sympathisers argued in reply that the Church could not rightly be turned inside out in this way by the State without at least being consulted concerning her future. Even if the secular power had the right to take away her property (which they mostly denied) it had no right to remodel her order and discipline. A National Council of the Gallican Church should have been set up to consider her reform and the views of the Pope should have been obtained. Although many of the lower clergy believed that the State did have important rights in the regulation of the Church the majority of those assembled at Versailles supported these counter-arguments, which were ably put forward by Jean-Siffrein Maury – whom the Pope would soon make a cardinal, and Napoleon would later make Archbishop of Paris.

The King, as we have seen, reluctantly approved the Civil Constitution, on July 22, 1790, and the next day came Pius's letter of July 10 warning him of the grave danger in which he stood of leading France into error and heresy, and advising him to consult with the archbishops of Aix and Bordeaux.[1] Neither Louis, nor Pius, nor the archbishops were anxious to take the initiative in condemning what each nevertheless knew the Church could not finally accept without putting herself into the power of the lay public. Each hoped that one of the other two would take the responsibility. But meanwhile the clergy of France had to decide what to do about it, and as they hesitated, and all but two of the bishop-deputies declared themselves against it, the Assembly grew angry and demanded that all the clergy should take a public oath swearing their acceptance of it or be deprived of their cures.

What followed is creditable to the clergy of France. When it is remembered that, under the terms of the Civil Constitution, the curé would at least double his stipend, and would enjoy a much better status *vis à vis* his bishop; that if he refused to take the oath he would lose his cure altogether; that the King had approved the Constitution and sanctioned the taking of the oath; and that the Pope had not yet officially pronounced himself, it is rather remarkable that so many of the curés refused to swear. Less than a third of the 300 clergy in the Assembly, and only two bishops, ended by

---

[1] A. Theiner *Documents inédits relatifs aux Affaires Religieuses de la France, 1790 à 1800*, Paris, 1857, Vol. i, p. 5.

taking the oath unconditionally; in the country as a whole the proportion who did so was similar, though about a half of the curés were prepared to do so.

That the bishops should refuse to take the oath was to be expected. They were hardly likely to favour a reorganization which undermined their authority over the lower clergy, reduced their income, and subjected them to lay election and lay control. Only seven out of some 160 bishops in the country as a whole took the oath. One was Talleyrand, who was useful (till the Pope excommunicated him) in consecrating new constitutional bishops and so passing on the apostolic succession to the constitutional clergy. Another was Gobel, who performed the same function after Talleyrand had resigned his bishopric and embraced politics. Gobel was elected Constitutional Bishop of Paris; but when later the Revolution turned against even the constitutional clergy he too hastened to resign, putting on the red bonnet in place of the mitre and pulling off his episcopal ring. A third was the astute Cardinal Loménie de Brienne, who had been one of those able politicians who had tried, in vain, to save the government before 1789. None of these new bishops was likely to provide the new Church with the moral fervour which its partisans hoped to see in it; for that it would have to wait for another of its elected bishops, Henri Grégoire, of Loir et Cher.

On the other hand moral fervour and religious zeal characterized only some of those many bishops who refused the oath, and who soon found themselves obliged to flee abroad to save their lives. Some – Jouffroy de Goussans of Le Mans for example – were great men, whose moral quality the Assembly had been compelled to acknowledge; very few were altogether unworthy. But they had been drawn too exclusively from the nobility, which limited their sympathies, while too many were worldly, in a utilitarian sense, being preoccupied, in the spirit of the times, with the economic administration of their dioceses, with agricultural improvements, canals, drainage, and the like; 'administrators of dioceses rather than of the sacraments' it was unkindly said. In this they resembled the Ecclesiastical Electors of the Rhineland, or even the Pope himself, though without the excuse of being temporal as well as spiritual rulers. They regarded their temporal authority as derived from the King, and their spiritual authority as derived either from God direct or mediately through the Pope. Neither authority, they were quite sure, could be derived from the People or from the Assembly. As soon as the King had broken with the Assembly they would go into exile, and many of them would show, in the end, when Pius VII tried to bring them back to Napoleon's France, that they rated their allegiance to the King above their allegiance to Rome. Meanwhile life at the German courts, or in Italy (till the Revolution overran both), or even in London (where many of them spent their last years of exile) was not too intolerable in those eighteenth-century days when the upper crust of European society was cosmopolitan in a sense in which it has not been since. They could count on the hospitality of their class, and they would need to; out of thirty French bishops in London twenty-five were living on charity.[1]

Far harder would be the lot of the 'non-jurors' amongst the lower clergy, who were not normally in a position to pay for their journey into exile, let alone for their maintenance while abroad. Yet between 30,000 and 40,000 of them emigrated in the course of the coming decade. It has been estimated that 5,000 were maintained in the Papal States, 5,000 in Switzerland, and no less than 10,000 in England – nearly 5,000 in London alone. After allowing for those turned out of the monasteries, and others belonging to Orders or to cathedral chapters, many of whom emigrated, we are still left with some 15-20,000 curés, out of about 50,000, who managed to find their way abroad, or more than half of the 25,000 odd who had refused to take the oath. Those who failed to emigrate were usually deprived of their livings, becoming dependent upon the charity of their neighbours; later they had to go into hiding, or else suffer imprisonment or deportation to French Guiana; im-

[1] Based on estimates made by Pastor, Vol. XL, p. 272, and A. Sicard *Le clergé de France pendant la Révolution*, Vol. 3, p. 10, etc. Theiner, in his *Documents, op. cit.*, Vol. I, p. 366, prints the Abbé de Barruel's letter to Cardinal Zelada of September 26, 1792, in which the Abbé says that, even by that date, there were 1,500 French priests, including thirteen bishops, in London, 600 to 700 in the English ports, and 2,500 in Jersey. He also prints (p. 159) Pius VI's letter of September 7, 1792, to King George III, thanking him for the hospitality shown in Britain to these priests.

prisonment was liable to lead to death from the guillotine, deportation to death 'from natural causes'.

Those clergy who did take the oath, together with the seven bishops who did so, provided the nucleus for the Constitutional Church. But it was necessary to go through hurried consecrations (leaving out the references to Rome in the ceremony) in order to find occupants for the new Sees, and to hunt the hedges and byways to find candidates for election to the livings in order to achieve the 30,000 effectives which that Church ultimately mustered. Sometimes a mere three months' training was treated as sufficient for a new ordinand; sometimes the secularized monks were willing to oblige. But by one means or another the object of establishing a Constitutional Church was achieved, even though a large proportion of the livings and a still larger proportion of the bishoprics were not filled. Alongside the constitutional clergy the non-jurors would often be living in semi-secrecy, ejected from their presbyteries, but sometimes allowed to say their own Mass in the Churches, though not to administer the sacraments or assume any parochial duties. Already, in November 1791, the Communes had been empowered by law to eject them in the event of any disturbances and a more drastic law, in May 1792, enabled the district authorities to deport any non-juror denounced by twenty active citizens.

CHAPTER FOUR

Pius VI and the French Persecution

By the summer then of 1792 there were two Churches in France both claiming to be Catholic, one sustained by the State and the other persecuted by it.

Why had the new régime, which had proclaimed liberty of conscience in its Declaration of the Rights of Man, denied that liberty to a body of priests who probably still represented the majority of religious opinion in France?

Only a few fanatics embarked on the persecution out of their zeal to restore the Church to her primitive simplicity, or out of their hatred of Rome and superstition, though those few were very vocal. The governments of 1792–93 had the more solid grounds that the State which the Revolution had created was menaced by enemies both at home and abroad and they thought, not without good reason, that the non-juring clergy were in sympathy with those enemies. This was far from always true but, in the nature of the case, once Pius VI had formally condemned the Civil Constitution in March 1791, those who took their stand with Rome could hardly hope to be regarded as reliable friends of the new régime, and when that régime was in danger from forces abroad known to have the secret support of the Pope (and by the spring of the year 1792 this was the case) then the hostility of the government towards the non-jurors naturally became acute.

The military odds in favour of Austria and Prussia, in their war with revolutionary France in 1792, seemed heavy; those in favour of the First Coalition, in the following year, seemed heavier still; so the persecution continued.

The analogy between this situation and that which prevailed in England at the time of the Spanish Armada, when the Queen's régime was threatened by the Hapsburgs of Spain, as Paris was now threatened by the Hapsburgs of Austria, has been drawn more than once. It is pertinent because in both cases Rome was known to be sympathetic with the Hapsburgs, and hoping for their victory, so that the threatened governments treated the clergy loyal to Rome as potential enemies. Pius VI himself had the parallel in mind; he wanted very much to avoid a repetition, in regard to France, of that which had proved so disastrous in the case of England; he was naturally anxious to avoid the threat of schism. In the event there was both a schism and a persecution, and if the Pope could hardly have avoided the former his policy had its share in bringing about the latter.

He cannot be blamed for the schism because he never had the chance to negotiate with Paris over the Civil Constitution. Not only did the National Assembly present him with a *fait accompli* but so did the Gallican Church. Four months after the Civil Constitution had been decreed by the Assembly, and likewise four months before Pius gave his ruling on it, the Gallican Church, through the mouth of her bishops, had pronounced it to be unacceptable. When the Pope finally condemned the Civil Constitution the majority of the French clergy had already made up their minds to follow their bishops in resisting; and we can be sure that the firm language of the papal Brief *Quod Aliquantum*, of March 10, 1791, which denounced the measure root and branch,[1] would never have issued from Rome had the Gallican Church not made it clear by then where its belief lay. The bishops' document was called an Exposition of Principles, and it was drawn up and signed at the end of October 1790 by all bishops in the National Assembly except for Talleyrand and Gobel. To this Exposition the bishops outside the Assembly soon openly adhered, no less than ninety-three of them giving it their explicit support. The burden of the document was that it was unconstitutional and impermissible for the Assembly to reform and reorder the Church without consulting her. 'When the civil power seeks to make changes in the ordering of religion without the help of the Church she only opposes sound principles without destroying them; she opposes sound principles and destroys the means by which her views could be put into effect.' This forthright statement had been the cause of

[1] Printed in Theiner, *Documents*, Vol. 1, pp. 32–71.

the Assembly requiring the clergy openly to take an oath in support
of the Constitution. When, by January 1791, the majority of the
clergy had refused, as we saw, to take this oath, their only guidance
on the theological aspects of the matter had been their bishops'
statement. Rome had not spoken. Only when the French clergy
had demonstrated, by some two to one, that they would not take
this oath, and therefore that they supported the attitude of their
bishops, had Pius issued his brief of condemnation.

So we cannot lay only on the shoulders of Pius VI responsibility
for creating a schism in France. That responsibility is also shared
between an Assembly which acted beyond its legitimate powers
and a clergy which resisted, insisting on the autonomy and independence of the spiritual power from secular control. The Pope
was only guilty of supporting – rather tardily – the French clergy,
which was something he could hardly avoid doing. Later, he was
guilty of harbouring French priests and other refugees at Rome, and
later still of the much graver action of making clear his moral
support for the armies of the First Coalition. In this way he had his
share in sharpening the persecution.

The determination shown by the French clergy had been the
more notable in that, given little lead by the Pope, they had been
given none at all by the King. Indeed Louis XVI, greatly as he disliked it, had informally approved the Civil Constitution ten days
after it had been placed before him, and had later signed it after the
month allowed him in which to consult with Rome, and before the
Pope had given his ruling. And he had done all this without consulting the French bishops. He had likewise signed the Assembly's
decree demanding the oath of allegiance. Not till the following
year (1791), after Rome had denounced the Constitution, did he
show a more spirited resistance. Certainly he was at little pains to
conceal his dislike of the new plan, insisting on having non-juring
priests as his confessors and receiving the sacrament from them.
But he gave no help to the resistance until after the Pope had published his Brief of Condemnation in March 1791. Then his attitude
changed. Believing profoundly, as he did, in his duty to maintain
the 'Catholic, Roman, and Apostolic faith,' he drew rapidly away
from the Revolution and along the road which led to Varennes.

Only a month after he received the Brief he made an attempt to escape from Paris and spend Easter at Saint Cloud. He wanted to attend the Holy Week ceremonies and to receive his Easter Communion from the hands of 'Roman' clergy, which was becoming very difficult for him at the Tuileries. But the crowd refused to let the royal couple go; for two hours their carriage stood surrounded, and eventually it was forced to turn round and take them back to the Tuileries. That was the night which steeled the Queen's resolution to escape and, through her, the resolution of the King.

In June the King tried to reach the allies at Varennes; when his subjects sent him back this time it was the beginning of the end. Louis XVI, whose weakness on the religious issue in the face of the Assembly had made matters more difficult for the French clergy, nevertheless, in the end, ruined his own cause for the sake of his religion.

If the French clergy, in the early and critical days, had been given no lead by their King, they were also inclined (as many historians have been since) to complain of the lack of an early lead from Rome. But the force of French complaint against Roman procrastination is weakened by the fact that for two centuries their hierarchy had been warning the Pope against any attempts to interfere with their Gallican liberties, and whatever else those liberties meant they certainly meant the ordering of the Church in France. Clearly it was for the French bishops to express their views to Rome on the Civil Constitution before Rome was in a proper position to make a pronouncement; courtesy and precedent demanded as much in any country, let alone in one which claimed the Gallican liberties. It would have been altogether inappropriate for the Pope to condemn or to approve the Civil Constitution until he had heard what the French bishops had to say – until, that is, he had received their Exposition of Principles at the beginning of November 1790. The delay attributable to the Pope was his delay of four months *after* receiving that Exposition, not a delay of 'eight interminable months'.[1] There were, indeed,

---

[1] The phrase is used by A. Latreille *L'Église Catholique et la Révolution*, Hachette, 1946, I. 90.

'eight interminable months' between the time when Louis XVI first sent the Constitution to the Pope and the time when the Pope sent his brief condemning it on March 10, 1791. But half the delay was due to his waiting for the verdict of the French bishops, and in waiting for that verdict he was only acting as the French bishops had perennially tried to convince him he should act.

His diplomatic reticence had not, however, prevented the Pope from letting it be known unofficially what were his sentiments concerning the religious work of the National Assembly. That he did not say more was largely due to the restraint urged upon him by the French ambassador at Rome, the Cardinal de Bernis. Bernis understood very well how important it was not to embarrass Louis too seriously, and how real was the danger that the new régime at Paris might break off relations altogether with Rome. He also possessed by now an unrivalled knowledge of Roman affairs, dating from before the suppression of the Jesuits, and an influence over policy greater than that of any other member of the diplomatic corps. His aim was always to urge restraint on the Pope so as to deprive the French government of the excuse to take more drastic steps. So far as his personal sentiments went it would be hard to say whether he or the Pope disliked the Assembly the more. Both were men of the ancien régime, and both believed, as the Pope expressed it, that 'the safety of kingdoms reposes mainly upon the doctrines of Christianity, and their happiness is best secured when sovereigns are obeyed with unanimous consent, according to the express teaching of Saint Augustine'.[1] But both could appreciate the dangers of too hasty a condemnation.

It was Bernis who persuaded Pius to maintain his restraint even after the distressing news had reached Rome of the dissolution of the French Monastic Orders. By the end of March 1790 the Pope conceived that the time had come when he must express himself in some way about the repeated violations of the rights of the Church in France; the Cardinal however was still able to persuade him to confine his remarks to an allocution in secret consistory. On account of the privacy of the occasion Pius was able to speak his mind fully, and he did not mince his words. He noted that the property and

---

[1] Allocution of March 29, 1790, Theiner, *Documents*, Vol. I, p. I.

income of the French Church had been appropriated by the State, that the monasteries had been closed and religious vows made invalid. But further, scorning the claim of the revolutionaries that they were restoring religion to its primitive simplicity, he insisted on taking the issue back to its foundations, back to the anti-Catholic philosophy which underlay the attack. The revolutionaries had been 'miserably seduced by an empty phantom of liberty and enslaved by a band of philosophers who contradict and abuse each other'. He rejected the claim that all men had the natural right to participate in the making of the laws, or to publish whatever they pleased about religion, or to debate about the status of the Church in France. He said this was a monstrous perversion of true order and true liberty, and he told the cardinals he was only prevented from sending a brief to France by the impossibility of finding a suitable person to send it to, the bishops and clergy being scattered, and the King 'in subjection to the Assembly'. Perhaps these difficulties would have been overcome but for the danger of schism, stressed by Bernis, and the Gallican traditions, opposed to such papal initiative.

An allocution in Consistory, while it is a formal expression of papal opinion, is neither an order nor a final ruling; another year would pass before the Pope would pronounce a verdict on the Revolution and the Civil Constitution. During the interval we find him, in his letters to the King, sympathizing with his difficulties, urging him to defend the rights of the Church, pointing out that the Civil Constitution could not be formally approved in the form in which it had taken shape, and stressing that he should take the advice of the episcopal members of his Council, who would be able to explain to him what was theologically permissible. During the summer of 1790 the hope of a settlement acceptable to Paris and to Rome was still alive, though it was fading fast; still hoping that the King would resist, the Pope was disillusioned when Louis signed the Civil Constitution on August 24. The following winter brought the rally of the French bishops against the new project, and then the refusal of the majority of the clergy to take the oath in support of it; the French Church having now spoken the Pope, without much further delay, issued his brief, *Quod aliquantum*, on March 10, 1791, which was technically a reply to the French bishop-deputies' *Exposition de Principes*, and which contained a formal denunciation, root and branch, of the Civil Constitution. This he followed up with his long letter, *Caritas*, on April 13, to the bishops, clergy, and people of France, which denounced Talleyrand's consecration of the new bishops, suspended him and the others concerned in the 'execrable consecrations' from all employment of their episcopal powers, condemned the 'so-called Constitutional Church', and suspended all clergy, of whatever rank, who had taken the oath, unless they should retract it within forty days.[1]

There were some moderately minded ecclesiastics like Cardinal Loménie de Brienne or Boisgelin, the Archbishop of Aix (both of whom wrote many letters to the Pope) who felt that Pius would do well to be more accommodating, and that he need not have condemned the Civil Constitution out of hand; and there have been historians who have followed them. It has been claimed that Pius was influenced unduly by his personal dislike of the principles of the revolution and of the character of the revolutionaries; that he listened too readily to the stories of the émigré priests and their sympathizers who swarmed into Rome, and to the Spanish ambassador Azara, whose government was about to enter the First Coalition against France, and who was therefore freer than Bernis – still France's ambassador – to move the mind of the Pope against the revolutionary government. We are reminded, too, that certain extraneous events stiffened the Pope's resolution. One was the collapse in 1790 of the Josephist reorganization of the Church in the Netherlands, which suggested that, if Rome stood firm, these secular attempts to reorganize religion to the liking of the State would fail. Another was the peculiar position in regard to the papal possessions which formed an *enclave* in France – Avignon and the Comtat Venaissin. The example of the revolution which was taking place all around the *enclave* naturally had not failed to have its effect within, nor did French revolutionary enthusiasts in surrounding Provence intend that it should fail. The Pope's subjects were encouraged to revolt and were soon making overtures to the French Assembly with a view to securing incorporation into France,

[1] Theiner, *Documents*, Vol. 1, p. 75.

towards which the Assembly took the decisive step when it set up the Avignon Committee in July, 1790.[1]

All these influences were at work at Rome, and all helped to colour the attitude of the Curia. But it is not necessary to attribute to any of them the line of policy adopted by Pius VI in dealing with the Civil Constitution of the Clergy. The reaction of Rome to that unilateral reorganization was characterized by just that caution, that delay, that hope of conciliation, and that final intransigence which have generally characterized her behaviour when confronted by a major challenge to her traditional rights. There was never any chance of her accepting the Constitution *in toto*; but there was room for discussion, and there was a definite need, in a matter so serious, for her to obtain first the views of the Gallican Church, in accordance with Gallican precedent. Once it had become clear that the Assembly would not negotiate on the matter with Rome, that the King was powerless, that a new Constitutional Church was being created, and that the French clergy as a whole were opposed to what was being done, then it was hardly possible for the Pope to delay longer in giving his verdict, and it was evident what that verdict would be. The ancient Concordat, which had governed

[1] The French historian Albert Mathiez, in his *Rome et le Clergé Français sous la Constituante: La Constitution Civile du Clergé, L'Affaire d'Avignon* (Paris, 1911) argued that Pius's entire policy towards the French Revolution was conditioned by his determination to maintain his sovereignty over Avignon. The Pope's silence on the Civil Constitution during the summer of 1790 is regarded as a Machiavellian attempt to induce the Assembly to guarantee this temporal sovereignty by holding out the hope that, if they did, he might be prepared to approve the new Church arrangements; when the Assembly nevertheless does incorporate Avignon into France the Pope moves over to outright opposition and enters the camp of France's enemies. The argument is strained; even the dating is unconvincing because the most obvious papal delays came *after* the creation of the Avignon Committee. Nor is it helped by Mathiez's insistence (e.g. pp. 235–37) that Pius could easily have approved in France Church policies which he had been compelled to tolerate in Russia. Pius, we are told, was indifferent to the character of the Civil Constitution as such.

Mathiez evidently overstated his case. Nevertheless the reader of Secretary of State Cardinal Zelada's letters to the unofficial papal agent at Paris, Salamon (in *Correspondance secrète de l'Abbé de Salamon avec le Cardinal de Zelada (1791–92) publiée par le Vicomte de Richemont*, Paris, 1898) will not be inclined to minimize the influence of the *affaire Avignon* as a factor in prejudicing Rome against the new French régime.

the relations between Rome and Paris since the year 1515, had been unilaterally revoked, without consultation; the French Church had been first despoiled, then turned upside down, and finally nationalized without being consulted about its fate; the monasteries had been dissolved, and the priests were becoming the objects of persecution for no other crime than their refusal to agree to these changes. Any further delay on the part of Pius VI in pronouncing upon the Constitution would evidently have been a dereliction of duty and, although the fate of the proscribed priests was likely to be aggravated by his action, he could not rightly deny to them the certain knowledge that they were suffering in the cause of the Catholic Church, a knowledge they badly needed when they had had to make so hard a choice.

Was there a chance, later on, of reconciliation?

Hardly in the winter of 1793–94, for that was when the anticlerical campaign conducted by Fouché, Chaumette, and their friends amongst the députés-en-mission was in progress; when Hébert, in his Père Duchesne, was rousing the rabble with ridicule of religion; when cathedrals and churches might find themselves turned over to every excess of profane charade; when any priest became a suspect who refused to take a wife; when constitutional bishops might be seen putting on the bonnet rouge; when donkeys were dolled up in cope and mitre. Nor yet after the fall of Robespierre, in the summer of 1794, for the reduced activity of the guillotine, after the Convention and Committee of Public Safety had yielded place to the régime of the Thermidorians, did not help to bring back religion. The cathedrals and churches were still generally without the Mass, and if patronized at all were only witnesses of 'Tenth Day', 'Theophilanthropist', or Deist celebrations.

The non-jurors were still proscribed; but by 1794 the Constitutional Church too was in trouble. Its clergy, though still at large, and even at liberty to say Mass in the churches if they could fit one in between the other activities occupying the building, were now without any means of support; for as a gesture of impartiality towards all religions the Convention had withdrawn all State sponsorship from that Church which the Revolution had created. Having confiscated the property of the Church of the ancien régime, and set up a state-salaried priesthood in its place, the Revolution had now decided to economize by ceasing to pay salaries.

The hard fate of the constitutional clergy, who had accepted so much (even wives) in order to obey a government which was not really interested in them, was of less immediate significance to Rome than was the great revolt in the Vendée. In that western province of France, where the insurgents placed the freedom of the Church in the forefront of their demands, and the non-jurors were everywhere succoured, lay the only living hope of the renewal of religion in France. As month followed month, and the government forces made no headway against the insurgents, the gleam of that hope grew steadily brighter. It was in February 1795 at La Jaunaye that the emissaries of the Republic at last made terms with the men of the Vendée, and one of the terms agreed was the liberty of the Catholic Church. The similar rising of the *Chouans* in Brittany having met with a similar success it began to appear that a toleration which had been won by force of arms in two provinces might be extended over the whole country. Though fighting was resumed in both provinces, life in France generally, from the spring of 1795 to the autumn of 1797, became a little less terrible for the non-jurors. If they would take an oath of obedience to the laws of the Republic they were not deported; and this oath was easier to take now that it no longer involved recognition of a schismatic Church. And the government was in a more lenient mood, partly because it had lost its special interest in the Constitutional Church, partly because the collapse of the First Coalition had made it feel more secure. It was not forgotten that the Pope had made little secret of his support for the First Coalition (a matter to which we must return in the next chapter) and diplomatic relations with Rome had been broken since the summer of 1791. Even so, a moment had come at last when there was some possibility of a reconciliation between Paris and Rome in regard to the ordering of the Church in France, and when Rome might give a positive lead to the many French clergy still faithful to her.

But the opportunity was lost.

Who was to blame?

The Pope, after some delay, addressed a brief, *Pastoralis Sollici-*

tudo (June 8, 1796), to the clergy of France, exhorting them to obey their new government. But it was never published in France. This was because the new French government, the Directory, prompted by the Head of the Constitutional clergy, Bishop Henri Grégoire of Loir-et-Cher, demanded that the Pope should first be required to withdraw all that he had published in opposition to the Revolution, and especially, of course, his condemnation of the Civil Constitution of the clergy, which still provided Grégoire and his followers with their title deed, even though the government had abandoned it. This Pius VI refused to do. He would in no wise seem to countenance the schismatic Church, even if his refusal meant – as it did – that the non-jurors continued to be proscribed. For many non-jurors the position in fact became worse in the summer of 1797 because the government demanded a new 'Oath of Hatred' against the monarchy, which was a very much more difficult oath to take than was an oath to obey the laws of the Republic, and many non-jurors were not prepared to take it. So the distressful exodus began once more, and priests who had returned to France over the Alpine passes from Italy, or across the Rhine, the English channel, or the Atlantic, were crowding the same routes once more, out of the country, or were going into a dangerous hiding, where discovery meant transportation to a likely death on the Isle of Oleron or in distant French Guiana. Under the influence of the Director Rewbell, assisted by the theophilan-thropist Larevellière, the government of the Directory, purged of its more moderate elements by the *coup d'état* of Fructidor 1797, acquired a new lease of life, and with it the Church suffered as severely as she had suffered under the Convention. Not until after Bonaparte returned from Egypt, in October of 1799, did France acquire a ruler who could recognize the folly of continuing to persecute the religion of the majority of her people.

But by then Pius VI was dead.

CHAPTER FIVE

The Revolution penetrates Rome

It's an ill wind that blows the Church no good. The alarming accounts of what was happening in France came with something of the force of revelation to Josephist and Febronian princes. They saw now what happened to religion (and to princes) when National Assemblies assumed control of the Church. And what they saw threw a new light on the Jansenist 'Great Synod' of Utrecht, on Ricci's 'Synod of Pistoia', on the National Councils invoked by Febronius. Were not these proposed assemblies, comprising lower clergy and lay representatives, very like the French National Assembly, looked at in its role as a body for Church reform? Would they not engender Civil Constitutions of the Clergy in the Netherlands, in Tuscany, and in the German States? The Emperor Leopold who, as Grand Duke of Tuscany, had sponsored Ricci, was glad now, as Emperor, to forget about the Josephist reforms in the Netherlands and to abolish the state seminaries in his hereditary dominions; his son Ferdinand, succeeding him at Florence, dropped the plans he had inherited for secularist reform. The fall of Ricci, and his later submission to Rome, were the natural consequence of events at Paris.

When in 1792 Leopold died, and was succeeded at Vienna by his son Francis II, the Pope took the opportunity to try to drive home to the new Emperor the lesson that the welfare of princes demanded that they should not interfere with the sovereign rights of the Church. An occasion for him to do this was provided by the Diet of Frankfurt, in June of that year, to which the Pope sent a special legate, who was none other than Maury, hot from his defence of the ancient Church in the French National Assembly, whom the Pope created cardinal and packed off to Germany.

If it was one of the tasks of the Cardinal Legate to clarify the mind of the Emperor on the implications everywhere of the Civil Constitution, it was also intended that he should warn him of what the French seizure of Avignon implied for all rulers. In the words of the Papal Secretary of State, Cardinal Zelada, 'What sovereign in future will feel secure in the possession of his states if, to make conquests of that kind legitimate, it is only necessary to stir up an insurrection in those states, to foment disturbances, to promise immunity to the leaders of the revolt, and to persuade the peoples to express a wish to unite themselves to a foreign rule?'[1] Here, indeed, was a very pertinent question raised by the papal government. For a new technique was emerging in European affairs: the technique of infiltration, the stirring up of faction, and then the establishment of a new régime 'in accordance with the will of the people'. Already there were signs that something of the sort might happen in Rome itself, and within six years a Roman Republic, satellite of France, would indeed have been created in this way. Considering the later developments of the technique, in the nineteenth and twentieth centuries, this warning given by the Papal Secretary of State when it was first used by the French Revolution is of more than passing interest. Doubtless the day for such *enclaves* as Avignon was over; by some diplomatic arrangement of the kind in which the eighteenth century was fertile it was desirable that Avignon should be transferred to French sovereignty. Nor was there anything new about infiltration as such; it was a time-honoured means, recommended by Machiavelli, for weakening or unseating rulers whom it was proposed to remove. What was new was the justification of such measures by appealing to the will of the people. Rousseau had made this will the sovereign, and the American and French revolutions had both invoked it as their justification; but at Avignon it was being invoked, in the place of the ancient principle of legitimacy, as the justification of a change of territorial sovereignty in Europe. It was particularly relevant for the Pope to warn the Hapsburg Emperor of what this implied, for no ruler's position would be more surely undermined than his

[1] De Richemont *Correspondance secrète de l'Abbé de Salamon avec le Cardinal de Zelada (1791-92)*, Paris, 1898, p. 56.

when the new principle of authority came to be generally accepted.

Cardinal Maury was not a fortunate choice as Legate at Frankfurt. Perhaps if Bernis had still been French ambassador at Rome he would have persuaded the Pope not to send Maury; but in March 1791 Bernis had been relieved of his position for refusing to take the oath in support of the Civil Constitution and diplomatic relations between the two governments had been broken off. Although Bernis remained in Rome (a favourite with the Pope and the best host in the city) diplomatic influence over the papal government was passing into the hands of the Spanish ambassador Azara and the Pope's attitude to events was becoming less restrained. It was however long since Rome had openly taken sides in a major European conflict, and Pius VI was far removed from contemplating doing that, even in 1792; moreover he never despaired of seeing a settlement of the religious dispute in France and was still anxious to do nothing to prejudice its chances. If the legate he despatched to Germany had been a man of discretion there was no reason why his presence there amongst the allied leaders should have seemed to put the papacy into their camp; but unfortunately the Cardinal made no secret of his own or of the Pope's personal fears and hopes in the impending struggle. An irascible and volatile abbé, with great gifts as an orator, Maury had been at his best in denouncing the Civil Constitution in the Assembly; but the gifts he had displayed there were the very opposite to those required in a discreet legate at a delicate moment. It was at the military camp at Mainz that he made his famous reply to the émigré Prince de Condé, who had asked him when the Pope was going to excommunicate the constitutional clergy: 'The Bull', he said, 'will be published when they [the allies] have defeated and scattered the [revolutionary] army; the Pope has need of their swords to sharpen his pen'.[1] The revolutionary government at Paris, well informed about the diplomatic moves at the enemy camp, was soon able to arrive at the correct conclusion

---

[1] *Correspondance et Mémoires inédits du Cardinal Maury* (1891), Vol. 1, p. 35. From Coblentz he had written on November 7, 1791, 'I have made every effort to bring together Coblentz and the Tuileries; we must hope that that understanding, which is so necessary, will take place' (De Richemont, *op. cit.*, p. 518).

that the Pope was lending his moral support to the plans of the
Austro-Prussian alliance to rescue Louis XVI and Marie-Antoinette
from the Revolution.

However, the French won.

The alliance had failed, and the subsequent coalition proved in-
effective against armies defending French territory and fighting on
interior lines. Prussia, then Austria, became preoccupied with par-
titioning Poland; Spain, having joined the coalition in 1793, withdrew from it in 1795. By the spring of 1796 the outlook had entirely
changed. The Revolution had secured itself at home and had beaten
off the attempts from abroad to maintain legitimacy; assuming the
offensive, it had carried its new message to the Scheldt and to the
Rhine. And now – even more interesting to Rome – it was about to
descend into the plain of Lombardy, led by the youngest of the new
generals, Napoleon Bonaparte.

With Bonaparte's invasion the Revolution made its effective
entry into Italy. But as an ideology it had entered earlier. Milan,
lying at the foot of the principal Alpine passes, the city most susceptible to the new ideas from the north, was already sufficiently
enlightened to harbour a coterie of intellectuals amongst whom the
Corsican general would find in Melzi d'Eril a congenial spirit
whom he would use as organizer of a new republic.

The soil of Rome was less well prepared. It was not, however,
free from 'infection' because it harboured so many colonies of
writers, students, and artists, from different countries, and in no age
are such people easily controlled, ideologically speaking. Pius VI
had done his best. He had adhered to the ban imposed by his predecessors on the Freemasons – the chief source of revolutionary
political ideas in the eighteenth century – and he had maintained
the customary censorship over books and periodicals. All the same
he was a man of considerable culture as well as courtesy, who enjoyed extending a welcome at Rome to the great literary luminaries
of the age, and it was not practicable for him to enquire too closely
about the speculations into which fashionable Roman intellectual
society had been led by a visiting Goethe or by a freethinker like the

Spanish ambassador Azara. Amongst the foreign colonies in Rome much the most vigorous and advanced was the French Academy in the Corso. Imbued with the fashionable Parisian spirit of mockery, it was already a problem, before the Revolution, to the Cardinal de Bernis at his palace near by; after the Revolution, and especially after France had dethroned and executed her king, its romantic republicanism knew no bounds. Not unnaturally the Romans, though ready enough to lampoon the papal government in their pasquinades, and splendidly sceptical about the efficiency and honesty of the administration, disliked having their ruler attacked by foreigners. And especially they disliked being criticized or instructed by the French – their common Latin background made them take the French seriously, whereas to the Germans or the British they extended the warmth of their hospitality but seldom the subtle intercourse of their ideas.

The early months of the Revolution had already produced some sharp reactions in Rome. The French students had formed a Masonic Lodge, promptly suppressed by the police. The charlatan Cagliostro had acquired a following, prophesied the impending collapse of the papacy, and been duly shut up in the Sant' Angelo. Some Frenchmen had misbehaved in Saint Peter's at Christmas; banned from subsequent ceremonies, they had recompensed themselves by appearing in the streets sporting tricolour cockades. And so it had continued; there were scuffles in the streets, protests, occasional expulsions. But in the winter of 1791–92 the situation became more serious on account of the papal denunciation of the Civil Constitution, the French seizure of Avignon, the burning of the Pope in effigy in Paris, the withdrawal of the Papal Nuncio from France, and the persecution of the French priests. The feelings of the Romans became embittered against the Revolution by the arrival of the destitute immigrant clergy from France, in ever increasing numbers, till they totalled some 5,000. For these, and for their secular companions in misfortune, the Papal government (more efficient in works of charity than in the ordinary business of governmental administration) organized the *Opera pia della ospitalità francese*, which distributed the refugees over the whole territory according to the extent to which the various monasteries, convents or diocesan institutions expressed their willingness to receive them. Much of the money needed was raised by making another raid on the convenient 'treasure of Sixtus V'. Meanwhile the more aristocratic émigrés, including two aunts of Louis XVI, settled down in Rome; Roman notions about life in revolutionary Paris gained some vivid colouring from their accounts.

With the establishment of the French Republic in August 1792 the tension in Rome increased further[1] and anxiety grew as it became clear that the Austro-Prussian alliance, despite the encouragement given to it by Cardinal Maury, would not succeed in slaying the dragon. A flamboyant letter was received from that gesture-loving citizeness Madame Roland. It warned the 'Prince-Bishop of Rome' that the 'centuries of ignorance' were over; men henceforth were going to be 'ruled only by conviction, led by truth, and bound together by their own good'; the French Republic was raising its voice 'in the name of justice, the arts, reason, and the nation'. It was time for the Pope to return to the 'disinterested profession of the evangelical principles'.[2]

To help him to do so there had arrived in Rome a young man, Hugon de Bassville, who was evangelically devoid of office or rank, save that of secretary to the French envoy at Naples. In the true spirit of equality he had placed himself on an equal footing in Rome with that of the ambassadors, had patronized the veteran Spanish ambassador Azara, and had made a quantity of demands on the Papal government, including one for the release of certain French students imprisoned for disturbances. Since the French fleet was known to be cruising about in the Tyrrhenian sea, and was expected at any time to make a descent on the coasts of the Papal States, he was granted most of his demands. He only came seriously

---

[1] The Congregation of State was meeting every few days, and was passing a bewildering series of resolutions to the Secretary of State, Cardinal Zelada, for execution. They range from a general levy of gold and jewelry (except that in the churches) to the strengthening of the locks on the doors of the French Academy in the Corso. More Swiss are to be recruited, a new galley is to be built, the coastal fortifications are to be looked to, and those of the Sant' Angelo. Foundries are to be set up at Rome and an arsenal at the Vatican. But the orders mostly concern imprisonment of suspects, or releases following pressure from the French. (Vat. Arch. *Epoca Napoleonica Italia.* Busta VI, Fasc 4.)

[2] Pastor, Vol. XL, p. 232.

up against the government when he insisted on replacing the fleurs de lys, on the various French buildings in Rome, by the emblem of the new French Republic, a figure of Liberty wearing the Phrygian cap. To this action, however logical, the Papal government took the gravest exception, both because the display of such emblems in Rome constituted and was intended to constitute an ideological challenge, and because Rome still recognized Louis XVI as King of France. Moreover the papal emblems had already been pulled down in Paris.

In January 1793 Bassville was joined at Rome by a French naval officer from Naples, La Flotte, whose high spirits had the effect of removing such vestiges of commonsense as the unofficial ambassador had hitherto shown. The two representatives of the French Republic now decided to drive down the Corso in an open carriage, with a few friends, and with Bassville's wife and child, the whole party sporting tricolour cockades and waving republican flags. This proved altogether too much for the Romans. Stones were thrown, and Bassville was chased into a courtyard and stabbed. La Flotte managed to dive through a window and later escaped with Bassville's family; but Bassville died two days later renouncing – rather surprisingly – with his dying breath, the Civil Constitution of the Clergy, so that he might receive the Last Sacraments. Technically, then, he can hardly be said to have died a martyr to the new faith which it was his object to further at Rome; but that did not prevent his being declared to be such in Paris. The new French envoy to Rome, François Cacault, was instructed to present humiliating demands for apology and compensation; but the Pope would not receive him.

There was no immediate sequel to these events because the early months of 1793 were an anxious time for the French Republic. Confronted by the First Coalition she was in no position to pursue her vendetta with Rome. As the summer progressed the tension in the city relaxed because the French navy had disappeared, being penned into Toulon by the British. But the respite was brief. The French successes in Belgium in 1794 (which brought into that country the full force of the anti-clerical legislation, with much plunder of Church property) and French penetration of the

G

Catholic Rhineland provided bleak news for Rome. Bleaker still was the separate peace made by Prussia in the following year and, even worse, by Spain; the understanding reached by the Spanish and French governments had the frightening effect of driving the British navy back upon Gibraltar, thus exposing the coast-line of the Papal States once again to the French.[1]

So when Bonaparte crushed the Piedmontese army in the spring of 1796 and made his way into Austrian Milan in May the Papal States lay wide open to the French, with no protection save some useless and expensive fortifications at Cività Vecchia, a handful of ill-paid soldiers, and a few Swiss Guards. The general had been invited by his government to destroy the 'centre of fanaticism' and to avenge Bassville. So on May 21, from Milan, he made a speech calculated to satisfy Paris, implying his intention of marching on Rome, and making suitable references to Brutus, to whom the French students in the Corso were busy putting up a statue to replace the one of Louis XIV which they had destroyed. Bonaparte would 'free the Roman people from their long slavery' – but not, it seemed, just yet. For although it would be easy enough for him to march on Rome, the Austrian withdrawal from Milan did not

---

[1] Both Austria and England complained that the Pope had not given much help. But in February 1794 Zelada had outlined the papal position in the following terms: 'The Pope, as Common Father of the Faithful, must strive for the conversion, not the death of him who has become an enemy of Religion and of the Church, and for this purpose must not use arms other than those given to him by his supreme spiritual authority. This special authority, which must always be linked with his temporal power, means that as sovereign of his states, he ought to try in every way to guard and defend them against invasion but not to carry the terror, desolation and horrors of war into other countries.' Logical or illogical, this was in fact the line followed by the papacy throughout the disturbed events in Italy of the time of Napoleon, the Concert of Europe, and the Risorgimento. To the British government it seemed that, if the Pope was not in a position to help the allies materially, he might at least give them his spiritual blessing. Zelada's reply to this suggestion was perhaps ironical, seeing that the suggestion came from London: 'It is true that there was a time when the voice of the Roman Pontiff was heard, respected, and obeyed; now (it must be said with feelings of the deepest grief) it is scarcely ever listened to, and never has any effect.' It is better, he argues, for Rome to stick to neutrality in the European conflict – and this was the line which she maintained both with Napoleon (who was only excommunicated when he seized the Papal States) and with the Concert of Europe, from which she withheld her blessing. (Vat. Arch. *Epoca Napoleonica Italia.* Busta VI, Fasc.5.)

mean that Austria had ceased to be a danger to him. It was court-
ing military disaster for him to march down the peninsula in
sufficient strength to deal with the Neapolitan army (which was
showing signs of coming to the support of the Pope) while leaving
the Austrian army in his rear. So he only overran the Legations
(Ravenna, Ferrara, and Bologna) which he could conveniently add
to the new Republic he was forming at Milan; after doing this he
concluded an armistice at Bologna. It was negotiated with the
Spanish ambassador, Azara, who acted on behalf of the Pope
because Rome still did not recognize the French Republic and
because Spain had undertaken, when she made peace with France
in the previous year, to act on behalf of the Holy See in her business
with Paris. The armistice gave the French the Legations of Ravenna
and Bologna, also Ancona, and the right of entry into any of the
Pope's ports. It also gave them 21,000,000 crowns, 100 works of
art, and 500 manuscripts. The terms were severe; but it was not
yet annihilation for Rome.

That shrewd old cynic Azara, the most experienced statesman at
Rome since the death of Cardinal Bernis in 1794, who now exerted
an influence over papal policy greater than was exerted by any
member of the Pope's own government, understood what was the
real situation. So long as the Austrians remained in the mountains
above Lake Garda, and a garrison of 15,000 of them still held the
key fortress of Mantua, Bonaparte would not undertake the march
on Rome; but if once that threat were removed he would be able
to dictate what terms he chose to the Pope. Neither Azara nor anybody else could be sure what the outcome of the war in Lombardy
would be, for the Austrian position was geographically strong,
and the armies which general Würmser was organizing in the
mountain passes would outnumber Bonaparte's by almost two to
one. The Papal government, after again raiding the treasure of
Sixtus V to pay the first instalment of the indemnity, began to be
hopeful that Würmser would win, and held back on further surrenders required by the armistice; paintings which had been packed
up for despatch to Paris were unpacked once more. And as the
military difficulties of the French became yet more apparent the
new Papal Secretary of State, Cardinal Busca, who had succeeded

the aged Cardinal Zelada in August 1796, set to work with vast
energy, but with less wisdom, to raise a respectable army. The only
chance of success, militarily speaking, lay in securing the support
of the Neapolitan army which, if backed by something like a
levée-en-masse of the population of the Papal States – a Vendée, as it
was said – might perhaps have been able to embarrass Bonaparte
while the Austrians mustered in his rear. But that was never
achieved because the many points of quarrel between Rome and
Naples, dating from the days of Tanucci, had not been resolved,
and confidence and co-operation between the two governments
were quite lacking. The ultimate salvation of the Eternal City may
indeed have owed more (it could hardly have owed less) to just
those efforts of spiritual intercession which so infuriated the cynical
Azara than it did to any military planning. The forty-hour prayers
and other intercessions organized throughout the city, which have
provoked the mirth of many historians, at least tended towards a
stronger spirituality in Rome which would make it easier, in the
long run, for the saintly Pius VII to take up his place there in the
year 1800, and to be restored to the whole of his states in 1815.

But this is to anticipate. In the year 1796 the rather hectic efforts
of Cardinal Busca to raise an army to defend the papal territories
were even more obviously futile, in the face of Bonaparte, than the
similar efforts of Mgr de Mérode were to prove, in 1860, when he
tried to defend those states against the Piedmontese. If the Papal
government's civil administration was inefficient, its military
administration was even worse. Whatever the justification, in the
special case of Rome, for a theocratic government, theocracies are
not seen at their best when they are waging war.

As the Austrian armies, intended by Würmser for the relief of
Mantua, descended on either side of Lake Garda, Bonaparte was
hard pressed; as they scanned their news-sheets the Romans held
their breath. For the young French general it proved a close thing;
but in this classic campaign he was saved by his mobility, which
enabled him to tackle the opposing armies singly. When his victory
at Rivoli compelled Würmser to surrender Mantua (February 2,
1797) Bonaparte had not only secured the Milanese against
Austria, he had put the Pope at his mercy. This fact General Colli,

Austrian commander of the Papal forces, quickly appreciated, and the opposition he offered was negligible. Almost unopposed the French advanced to Ancona, then moved inland, picking up at Loretto what remained of the treasure bestowed on the famous shrine – the government had managed to remove most of it to safety. At Tolentino, on February 17, Bonaparte met Cardinal Mattei and the Pope's nephew, Duke Braschi. There was little the Roman delegates could do but accept his terms; yet on one significant point they proved obdurate. The general suggested that in future France, and France alone, should enjoy the 'Exclusive' (the right of veto at a Papal election) and that she should enjoy it even after the cardinals had made their choice. This the Papal delegation rejected as being a demand made on the spiritual as distinct from the temporal power, and therefore impermissible. They were there to consider the future of the Papal States, not of the papacy. Bonaparte grudgingly agreed, and proceeded to dictate his temporal terms. These proved to be an aggravation of the conditions of the Bologna armistice; Rome must recognize the cession to France of Avignon and the Comtat Venaissin, and yield Ferrara as well as the other two legations. She must also pay a further 15,000,000 crowns and hand over some more works of art. Onerous conditions, yet the really significant thing about the settlement at Tolentino was that Bonaparte made it at all, that even now he did not march on and occupy Rome. The Directors at the head of the government at Paris had the idea that it would be quite easy to wind up the Papal government altogether and to establish a Roman Republic under French tutelage, and certainly they were to achieve this easily enough in the following year. But Bonaparte thought an occupation of Rome would have to be undertaken in force, that it would bring no military advantages, and that his army would become tied down, keeping order in the Papal States, so that he would be prevented from securing his hold on northern Italy, which could only be achieved by his pushing on to a final settlement with Austria.

It is interesting too to notice that Bonaparte did not see the Roman question from the same ideological angle as did the politicians in Paris. The Directory (especially the Director

Rewbell), being imbued with a sense of their own enlightenment, thought that the advantages to be gained by overthrowing the 'Prince of Darkness' would be overwhelming. It would set the seal of success, in the new Europe, on their Revolution, ushering in unmistakably the reign of Liberty, Equality, Fraternity, and the rest. They also thought, in more practical terms, that the security of their own régime would best be advanced by eliminating its most obstinate opponent, an opponent who, however weak, could not be expected to rest until the independent spiritual authority of the Church in France had been reasserted.

But where the more philosophically minded Directors saw a clear conflict of principle, a new moral allegiance which they were trying to create by destroying the old one, Bonaparte was already thinking more in terms of power than of principle. He was, after all, a soldier. He was beginning, certainly, to be a politician, signing treaties on his own initiative and planning the creation of new republics in Italy. But all this was within a strictly military context. Austria remained the enemy because her army remained formidable; if there were to be French satellite states in northern Italy they could only be set up against the background of a defeated Austria, an Austria induced to give up the attempt to try conclusions with the French in Lombardy. Soon his sense of *realpolitik* would induce him to give Venice to Vienna, as compensation for her losses elsewhere; the arrangement might not harmonize very well with the revolutionary principle of the freedom of peoples but it would certainly be convenient.

The same sort of thinking governed his approach to Rome. The Papal States concerned him, but for different reasons from those which made them interesting to his government. He did not see them as something to be destroyed because, as the Directors told him, they were a 'scourge in the hands of fanaticism'. His interest in them was practical and military. He wanted the legations because geography and economic interest made them face towards the north, where he could embody them in his new republic. And he wanted, for military reasons, to control the papal ports, Ancona on the east coast and Cività Vecchia on the west. But he was not interested, as were French enthusiasts both at Rome and at Paris, in the sporting of republican cockades on the Corso, in setting up a statue of Brutus on the Janiculum, or in planting a Tree of Liberty on the Capitol. He could see that such antics would exasperate not only the Romans but also the underground Catholic opposition in France, Belgium, and especially northern Italy, which he was planning to reconcile; and he could not see their military advantages.

CHAPTER SIX

The Revolution in Power at Milan and at Rome

In so far as Bonaparte was yet concerning himself seriously with the Roman religion, in which his mother had educated him, it was from an angle which differed markedly from the one which the Revolution had made fashionable at Paris. Whether that religion was true or false, Christ or anti-Christ, superseded or perennial, was not a question he asked himself. What interested him was that it was a fact. He had noticed that the Faith was tenacious – the lesson of the Vendée was not lost on him. And he had found Italy saturated in it. His policy in that country, from the first, indicated that he did not think it made political or military sense to oppose the Roman religion à l'outrance, as his government wanted him to.

We find him, in 1796, working quite amicably with the rather intransigent Cardinal Archbishop of Ferrara, Mattei, with whom he signed the treaty of Tolentino in the following February, and giving him assurances, in which there was more than a grain of truth, that if only they could see things aright at Rome they would realize that he was no ogre but really their friend. He notes with approval that, during the disturbances and fighting, the Cardinal Bishop of Imola, Chiaramonti (the future Pope Pius VII), had remained at his post and co-operated with the revolutionary authorities of the Cispadane Republic, and he recommends the same behaviour to the Archbishop of Ancona, who had fled as the French armies approached. He spends a long time examining the wonder-working statue of Our Lady at Ancona, and having decided that there is no fake mechanism connected with it restores to the neck the string of fine pearls he has removed from it.[1] In short he was looking at the Roman religion in Italy, looking at it

[1] Artaud de Montor, *Histoire du Pape Pie VII* (Paris, 1837), Vol. I, pp. 28–30.

dispassionately, and coming to the conclusion that it was a force not to be destroyed but to be enlisted in his support.

It seemed a more constructive approach than the Revolution had yet shown. But was it really a more perceptive one?

In one sense the fanatics at Paris showed a shrewder understanding of the reality than did the general. For they were right in supposing that the Roman religion was irreconcilable with the naturalism and pantheism on which they sought to base a new society. And the general was wrong (when he later became First Consul and then Emperor) in supposing he could so gain control over the Church as to make her his servant. Her enemies sometimes understood her better than did her patrons. In the long run she could no more stand in permanent subjection to a new Emperor of the French than she could stand in subjection to an old Emperor of Austria. Rousseau, Diderot, d'Alembert before the Revolution; Hébert, Chaumette, Larevellière, Rewbell as the Revolution ran its course, were at least paying Rome the compliment of recognizing her authority as a rival to their own. They understood that her principles were irreconcilable with those on which they intended to refashion society. By contrast Joseph II of Austria and Napoleon both supposed that they could take the Church under their wing, that they could run her to suit their own convenience.

During those summer months of the year 1797, when the young general 'held court' with Josephine at the palace of Mombello outside Milan, we see a curious curtain-raiser, in his relations with the Church, to what would come later when he had won supreme power at Paris. The Cisalpine Republic, which he had constituted in May, he extended in July to embrace the three legations which he had taken from the Papal States. It was his own creation; he appointed its five Directors, its Council of Seniors, and its Council of Juniors; and he remained on the spot, himself, till November, lest they should not do what he wanted. So in this small but important experimental State, with its $3\frac{1}{2}$ million inhabitants, Catholic in tradition, we first see him, as a civil ruler, confronting the Church. And on the opposite side we see three Cardinals, namely the Archbishops of Ferrara and Bologna, and the Bishop of

Imola. And the special interest of the situation arises from the fact
that the Bishop of Imola was Cardinal Chiaramonti, who in three
years' time would become Pope Pius VII and confront Napoleon
on a wider stage.

The two archbishops fought the new régime at every step.
Chiaramonti, on the other hand, co-operated with it. As Bishop of
Imola this quiet Benedictine showed already the balance he would
later display as an example to the world, a balance which enabled
him to combine proper respect for any existing civil government
with an absolute spiritual integrity. Whereas his brother Cardinals
at Ferrara and Bologna declared the secularist and egalitarian constitution of the new Cisalpine Republic to be incompatible with the
rights of the Catholic Church Chiaramonti, at Imola, accepted that
constitution and tried to 'baptize' it.[1] It was his way. In the previous
year, when Bonaparte had first invaded Lombardy, and Chiaramonti's diocese had fallen under the French, the Cardinal had told
his flock to accept the new order, and had tried to dissuade those
who had staged a futile revolt against it. For this he had been called
a Jacobin; but his real objectives were calm, order, and mercy, as
he showed when he pleaded with the brutal French General
Augereau for the lives of those captured leaders of the revolt who
had ignored his own advice. When the constitution of the Cisalpine
Republic abolished all titles and privileges he was ready to give up

---

[1] What follows is based on (1) the papers in the Vatican Archives (*Ep. Nap.
Italia*, Busta IX, Fasc. 1. *Carteggio del Governo Cisalpino al Sig. Card. Chiaramonti,
Vescovo d'Imola*) and (2) on the information given by J. Leflon in his article *Le
Cardinal Chiaramonti, évêque d'Imola, et la République Cisalpine*, in the *Rassegna
Storica del Risorgimento* (Fasc. III, 1956) which makes use of the archives of the
French Ministry of War. On this information the French historian has since com-
mented more fully in chapters VI–X of his *Pie VII*, Vol. 1 (Plon, 1958).

The attitude of the more conservative bishops in the Cisalpine towards the constitution of that republic was summed up by the Archbishop of Bologna in a letter
in the Vatican *Carteggio* referred on August 22, 1797, to the Congregation di
Pietro. He complains that it says 'nothing about the Catholic religion, treating all
religious attitudes as the same . . . so extends the idea of equality that the idea given
us by the Gospel and by Tradition of the aristocratic-monarchical government of
the Church is eliminated . . . is best suited to a republic of unbelievers, the Jew, the
Gentile, and the Heretic enjoying equal authority . . . thinks little or nothing of
good customs; rather seems to desire their destruction by permitting free speech,
writing, printing'.

his estates, to abandon his title of Monsignor, and to style himself Citizen-Cardinal. He saw that these things did not matter. What mattered was to save the essentials. Moreover he thought that the principles of the Revolution could be interpreted in a Christian sense, a belief which he illustrated rather amusingly by heading his note-paper with 'Liberty' in the left-hand corner and 'Equality' in the right, only insisting on putting in the centre not 'Fraternity' but 'And Peace in Our Lord Jesus Christ'. In this odd and rather disarming way he symbolized his attempt to reconcile the Revolution with religion. In his view the Church could have no quarrel with political liberty or with social equality; but for fraternity – i.e. for the ideal of society held together only by the bond of natural human affection – he preferred to substitute the peace of God, or the bond which arose from being His children.

In practice the Cardinal found there were two principal occasions when he was in difficulty in trying to collaborate with the French. One was when they tried to introduce into Italy something analogous to the Civil Constitution of the Clergy, excluding the Pope from his canonical investiture of the bishops and from all other rights in the Cisalpine Church, and introducing election of parish priests. This was a rather arbitrary and doctrinaire enterprise on the part of the new régime; by the year 1797 even the government at Paris had lost its interest in establishing this kind of a Church. Chiaramonti, perhaps aware that Bonaparte's heart was not in the matter, and certainly knowing that it was quite impracticable to introduce such a system in a hurry into the Milanese or the Legations, turned a blind eye to what was proposed. He contented himself with affirming that perceptive men, like the new Directors of the Cisalpine, who professed themselves so solicitous for the dogmas and discipline of the Catholic Church, would be sure to appreciate that her reorganization must rest with her own ecclesiastical hierarchy. Had the Cisalpine lasted longer this mixture of flattery and resistance might not have continued to satisfy the Milanese Directors. As it was, however, it sufficed until the wheel of political change at Milan moved on to its next position.

The other main occasion of conflict proved more difficult for the Cardinal to handle. The government decided to adopt the French

Declaration of the Rights of Man, proclaiming religious indifference on the part of the State, disestablishing the Catholic Church, and putting every sect, Christian, non-Christian, and anti-Christian, on a footing of absolute equality. In December 1797 the Cardinal was required to lend his support to this move by publishing a pastoral letter which would show that 'the spirit of the gospel is founded on the maxims of Liberty, Equality and Fraternity, and is in no wise contrary to Democracy'. It was a requirement which his brother-cardinal Mattei at Ravenna met with a blank refusal. Chiaramonti, however, in a Christmas homily which later became famous, set himself to show that, if only they were properly understood in a Christian sense, there was nothing irreconcilable between the new revolutionary ideas and those of the Church. And taking his argument a stage further he insisted that the new ideas could only be carried out effectively if they were interpreted in a Christian sense. He had been told to demonstrate that the gospel was founded upon the maxims of liberty, equality and fraternity and was in no wise contrary to democracy; very well, he would invert the demand and show that liberty, equality, fraternity and democracy could only be founded on Christianity. And he would take his argument a step further; he would show that of all kinds of society a democratic one was the kind which stood most urgently in need of the supernatural graces of the Church. For under the ancien régime, he pointed out, a man had only been obliged to obey the government blindly, whereas in a republican democracy a higher degree of virtue was called for on the part of the citizen. In the place of absolutism and obedience democracy put the voluntary principle, free will exercising choice in the making of the laws. And precisely because of this new responsibility supernatural grace and the guidance of the Church were more necessary than ever. It was all very well, as was the fashion of the times, to praise the ancient Laws of Solon, or the days of the Roman Republic; but democracy in ancient times had failed for lack of Christian baptism. In other words the Revolution, far from superseding the Church, had made her more necessary than ever: 'Ordinary virtue might, perhaps, suffice to guarantee the lasting prosperity of other forms of government. Our form requires something more. Strive to attain to the full height of virtue and you will be true democrats. Fulfil faithfully the precepts of the gospel and you will be the joy of the Republic. Be good Catholics, and you will be good democrats.'[1]

This homily, published by the future Pius VII, has some claim to be regarded as one of the key documents of modern Catholic history. For in the eighteenth century the assumptions of Bossuet, who had taken it for granted that monarchical government was of divine right, had held the field amongst orthodox Catholics. It is true that the constitutional bishops in France had also accepted the 'principles of 1789'; but then they had gone too far and lost sight of the unity and authority necessary to the Church. Chiaramonti, abandoning inessential externals, and turning a blind eye towards the endless insults of the revolutionaries, accepted their political and social democracy but at the same time affirmed, à l'outrance, the absolute need of the supernatural grace and spiritual guidance of which the Church was custodian, and therefore the need for her to be independent in her organization and spiritual authority. He foreshadowed the line of liberal Catholic thought in the nineteenth century, being echoed by Bishop Dupanloup of Orleans when he cried: 'We accept, we invoke, the principles and the liberties proclaimed in '89. . . . You made the revolution of 1789 without us and against us, but for us, God wishing it so in spite of you', and by Montalembert who, in his speech at the Malines Congress of 1863, quoted these words of Dupanloup, and expressed exactly Chiaramonti's thought by saying: 'The more one is a democrat the more it is necessary to be a Christian; the fervent and practical cult of God made man is the indispensable counter-weight of that perpetual tendency of democracy to establish the cult of man believing himself God.'[2] Even more interesting, the bearing of Chiaramonti at Imola under the Revolution was to prove the inspiration of a later Bishop of Imola, a bishop who, like Chiaramonti, would be elected Pope, and would take the name of Pius in honour of his

---

[1] The Bishop sent four copies of his homily, which was printed on sixteen quarto pages, to the Commissioners of the Executive for the organization of Emilia. There is a copy in the Vatican Archives (*Ref. Cit.*).

[2] C. de Montalembert, *L'Église libre dans l'État libre*, Paris, 1863, p. 55.

predecessor Pius VII. Pius IX, in his early years as 'the liberal Pope', was inspired by the sympathies of Chiaramonti, just as later, in the time of his troubles, he would repeat the very words used by Pius VII in his afflictions.

Chiaramonti's Christmas homily of 1797 has, then, its place in history. But it would be a mistake to claim for it any very great importance at the time it was issued. It merely outlined a *modus vivendi* for the Church in the Cisalpine during the brief eighteen months of life which remained to that republic. When the Austrians returned and occupied northern Italy in 1799, while Bonaparte was in Egypt, the homily was quietly forgotten. And so far as it was remembered at Rome when the Cardinal became Pope in 1800 it was generally held against him, especially when he became suspect with the conservatives by signing the Concordat with Napoleon and when he went to Paris to crown him. The view of Barruel that the Revolution was satanic had been repeated by de Maistre,[1] and was the view generally adopted at Rome; and when Napoleon later kidnapped and imprisoned the Pope its validity seemed to be confirmed. When the life of Pius VII came to be published in 1837 by Artaud de Montor the biographer tried to explain away the passages in the homily on the subject of the revolution and democracy. He thought they had been inserted by the hands of others who were anxious to please the French. '. . . *les hommes timides qui environnaient le cardinal ont pris ici la plume des mains de son Éminence.*'[2] There is no reason to suppose that that was so; these passages in the homily represent a point of view entirely characteristic of Chiaramonti ever since the time when, as a young man, he had begun his active life by defending the novices of a monastery in Rome against the oppressive rule of their masters.

The practical significance of the Cardinal's attitude at the time lay in the indirect influence it may be assumed to have had on Bonaparte. We need not suppose that the young general ever read the homily – indeed he had left for Paris during the month before it was published. But because its author was stamped as a liberal (in the parlance of the time such men were classed as 'patriots', to dis-

---

[1] *Considérations sur La France*, 1796, chapter 5.
[2] Vol. 1, p. 68.

tinguish them from the 'aristocrats'[1]) Bonaparte, when he returned
from Egypt, would be encouraged to open negotiations with him
for a new concordat with France.

By comparison with these suggestive events in the Cisalpine
Republic, which seemed to imply not only that a *modus vivendi*
could be found between the Church and the Revolution but that,
with a proper understanding on both sides, their marriage might
benefit both, the events in this same year (1797) at Rome were
banal. The Revolution, when it chose, could harmonize its principles with those of the Church, and greatly gain by doing so.
What the Revolution could not do was to harmonize itself with
Rome. For the Revolution was republican and Rome, at this date,
was regal. The Pope was not only Head of the Church but a
temporal sovereign, with a principality and a court. However carefully he might keep the door open for a settlement with the
Republic about Church affairs in France he could not disguise his
sentiments nor cease to protect the royal and aristocratic émigrés.
The blade which severed the head of Louis XVI severed, too, all
bonds of sympathy between the Pope and the new rulers. As far
back as the year 1793 he had referred to the executed king as a
martyr and had arranged for the veteran Cardinal Bernis (no longer
French ambassador but belonging, like Louis XV's two nieces, to
the respected group of French aristocratic émigrés at Rome) to say
a Requiem Mass for him at the Quirinal. Nor was monarchical
sentiment at Rome confined to the Curia. So great a popular
indignation was felt in the city when the execution at Paris of Marie
Antoinette followed that of her husband that precautionary police
measures had to be taken to protect the French artists and students
there.

The assassination of Bassville by the Roman mob had occurred
as far back as 1793. Paris had been in no position at the time to
avenge her unofficial envoy, but she made a martyr of him, which
set him off suitably against the martyr-king. Meanwhile 'avenging
Bassville' had become an ideal nursed in revolutionary circles by

[1] Chiaramonti had already been listed as a 'patriot' by Bonaparte's agents (cf.
Leflon's *Rassegna* article, p. 427).

those who wanted to see Bonaparte take his army to Rome. In the city itself this ideal was shared mainly by the French revolutionary colony, centred on the French Academy at the Palazzo Salviati in the Corso, and by the limited number of Italian Jacobins who attached themselves to the French. Those responsible for policy, on both sides, showed a marked desire to maintain the peace, the French ambassador, François Cacault, trying to interpret in a humane manner the mortifying stipulations of the treaty of Tolentino concerning the seizure of Roman works of art, and both Pope and cardinals showing a commendable zeal in stripping themselves of their jewelry to pay the French indemnity. But with the removal of Cacault in August, and the appearance of Joseph Bonaparte as ambassador at the Corsini palace in the Trastevere, French propaganda acquired a more significant centre and more effective backing – even though Joseph himself seemed inclined to discourage the extremists.

The mood of the Romans now became more receptive to the French propaganda; they were losing confidence in the power of the papal government to protect them.[1] When the Secretary of State, Cardinal Busca, in 1796 had been doubling the army, encouraging a *levée en masse* to oppose the French, and making forty-hour devotions the order of the day, the *élan* of it all had carried the crowd along. But since Tolentino the whole situation had been reversed. Cardinal Busca himself had been compelled to resign, at the instigation of Azara, who resented the Cardinal's criticisms of

[1] But the most useful analysis which we have of Roman opinion at this time, that of V. E. Giuntella *La Giacobina Repubblica Romana* in *Archivio della Società romana di storia patria*, Vol. LXXIII (1950), suggests (p. 5) that it was still in sympathy with the papal régime. 'The population of the ex-Papal States, in the great majority, and that of Rome in particular, was faithful to the old régime. They delighted themselves in mockery and satire, which spared nobody, not even the sovereign, but they were certainly not disposed to see in the mild old invalid, who was Pius VI in the last years of his pontificate, the despotic tyrant of the vociferous exhortations of the Jacobins.' After describing the preoccupation of the Roman population with pleasure, Giuntella adds: 'The French revolution had upset this lazy and attractive way of life, and the advance of the French soldiers south of the Alps had set up a condition of fear and irritation. The various outbreaks of violence at Rome against the French, even the episode of Bassville itself, were the expression of popular reaction against the threatening novelties – an attempt to ward off by violence the feared crisis.'

his own efforts to act as mediator between Rome and Paris. The new Secretary, Cardinal Doria (known, for his small stature, as the 'Pope's Brief'), made it his object to appease the French. The efforts of the previous year, together with the French occupation of the provinces and their exactions all had to be paid for, with consequent increase in taxation and a further decline in the value of the paper money. The Pope was both old and ill, and his government seemed to be becoming powerless not only to protect but also to provide for its subjects. The port of Ancona, released in October by the French, voted itself an independent republic. It was becoming difficult to see how the temporal power could survive in an Italy which was everywhere beginning to plant trees of liberty, and the French in Rome, now freely sporting their republican cockades and ridiculing the government, acquired an Italian following more substantial than they had enjoyed five years earlier when Bassville had driven down the Corso.

And now a new Bassville was at hand in the more elegant shape of General Duphot, a friend of Joseph Bonaparte, and his guest at the Corsini palace. Generals were young in that decade; Duphot was only twenty-eight, and he was engaged to Joseph's sister-in-law Désirée, who was also a guest at the Corsini. Another guest was Napoleon's brother-in-law, Eugène de Beauharnais. These attractive representatives of the revolutionary power acted like a magnet on the Roman Jacobins two bands of whom made their way to the Corsini on December 28, 1797. The first was sent packing by the ambassador, who correctly went to report the affair to Cardinal Doria. The second was more successful, penetrating into the palace gardens, whereupon the papal dragoons (part of a force called up by Cardinal Consalvi – the future Secretary of State – to maintain order in the city) pushed their way in after the Roman Jacobins. But the latter had now been joined by General Duphot, who helped them to chase the dragoons down to the Porta Settimiana, where the general was hit and killed by a bullet from a papal police post.[1]

[1] Doria had hired a new Austrian general, Provera, to replace the unsuccessful Colli. But, when Joseph Bonaparte protested, Doria proceeded to expel Provera from Rome in November 1797. (Vat. Arch. Ep. Nap. Italia, Busta VI, Fasc. 6.)

H

Though the papal dragoons had put themselves in the wrong by entering the embassy grounds, Duphot had hardly acted correctly in joining the Roman Jacobins in the street. But it was the second time within five years that a prominent Frenchman had been killed in the streets of Rome, and with Désirée lying senseless with grief at the embassy, and Beauharnais at Joseph's elbow to remind him of the conduct to be expected of the Bonaparte family, the ambassador did not hesitate for long. He knew that Paris was only looking for an excuse to overturn the Papal government so, ignoring the advice of Azara, and the apologies tendered by Cardinal Doria, he demanded his passports and left.

He was replaced by General Berthier, at the head of a French army, with orders to occupy Rome, remove the Pope, and set up a Roman Republic. By February 9, 1798, Berthier had reached the outskirts of the city unopposed; there he received Cardinal Doria, the Pope's nephew Duke Braschi, and the Spanish ambassador Azara. Concealing his real intentions, and promising to respect religion, the Pope, and the papal properties, Berthier received from Doria the military surrender of the city. Meanwhile he continued to wait, with this troops, without the gates, for the revolution he was daily expecting would take place within. But nothing happened. Disillusioned he wrote to Bonaparte that only one patriot had come over to him. The Romans, after thronging Saint Peter's and the other major basilicas for a series of intercessionary services, now awaited their fate; but they would not lift a finger for the French.

On February 15, when the cardinals were solemnly celebrating the twenty-third anniversary of the Pope's election, the general allowed his troops to enter. 'I found nothing but stupor, and not a trace of patriotic feeling' he reported to Talleyrand. But the Roman 'patriots' now felt it safe to emerge into the open; mingling with the French troops they applauded Berthier, on the Capitol, as he planted the customary tree of liberty, made suitable references to Cato, Brutus and Pompey, declared the Pope deposed, and accepted an 'Act of the Sovereign People', setting up a consular régime, the document having been hastily drawn up by a scratch gathering of patriots the same morning.

The cardinals who had been taking part in the papal ceremonies that morning were arrested and taken first to a Roman penitentiary and later to Città Vecchia. The French Commissioner Haller (a Swiss banker, who was in charge of the expedition's finances, and therefore its most important figure) bluntly informed the octogenarian Pope that he would have to leave in three days. He claimed the two rings the Pope was wearing, but when Pius explained that he had to retain the Fisherman's, to pass on to his successor, he was allowed to do so although neither Berthier nor his companions believed that there would ever be a successor. When Pius asked to be allowed to die in Rome the general replied: 'One can die anywhere.'[1]

So 'Citizen Pope', with his half paralysed legs, was trundled off, to suffer for eighteen months more and then to die in sordid circumstances at Valence while his books, and his plate, and his sacred vessels were likewise carried away, by the cartload. All he had the chance to do, before he left, was to nominate Cardinal Leonardo Antonelli, and six others, to form a special congregation to deal with immediate business on behalf of the Church.

[1] The most useful contemporary accounts of these events are in the *Diario* of Cardinal Giuseppe Antonio Sala (Vols. 1–3 of the *Scritti di G. Sala*, Ed. Cugnoni, *Società Romana di Storia Patria*, 1891) and in Cardinal Antonelli's unpublished *Relazione sull' avenuto in Roma dal 1797 al 1799* (Rome, *Biblioteca Vallicelliana*, Cat. of MSS Appendix III, Vol. 12). But for further references, and especially Azara's reports, see Pastor, Vol. XL, pp. 329–39.

CHAPTER SEVEN

The Sanfedist Counter-Revolution

The masters of the French Revolution at Rome, a Revolution supposed to eclipse the greatest glories of the ancient Romans, now settled down to exploit for their own benefit, and for the Directory at Paris, the supposedly fabulous wealth of the Eternal City. 'This Babylon', said Haller, 'gorged with the spoils of the universe, must feed us and pay our debts.' But Rome had already had to pay for the efforts of Cardinal Busca to defend her, as also the levies imposed at Bologna and Tolentino. And instead of the usual pilgrims and visitors, who normally brought something into her exchequer, she had harboured from abroad, over the last seven years, only penniless refugees requiring her support. She had taxed her clergy and had raised forced loans from her cardinals. She was now living on an ever depreciating paper currency.

Some spoils of the universe however remained, for there were still the gifts of the devout, who had endowed her many churches with their treasure – offerings of sacred vessels for the altars, or precious stones placed on holy images and relics, treasure which it was sacrilegious to remove. These were now taken from the churches which were rifled as the palaces had already been rifled. It was important for Haller and his friends to hurry, for they knew that fresh commissioners were on their way from Paris. Berthier had been quickly replaced at Rome by the more ruthless Masséna; under him the orgy of spoliation, for a few days, was quite without scruple.

Those on the spot naturally thought first of lining their own pockets. But for the Directory at Paris there was a real problem since there was no money to pay for the armies of occupation – not only for that occupying Rome but for those occupying the rest of Italy. In the Eternal City they had to try to find a new source of supply to replace the dwindling resources of Turin, Genoa, Milan and Bologna.

No doubt the French administration at Rome would have been less scandalous if Bonaparte had made it his concern. Unfortunately Italy was no longer his business; he was preparing to lead his hungry army to fresh fields of corn and treasure in Egypt. Had Rome been his business she might well have been squeezed just as dry (for he had already exploited the north of Italy and would exploit it still more thoroughly after he returned) but at least the French army as a whole might have benefited, and there might have been less wanton impiety. Under the chaotic conditions imposed by an incompetent government at Paris and a rule at Rome divided between Masséna, a host of French commissioners, and some puppet Italian 'consuls', the French soldiers continued to go unpaid and their officers might be seen in rags although a host of parasitic French civilians, outnumbering the army of occupation by two to one, trampled on each other in a scramble to get rich quickly.

The background of exploitation was however obscured by a bright shop-window display of republican emblems, by popular banquets, trees of liberty, statues of liberty, odes to liberty, and greetings across the centuries to the ancient republic of the Gracchi. There were those who enjoyed this heady wine, but the populace of the Trastevere were more concerned about one practical aspect of the new liberalism, namely the emancipation of the Jews. The removal of the traditional restrictions from these potential rivals of the small shop-keepers of the right bank of the river was a measure of immense and unwelcome economic significance to them. Soon they were out uprooting trees of liberty and assassinating any Frenchmen they could find. Some of the penniless French officers fraternized with the Roman malcontents; there was a mass meeting at the Pantheon; but the government, which could not check the speculators and the robbers, could and did check the attempted counter-revolution by means of firing squads in the *Piazza del Popolo*.

In April 1798 Masséna was replaced by a more likeable commander, Gouvion Saint-Cyr. But political power was moving away from the military and into the hands of the commissioners from

Paris, who were working in some sort of collaboration with the Roman consuls, while in the background were bankers and entrepreneurs – notably the Torlonia family – who bought up the confiscated land, property, and such *objets d'art* as were not carried off to Paris. When the artistic treasure of Rome was thus dumped on the market it naturally fetched a poor price; but the Roman government needed ready cash, even if it could only get a little. Times were therefore good for bankers, so long as they were large enough to forward some money to the government and hold on to the splendid security until normalcy should return and better prices be obtainable.

In a milieu of speculators the new military governor stood out as an honest man; but it cost him his position. When he insisted on the return of a valuable gold monstrance which had been seized from Prince Doria the commissioners secured his dismissal. He was succeeded in August by General Macdonald, who wisely refrained from trying conclusions with the commissioners.[1]

While the Romans, for the most part, were settling supinely into some sort of acquiescence in their exploitation, Pius VI was being moved, on June 1, one stage farther away from Rome. He was being carried from Siena, whither he had first been taken, to the Certosa, outside Florence. He was very feeble, and very disinclined to try to carry on any effective government of the Church; only once in his correspondence do we see him roused to anger and resolution, when he refuses the application of two cardinals at Rome (Altieri and Antici) to resign the purple because they find it is making life intolerable for them under the new conditions, and they feel powerless any longer to serve the Church.

Cardinal Antonelli, who was trying in some sort to 'hold the fort' for the Pope at Rome, was endeavouring to secure that at least a skeleton administrative staff, drawn from the *Dateria* (which dealt with the patronage of benefices) and from the Secretariat of Briefs, be moved out of Rome, with their papers, to join the Pope, because he was finding it impossible either to pay or to protect these

[1] Sala's *Diario*, Antonelli's *Relazione*, Giuntella's *Giacobina Repubblica Romana*, and Pastor, Vol. XL, pp. 339–47.

officials at Rome. But he met with little encouragement from Pius, who wanted neither cardinals nor officials around him at Siena and was allowed none by Grand Duke Ferdinand III of Tuscany (for fear of the French) when he was at the Certosa. Antonelli continued to insist that there were two practical matters, at least, with which the Pope should deal, having regard to the future needs of the Church. One was to create new cardinals, because their numbers had now fallen to fifty. The other was to issue instructions that the next Conclave should meet at Venice, to elect the new Pope, that being the Italian city which seemed most likely to enjoy tranquillity and protection since it now belonged to Austria. But the Pope would neither create new cardinals nor change the existing arrange-ments for the Conclave, and according to these arrangements the Cardinal Dean, Albani, with four others, was to make whatever provision seemed best when the time came. The special danger, however, of a French attempt to organize a schismatic Conclave at Rome Pius met in November 1798 by saying in a Bull that the true Conclave would be the one attended by the largest number of cardinals held in the territory of a catholic ruler.[1]

Albani had with him at Naples the largest group of cardinals. They were much less fearful for the future than were those at Rome or those in exile farther north. Although the Emperor Francis II urged that all the cardinals (together with the Pope, if he could escape the clutches of the French) should make their way to Venice, so as to be in readiness for a Conclave there, and although Antonelli urged the same course of action from Rome, and the Pope gave it his tacit support, the cardinals at Naples were altogether disinclined to move and persisted in the attitude that the next Conclave could yet be held at Rome. In this they were fortified by their hosts, the Bourbon King Ferdinand, and his Hapsburg Queen, Maria Carolina. To them the French régimes in northern and central Italy were a bubble which would soon be pricked by an Italian up-rising backed by Austrian and Neapolitan arms, and their optimism was vastly increased when the sensational news arrived that Nelson

[1] For the correspondence of Pope and Cardinals in 1798–99 see Bibl. Vallicel-liana, MSS Appendix III, Vol. 12, pp. 101–114.

had destroyed Bonaparte's ships at Aboukir bay on August 1, 1798.
The British admiral, already the darling not only of the British
ambassador's wife Emma Hamilton but of the Neapolitan court,
had learnt from his royal host the secret of Bonaparte's des-
tination. When he returned, having destroyed the French fleet and
cut off the most effective of French armies, the excitement at Naples
developed to such a pitch that Ferdinand decided to destroy the
Roman Republic and announced in November his intention of
restoring Rome to her rightful sovereign. This rash undertaking,
which meant war on France, did not seem so rash at the time, for
Nelson's victory had brought Turkey, then Russia, and reputedly
Austria into a new coalition against the French. Without waiting
for the Austrians to enter the plain of Lombardy Ferdinand took
the initiative, marching his troops on November 22 under General
Mack (imported from Vienna) straight up to Rome and beyond.
With fifty thousand men behind him Mack had found it easy to enter
Rome, where he and his troops received a delirious ovation. But the
young French general Championnet, sent by the Directory at Paris
to take charge over the head of Macdonald, their military governor
at Rome, knew how to meet the situation. Withdrawing into the
mountains north of Rome he allowed Mack to advance still farther;
then, though he had only 15,000 men, he counter-attacked, and
the Neapolitan army was driven not merely back to Rome but back
to the Neapolitan frontier. Nor did it halt there, but fell back
farther, across the Garigliano river, surrendering even the readily
defensible fortress of Gaeta. Soon it was across the Volturno. Not
till he reached Capua, a mere thirty miles from Naples, did the incompetent Mack, who still commanded an army three times the
size of Championnet's, make his stand; and even there he merely
shut himself in the fortress and waited on events.

They were tumultuous. Ferdinand, his Queen, and their friends,
together with the royal treasure and everything else of value they
could lay hands on in the city, got themselves on board Nelson's
ship the *Vanguard* and sailed for Sicily on December 23. The
Neapolitans were left to their fate.

Then something like a miracle occurred. For a whole month the
lazzaroni of the water-front and the priests and peasants of the

interior put up a resistance to the French which put to shame the miserable showing of the royal family, of the Austrian general, of the Neapolitan army. Not till January 20 did the astonished Championnet make his entry into the city and have the chance to surround himself with a handful of Jacobin 'patriots' and to impose a régime ideologically akin to that of the Roman Republic. As had already occurred at Rome the monasteries and convents were closed, their property was confiscated, and their inmates were 'released' and encouraged to marry. But the exploitation was less gross if only because there was less to exploit, the royal party having already filled two ships with what was most valuable and carried it off to Sicily. Moreover Championnet, though as obsessed with the current revolutionary ideology as were those in power at Rome or at Paris, was a humane man and even something of an idealist. He really believed that a new and better era for mankind was being opened by the satellite republics of the French Revolution and he was determined to add another which should not disgrace the ideals of Liberty, Equality and Fraternity. But he was playing a lone hand. The Directory at Paris did not intend, in the dangerous situation which confronted France in the Mediterranean since the Battle of the Nile, to add another satellite republic. It therefore refused to recognize the new Parthenopean Republic, recalled Championnet at the end of February, and put Macdonald in command of what it openly treated as a French military occupation.

The self-styled Parthenopean Republic lasted for less than six months. On May 7, 1799, Macdonald had to withdraw the French troops from Naples because of developments in the north of Italy where Austro-Russian forces had erased the Cisalpine Republic and threatened to cut the rest of the French in Italy off from France. In the north of the peninsula only Genoa seemed likely to remain in the hands of the French. Macdonald had therefore to beat his retreat as quickly as he could; nor had he only the Austro-Russian forces to fear. Before he abandoned Naples the popular crusade against the French had already begun and their rule, together with that of the Parthenopian republicans, had already ceased over most of the Neapolitan mainland. And as he made his way back through the

Papal States and through Tuscany he found that many places in these territories too were 'up', having thrown out the French and their Italian puppets. In a widespread rising Italians in Tuscany, in the Papal States, and in Naples had demonstrated the hatred which peasant and town-dweller alike felt for the French and for their friends the Italian Jacobins. They hated them for their exploitation, but they also hated them for their insults to religion, for the sacrilege of which they were guilty, and for the new symbols they were setting up. It was a first objective with the counter-revolution to uproot the Trees of Liberty, which were replaced with Crosses, to burn the offensive emblems, to repair the damage in the churches, to reopen the monasteries and convents. Nor was the lesson lost on the French. When Bonaparte restored French power in northern Italy, after his victory at Marengo in 1800, it rested not on a new ideology but on a restored Church.

To be the instrument of the struggle in 1799 against the new secularism in Italy was fashioned a new Congregation, the Congregation of the Holy Faith (the *Sanfedisti*), together with a new body of crusaders, the Army of the Holy Faith. Like the crusaders of old these new crusaders were not too nice in their methods; but then they believed that they were defending the holy emblems of their religion. Their Church had never taught that it was wrong to take up the sword in defence of the rights, liberties, or sacred properties of religion and she was quite prepared to help them to do so now. What could be achieved by peasants, armed with nothing but scythes and shot-guns, and by priests waving crucifixes, had already been shown in the Vendée. How they could drive an army right out of a great country would soon be shown in Spain. And the French generals at Rome had no illusions about what might happen in the provinces of the Papal States, because they had encountered a widespread revolt in the summer of 1798.[1]

The most striking episode in the north, in the counter-revolution of 1799, was the rising at Arezzo, when the Aretini threw out the local French and patriots and advanced across the countryside to Siena, where they placed themselves under the protection of

---

[1] See the graphic account in the *mémoires* of General Thiébault (Plon, 1894), Vol. II, ch. IX.

Archbishop Zondadari, who stood at the centre of a web of Sanfedist organization in Tuscany. This powerful prelate, who had received Pius VI at Siena on his expulsion from Rome, enjoyed a wide influence. He had already used it to persuade the Grand-Duke Ferdinand, at Florence, to withdraw some of his father Leopold's Josephist legislation. At Arezzo, where the Sanfedist uprising had started, his influence was built on the local opposition to the bishop, who was none other than Scipione de Ricci, of Council of Pistoia fame. In short, in the person of Archbishop Zondadari, anti-Jansenist and anti-Jacobin sentiment were combined.

In the Legations, in Umbria, and in the Marches, the local *Sanfedisti* would sometimes enrol under the banner of that strange Spanish figure Giuseppe Lahoz, who tried to unite the opposition to the French with opposition to the Austrians being fired, though a Spaniard, with the ideal of an independent Italy. An heir of Machiavelli's patriotism, and a precursor of Mazzini's, Lahoz yet secured support from the local *Sanfedisti* because he had a place for the Pope and for the Church in his vision of a new Italy; this was a region where that patriot-prince Pope Julius II was a legend still, and where the neo-Guelphs, of Pio Nono's younger days, would later flourish.

Local economic motives played their part in the counter-revolution. The French and Jacobin confiscations might directly have hit only the wealthier classes but they had ruined the traditional patrons of the poor without providing new employment for their dependents. This was particularly the case at Rome. The removal of the Pope and the scattering of the cardinals destroyed the city's principal *raison d'être* and a main source of her interest to foreign visitors. No doubt often the motives of the insurgents would be mixed; but the core of the resistance, in central and southern Italy, to all appearance was religious, and its leaders were often priests. Some were rather surprising priests. Zondadari endeavoured to control the movement in Tuscany from his palace apartments in Siena. By contrast Michele Pezza (the 'Fra Diavolo' of Auber's opera) roamed the Neapolitan countryside like a religious Robin Hood. But the most interesting, as he was also the most effective, Sanfedist leader was Cardinal Ruffo, the man mainly responsible for the overthrow of the Parthenopean Republic in the south.

Fabrizio Ruffo had been Treasurer in the papal government, an office in which he had shown an enlightened zeal (for instance in abolishing internal duties) which had earned him the unpopularity accorded to those who interfere with traditional privileges. Created a cardinal, he had withdrawn to his native kingdom of Naples and attached himself to the Bourbon court. On the arrival of the French he had sailed with the King and Queen to Sicily; but, unlike the court, he did not mean to stay there. Four days were enough for him. At a time when the royal Neapolitan army had been scattered and the royal family had appropriated what remained of the treasure Cardinal Ruffo, asking neither for arms nor for money, requested only to be allowed to return to the mainland and recover the kingdom from its new overlords.

He had been born and brought up in Calabria where his family owned large estates. So when he landed there from Sicily, with eight men, he was able quickly to gather round him, off the ancestral lands, a little band of two or three hundred, armed with shot-guns, or only with fork or flail. He had embarked on a hazardous enterprise of a kind which had signally failed when Cardinal Busca had tried to organize it in the Papal States two years earlier. But, apart from his own ability, he had a few points in his favour which Busca had not had. The mountainous country of Calabria and Apulia, which he knew from his youth, afforded far better protection for guerilla bands than did the flat open land between the Apennines and the Adriatic, where Busca's men had been helpless against Bonaparte's rapid advance. And Macdonald was not Bonaparte; nor was his army the Army of Italy of '96–'97. True, it had driven Mack and his army before it. But it had been held up outside Naples for a whole month by the obstinate resistance of the *lazzaroni*. It was from this resistance that Cardinal Ruffo now took his inspiration.

Wherever he went, wearing his cardinal's satin, he preached the crusade, raising his Christian Army of the Holy Faith. By the end of February his following was to be counted by tens of thousands and, despite appalling weather, he had recovered most of Calabria and had scattered the troops sent out by the Parthenopean Republic to recover the province. In Apulia the patriot Ettore Carafa, with French help, met with greater success against him; but when the French help was withdrawn he too was at the mercy of the *Sanfedisti*. After Ruffo had captured and sacked Altamura[1] (where his followers rescued alive three out of forty-eight priests and other unfortunates who had been chained together and dropped into a ditch) he advanced on Naples. But throughout the spring the city held out. Even after Macdonald had withdrawn at the beginning of May 1799, there remained French garrisons at the fortress of Sant' Elmo, above the city, and at Capua, while republican forces held other strong points which Ruffo's men were ill-suited and ill-equipped to tackle. The city itself was occupied by the *Sanfedisti* by the middle of June; but the terms for the surrender of the strong places around it were only agreed on the twenty-third of that month. Ruffo, to secure peace and avoid bloodshed, had granted generous terms to their garrisons; they were to be evacuated, if they chose, with full honours of war, to Toulon. This operation had already begun when, on June 24, Nelson with his navy made his appearance in the harbour.

His arrival at that moment was quite simply a disaster. Armed with royal powers given to him at Palermo, and bearing on board the British ambassador and, more important, Lady Hamilton, whose ruling idea was to avenge herself on her personal enemies at Naples, he refused to honour the Cardinal's signature and prevented the evacuation of the Jacobin garrisons. Instead of the reconciliation and reform which had been Ruffo's objective there followed a sanguinary series of executions and imprisonments which lasted for more than six months. Nelson, it is fair to remember, was engaged in fighting the French all over the Mediterranean; he could hardly welcome a capitulation which allowed their sympathizers to go to Toulon. To him the Italian Jacobins were merely friends of the French and therefore his country's enemies. Likewise to Ferdinand and Maria Carolina they were merely rebels and traitors. But Ruffo

---

[1] An account of this episode is given by Giacomo Racioppi in his *Storia dei popoli della Lucania e della Basilicata*, Vol. 2, pp. 268–272.

was a dignitary of the Church, bent on reconciliation, to whom the shedding of blood was only legitimate in the direct defence of Church or State, and he was also a realist, who wanted to restore the monarchy to a sounder footing than it had enjoyed in the years before the French invasion.

But Ruffo's hour was over. Even his personal following melted away as his peasants came into conflict with the *lazzaroni* of the Naples water-front and found themselves compelled by hunger to return to the lands they had left.

This rising of the *Sanfedisti* in 1799, which upset the republican régimes at Naples, Rome, and Florence, was a phenomenon which may be worthy of more consideration than it has been given. No doubt the motives which induced the peasants to rise behind Ruffo were no less mixed than were those which would prompt their grandchildren to rise behind Garibaldi; near-starvation, and the hope of easy plunder played their important parts in the movement. But the crusade was also strong in the towns (Arezzo, Siena, Bologna) and its proclaimed motives were to come to the rescue of the Church, to save Rome, and to restore 'Citizen Pope' to his proper position. Ruffo assured his followers that they were going to the rescue of the Holy Father, and wherever he went he allowed them to uproot the symbols of 1789 and to replace them by the Cross. But although there is no dispute about the fact that the populace was up in defence of its churches, images, Religious Orders, and all those traditions of life which it regarded as holy, leaders like Zondadari have come in for the historian's censure for organizing 'holy publicity stunts' and Cardinal Ruffo's campaign is widely regarded as a sort of sanctified brigandage.[1] We are reminded that the Church was arousing men's basest passions, promising them eternal life for their pains, playing on their superstitious beliefs about their images and relics. No doubt (as in all religious wars) opinion on the merits of this matter will differ in proportion as what was at stake seems important or unimportant. A holy war is assuredly a horrible thing, as the whole of history

[1] Cf., e.g. Angus Heriot, *The French in Italy, 1796–1799*, Chatto and Windus, 1957, pp. 264 and 267.

testifies; it is hard to justify any leader who raises it save when essentials are at stake, and there will be those who believe that even then it is wrong. But it is necessary to notice that the leaders believed essentials were at stake, that the faith itself was in jeopardy. Prominence has been given to the part played by images and relics; but these images and relics were, after all, the traditional channel through which spiritual strength was given to a people whose beliefs were now being affronted. Nor were these externals the only objects of Jacobin iconoclasm; the centre of the faith, the sacrament itself, was far from safe.

Not all the Italians were equally warlike. On the whole the Romans, apart from the populace of the Trastevere, were passive. In the years of Rome's danger, before Pius VI had been abducted and the Republic set up, it had been the habit of the Romans to rely rather upon immense efforts of collective intercession, such as the 'forty-hour prayer' – the *Quarant' Ore*. Perhaps this essentially pacific way of meeting the crisis was a more suitable procedure, in the circumstances, than was the organization of militant bands of *Sanfedisti*, in the manner of Cardinal Ruffo. Possibly those who took up their shot-guns were deserving of the rebuke given to the apostle who cut off the ear of the High Priest's servant. But it is inconsistent, though not unknown, to blame the Romans for depending on prayer, and to blame Cardinal Ruffo's followers for using the shot-gun and the flail.

The *Sanfedisti*, following like a forest fire in the wake of French armies compelled to retire before the Austro-Russian armies in the north, ended for the time being the Jacobin-Republican system in Italy. But they did not save the Pope. Since he had been moved in June 1798 from Siena to the Florentine Certosa he had been more closely confined. Not even his nephew the Duke Braschi was allowed to stay with him. The Carthusian monks kept him in tolerable comfort through the winter, but the paralysis of his legs grew worse, perhaps because he was not allowed outside for any exercise. For his contact with the world he depended on Mgr Spina (an efficient and devoted servant who would play an important role under his successor) and on the Nuncio at Florence, Archbishop

Odescalchi. During the winter of 1798–99 Odescalchi was, in fact, a sort of acting Secretary of State; but the possibility that the government of the Church should be set up at the Certosa was never seriously entertained, partly because the Pope did not want it and partly because Grand Duke Ferdinand at Florence was far too frightened of the French to allow such a thing to happen. He would permit no visitor to see the Pope for more than two consecutive days; even Odescalchi was only allowed to come out from Florence on three days a week. It was only as a concession to the Catholic powers that the French government allowed the Pope to remain on the neutral territory of the Grand Duchy, and Ferdinand's hospitality, such as it was, would help to bring about his own undoing. The French were continually threatening to remove the Pope to Sardinia; only the manifest impossibility of his surviving the voyage prevented them.

When in March 1799 the position of the French in the whole of Italy seemed to be becoming precarious they deemed the time had come to move their prisoner farther north to safer quarters. So the eighty-one year old Pius was moved across the Apennines to Bologna and thence on to Parma. Soon the Austro-Russian army was invading Lombardy, so 'Citizen Pope' had to be hurried across to Piedmont, thence to be taken over the Alps to Briançon, to Grenoble, to Valence. The Directory were planning to take him yet farther, to Lyons; but at Valence, in the dilapidated *Hôtel du Gouvernement*, in a bed which mercifully gave him a view over the river Rhône and the mountains, he died on August 29, with a last prayer for his enemies.

Pius VI had reigned for twenty-four years and six months, the longest pontificate since the traditional twenty-five years of Saint Peter. He had not been above nepotism, nor vanity, nor an over-preoccupation with the temporal affairs of his states. He had been something of a Renaissance Prince, something of an enlightened despot. He had been happiest amongst the treasures of his library and museum, or when watching the progress made in the draining of the Pontine marshes. An aristocrat, he had abhorred the Revolution.

The arrival of Pius VI at Valence, 1799. From an engraving by Scotti. (*Radio Times Hulton Picture Library.*)

His merit had been that, though in many ways a worldly man, he had understood very clearly what was essential to the Church and what was the nature of the challenge, in his times, to her position; there had never been any danger that he would yield on essential issues. He had confronted bravely the erastianism of the Emperor Joseph II and the secularism and impiety of the French Revolution. He had shown some small measure of diplomatic skill, and more patience, though not often an imaginative understanding.

But the importance of his personal failings and of his personal qualities pales before the importance of the times in which he lived. His death marked the end of an era. After the French Revolution, after the Italian revolutions, neither society nor the Church-in-society could be the same again. It was widely supposed that the papacy itself had at last come to an end. That had been supposed before, and would be supposed again – notably in 1870. But in 1799, when the paralysed pontiff died at Valence, and the cardinals were scattered, and the intellectuals were still talking about the new age of philosophy and reason, it did seem as though there might be something in it.

I

CHAPTER EIGHT

The Conclave of Venice

I n the high summer of 1799, when Pius VI lay dying at Valence, an enormous question mark hung over the affairs of Europe. The French Revolution had been driven out of Italy, it was in retreat on the Rhine, its best general had left his army cut off in Egypt. Austrian power was back in Lombardy and had occupied the Legations of the Papal States. The Roman Republic had collapsed, and the city itself was now occupied by Neapolitan troops. Although only the most extreme optimists among the émigrés entertained the hope that the revolutionary front was already beginning to crack in France herself, it did seem as though, over the greater part of western Europe, the ancien régime might be re-established.

At the head of the anti-French coalition stood the Emperor Francis II and his Chancellor Thugut. To them the Catholic Church seemed the natural ally of law and order, to which they felt she afforded a spiritual sanction. After all that had occurred in the last three years in Italy it hardly seemed possible at Vienna that the dignitaries of the Church could think otherwise. The Revolution was evidently anti-Christ; the Emperor was evidently Defender of the Faith.

Since the autumn of 1798 the Emperor had been urging that the scattered cardinals should collect under his protection at Venice, in preparation for the next Conclave. Pius VI, as we saw, had not been willing to press this course on the reluctant Dean of the Sacred College, Albani, who was at Naples with several other of its members, and who still hoped the Conclave would be held at Rome; but this little group had since been scattered by the appearance of Championnet and the Parthenopean Republic. Several cardinals, though they were now penniless, had managed, with the help of the Roman banker Torlonia, to make their way to Venice, where a fair nucleus for a Conclave had already formed itself by the time of the Pope's death. Although Neapolitan troops were now in occupation of Rome the political uncertainty there was such that most cardinals preferred to accept the Emperor's protection and stay where they now found themselves. So the island of San Giorgio, opposite the piazzetta, became the rendezvous for the election.

To the Emperor and his Chancellor Thugut, following in the Josephist traditions of Vienna, and hoping for the election of a compliant Pope, the arrangement seemed a happy one, and they were quite prepared to place some 40,000 ducats at the disposal of the cardinals while the Benedictines on the island gave them the use of their monastery. Thugut had good reason to be pleased. For here was an opportunity not merely to secure the election of a friendly Pope (he could surely assume that any new Pope must be opposed to the Revolution) but to secure one who would be willing to yield to the Austrian protector of the Italian peninsula what was necessary to make that protection effective, namely suzerainty over the legations of the Papal States.

Thugut had some ambitious plans. Just as the Revolution had set up in Italy a series of satellite republics dependent on France so, now that Austrian military power had replaced French, he planned an Austrian protective belt across northern Italy to include Venice, Ravenna, Bologna, Milan, Genoa, and even Nice. Austrian garrisons would hold this belt and so provide a ring of steel against further incursions by the French into Italy. In this plan for an Austrian plain of Lombardy, and an Austrian riviera, the Papal legations were important not only militarily but also economically, since Bologna and the rich surrounding plain north-east of the Apennines looked northwards towards Parma, Modena, Piacenza, Padua, and Milan, rather than southwards across the mountains to Rome. Not the river Po but the great Apennine range seemed the natural Austrian frontier. Bonaparte, likewise, had recognized the geographical unity of the whole plain when he created the Cisalpine Republic, and he would recognize it again when he created his Kingdom of Italy.

But, unfortunately for Thugut, the cardinals too knew what he wanted and why he wanted it. And they knew that they did not mean to let him have it. They were influenced by the fact that the legations were not only much the most prosperous part of the Papal States, without which the rest was unviable, but also by the fact that the whole plain was peculiarly rich in Roman and Papal tradition. The last four Popes – to go no further back than the middle of the eighteenth century – had all come from that region, or from neighbouring Venetia. Benedict XIV had been Archbishop of Bologna; Clement XIII, a Venetian, had been Bishop of Padua; Clement XIV had come from Rimini; Pius VI had come from Cesena. Their pride, their culture, even an underlying Italian national feeling made the cardinals ready to echo the cry of their illustrious predecessor, Julius II, who had first taken over the region of the legations: *fuori gli barbari!* From Pius VI to Pius IX an intense sensitivity about Austrian attempts to garrison the legations characterized the Popes and the Curia; in 1847 the newly elected Pio Nono would be willing to risk war to maintain their strict independence.

All the same, in 1799 Thugut was in a very strong position because his armies were in actual occupation of the area. And it was made still stronger by the fact that, at the treaty of Tolentino in 1797, the papal plenipotentiaries had themselves signed away the legations to Bonaparte, who had incorporated them in his Cispadane and later his Cisalpine Republic. If Rome could thus give the legations to Bonaparte why could she not transfer the gift to the Emperor to help him to defend the Roman religion? To this the cardinals could reply that, although Pius VI had been obliged to yield the legations to the conqueror, Bonaparte, he had never recognized the Cisalpine Republic; Tolentino had recognized a military *fait accompli* in time of war; it had not given papal blessing to a new order in northern Italy in time of peace. An Austrian military occupation might, for the time being, be inevitable; a formal transfer of sovereignty from Rome to Vienna would be another matter.

To change this Roman attitude about the legations was one of the objectives which the Austrian government hoped to secure by the election of the right Pope at the Conclave of Venice. And the cardinal most likely to effect the change, if elected, seemed to them to be Mattei, for Mattei had signed the treaty of Tolentino on behalf of Pius VI. Surely a cardinal who had himself already signed away the legations to Bonaparte would be ready now to sign them away to the Emperor Francis? And there was a further point in his favour. As Archbishop of Ravenna he had resolutely refused to accept the decrees of the Cisalpine government whereas, as we saw, his colleague Chiaramonti at Imola had lent his qualified support to the new régime. Mattei was therefore to be regarded as a resolute and reliable monarchist who would make no compromises with Austria's enemy, the Revolution.

If the issue lying behind the Conclave of 1769 had been the fate of the Jesuits the issue lying behind that of 1799 was little less than the ending of the temporal power, for nobody supposed that the Papal States could long survive without the legations, and in any case Austrian ambition did not end at Bologna; it stretched at least to Ancona, on the Adriatic coast, then occupied by Austrian troops. Moreover the Papal States, at that date, could hardly be said to exist as an independent sovereignty for the Neapolitans were occupying Rome and considerable portions of the Marches; if Austria were to acquire the northern portions of the territory a *quid pro quo* for the King of Naples in the southern portions was to be expected. No doubt it is arguable that this was the moment when the temporal power might, in the best interests of the papacy, have been brought to an end, freeing its energies for exclusive attention to its spiritual duties. On the other hand without a state, and with northern Italy under Austrian rule, Rome would, in fact, have been subject to Vienna. With a state, and with the Austrian army a comfortable 200 miles away to the north (which was the position after 1815), she could at least feel free from immediate domination at the hand of either Austria or France so long as the intense mutual rivalry between these two powers prevented either from allowing the other to make any important move in Italy. When, in 1860–70, the Papal States were at last eliminated, the new power which took their place was one which was not strong enough to defy Catholic Europe and to oppress the papacy with impunity as Francis II, who inherited the Josephist tradition, might well have done, had he been sole overlord of Rome, and as Napoleon soon did when he acquired that position.

The Conclave of Venice was then a critical Conclave. Fortunately we have more reliable information about it than we have about most conclaves because its secretary, Cardinal Consalvi, wrote an essay on it in his memoirs.[1] It is a very frank essay, and in some ways it gives an unedifying picture; but to Consalvi himself the events at Venice, which he often deplores, caused no fundamental disquiet because he could see what he believed to be the right result emerging in despite of the human agents' various preoccupations.

Opened on November 30, 1799, with thirty-four cardinals in attendance, the Conclave quickly showed a surprisingly large majority forming itself in favour of Cardinal Bellisomi, Bishop of Cesena, whose religious qualities were generally recognized and appreciated. But the Austrian Cardinal Herzan had come with the firm intention of securing the election of Mattei, and when it seemed certain that the very next day would see Bellisomi's election he pleaded, successfully, with the Dean of the Sacred College, Albani, that he should defer further ballots for a few days, until fresh instructions were received from Vienna. It was a shocking request, the more so since Herzan carried no imperial 'Exclusive' against Bellisomi, but only a general instruction to try to secure the election of Mattei. Albani, no doubt, should not have agreed to it; his attitude can only be explained by the extreme uncertainty of the political position in Italy and by the disasters which all the cardinals felt would be incurred by their offending the Emperor too deeply. The reply from Vienna only repeated the Emperor's support for

[1] Consalvi *Mémoires* (2nd Ed. 1866), Vol. 1, pp. 215–309. But his account was not written till 1812 and conflicts in minor respects with his own account written at the time in his letters to the Principessa Borghese, for which see E. Celani *I preliminari del conclave di Venezia* in *Archivio della Società Romana di storia patria*, Vol. XXXVI, 1913. For the negotiations with Vienna during the Conclave see C. van Duerm *un peu plus de lumière sur le conclave de Venise*, Louvain, 1896, which utilizes Chancellor Thugut's correspondence in the Vienna archives. Cardinal Maury, who was at the Conclave, wrote his recollections which appeared in Book 2, *Le Conclave de Venise*, in *Correspondance Diplomatique et Mémoires inédits du Cardinal Maury*, Ed. Richard, Lille, 1891, Vol. 1 (1837). J. Leflon (*Pie VII*, Ch. XII), using the diary of the unofficial Spanish envoy Mgr Despuig (*Libro de viages* . . .), has shown how Chiaramonti came to be elected. The Vatican papers are analysed in J. Schmidlin *Histoire des Papes*, Vol. 1, Part 1, *Pie VII* (Vitte, 1938, transl. from the German), pp. 22 and 23 notes.

Mattei; in the meantime a group of some ten cardinals formed it-self under the leadership of Antonelli and in support of Mattei. For long and weary weeks a stalemate ensued, some eighteen to twenty cardinals, under the leadership of Albani, continuing to support the candidature of Bellisomi, some ten supporting Mattei. The dead-lock was only eventually broken when two realists outside the Con-clave, its Secretary, Consalvi, and the Spanish envoy Mgr Despuig, put their heads together and devised an ingenious plan. If a member of the group supporting Mattei, they reasoned, were to select a can-didate from the group supporting Bellisomi, might not the honour of both groups be saved by their concurring in this new choice? And so it was agreed. Antonelli was chosen to do the selecting. And he was to be persuaded to select Chiaramonti, because the Benedictine Bishop of Imola had the necessary religious and personal qualities, and because there were objections to each of the other supporters of Bellisomi. Only two tenable objections could be raised against Chiaramonti, and they were both what were called 'extrinsic' (to do with circumstances beyond his control) as distinct from 'intrinsic' (to do with his personal character). The first objection was that he was young; he was only fifty-eight years old. The second objection was that he was a creation of, and very close to the last Pope, and after a pontificate of more than twenty-four years the cardinals were tired of the friends and relations of the Braschi family. Neither objection was considered paramount. Antonelli won over the other supporters of Mattei; Albani won over the other supporters of Bellisomi. Herzan felt he had done his best for Vienna and made little more trouble. So the compromise was accepted and a cardinal elected who combined, signally, the qualities of saintliness, simplicity, graciousness and humour. It was a popular choice and it did the Conclave credit. In the end the cardinals had overcome not only Vienna but also their own inclina-tion to elect a Pope who would not live too long and also their private antipathy to the Braschi connection.

But Vienna was not pleased, as the Emperor quickly showed. Permission was not given for the enthronement of the new Pope in the great Venetian cathedral of Saint Mark. This was more than an act of discourtesy, aimed at an uncongenial Pope; the ceremony of enthronement had its temporal as well as its spiritual aspect; it symbolized the Pope's assumption of his sovereignty over the Papal States, and this was the subject on which Vienna was now most sensitive. If she placed Saint Mark's at his disposal she would have to send an imposing official delegation, and she did not wish in this way to endorse his full temporal sovereignty. But Chiaramonti, who had assumed the title of Pius VII in honour of his predecessor, had no intention of playing down his temporal sovereignty by forgoing any of the customary ceremonial, so the enthronement was carried out in the usual way, though in the confined space of the monastic Church of San Giorgio, and was witnessed from outside by a considerable crowd, squeezed into the little piazza, while something of what was going on was witnessed by others, peering across the water with telescopes from the Venetian piazzetta.

Thugut did not rest content with making his influence felt in this rather negative way. Within three days of his election the Pope was being pressed by Cardinal Herzan to appoint as his Secretary of State an Austrian subject, the Venetian Cardinal Flangini. To this he replied, with some aptness, that since he was not yet in possession of a state he had no need for a Secretary of State, and he appointed Consalvi to the post of Secretary to the Pope. Next Herzan brought pressure on him to go to Vienna,[1] representing that it was vital that Pope and Emperor should confer on the state of affairs; the Emperor would pay all the expenses. But since Consalvi and the new Pope knew that what was required of them at Vienna was that they should make a formal cession of their right to the legations, and since Pius preferred to make his restoration to Rome rather than a visit to Vienna his first official act, this suggestion too was declined. Finally Thugut sent a special envoy, the Marquis Ghislieri, to demand outright the cession to Austria of the three legations; if her sovereignty over them were formally recognized then the remainder of those papal territories occupied by the Austrians would be restored. With polite astonishment Pope and Secretary replied that this was out of the question; they demanded the return of the whole

---

[1] See Boulay de la Meurthe *Documents sur la Négociation du Concordat*, Paris, 1891, Vol. I, pp. 14-20.

of the states; nor did their attitude alter when Ghislieri offered to surrender the Legation of Ravenna provided that Austria retained those of Ferrara and Bologna.

It now became necessary for the Austrian government to prevent what was likely to prove a triumphal progress on the part of the new Pope through those same legations on his way to Rome. Since Austrian troops were in occupation, and since the Pope and his entourage had no funds, it was easy for Vienna to arrange this journey as she chose; but it made a very poor impression when it was found that she proposed to ferry the Pope, with his little following of four cardinals and some secretaries and servants, by gondola to the port of Malamocco, where an ill-equipped and ill-manned frigate, *la Bellone*, would take them down the Adriatic as far as Pesaro, whence they could proceed to Rome by road. Consalvi was chiefly impressed by the fact that the *Bellone* possessed no cooking facilities, a deficiency which would have mattered less if the voyage had taken only the scheduled twenty-four hours instead of the twelve days which a series of storms and the ineptitude of the crew imposed on the helpless passengers. On the other hand Consalvi's narrative does little to support the widely circulated opinion that Ghislieri, who was present on the voyage, was commissioned to secure the death of the Pope.

When the little party reached Ancona, by coach from Pesaro, a new aspect was placed on its relations with Ghislieri by the news of Bonaparte's victory at Marengo (June 14, 1800). Ghislieri understood the significance of the news. When, at Foligno, he formally handed over to Pius VII sovereignty over the territories of the Papal States between Pesaro and Rome (not over the legations, nor over the southern territories occupied by the Neapolitans) he was no longer in a position to make a magnificent gesture of the transfer, for already the Austrian troops could be seen running for the north.[1]

By the time Pius VII made his formal entry into Rome on July 3 the whole balance of power in Europe had been changed once more. The Austrian troops were not only withdrawing from central Italy, they were withdrawing from the legations, from

---

[1] Consalvi *Mémoires* (2nd Ed.), Vol. 1, pp. 231–41.

Lombardy, from Venetia, from the whole of the peninsula. The Cisalpine was about to reappear under French tutelage. The new Pope was no longer fettered by the patronage of the Emperor and the instructions given to Ghislieri.

The papacy was once more confronted by Bonaparte.

CHAPTER NINE

The Concordat with Napoleon

When Pius VII entered Rome he did not proceed straight to the Quirinal. He went first to Saint Peter's to pay his homage at the shrine of the Apostle and to invoke the prayers of his first predecessor to protect his own pontificate. This was the traditional papal custom. But in the circumstances prevailing at the time of Pius VII's accession an appeal for protection might seem particularly prudent, for assuredly both the Pope's spiritual and his temporal position had never stood in greater need of it.

In France the Church, still disavowed and sometimes persecuted by the government, lived on only behind closed doors and seemed slowly dying for lack of the chance to train new priests. In Austria it was evident that the anti-Roman attitude still prevailed. In Spain the traditions of Charles III were maintained, while the Spanish ambassadors at Rome had become more powerful there than the Pope. And the Neapolitan Bourbons, far from being a source of protection, were an immediate threat; they had only removed their army from the city of Rome because Vienna did not like to see it there.

But only one figure now held the attention of the restored Pope – that of Bonaparte. Azara was no longer at Rome, to lord it over the Curia, for he had been moved to the Spanish embassy at Paris. Nor was the Austrian ambassador, Cardinal Herzan, any longer the over-powerful protector that he had been at Venice, for the military might of Vienna was now fenced off by the steel of French bayonets in northern Italy. The great question was what the new First Consul at Paris would do. He had revived the French satellite republics at Genoa and Milan; might he not be expected to revive those at Rome and at Naples? Pius VII had not notified the new

French consular government of his election; he had only notified Louis XVIII.[1] Nor had he been recognized by Bonaparte either as Pope or as ruler of Rome. He had little reason to expect anything better than the treatment handed out to his predecessor.

Yet some grounds, however slender, did exist for expecting better treatment for the new Pope than the last one had received. There was his reputation, known to Bonaparte, as one who had been prepared to collaborate with the Cisalpine Republic. And there was the further point that his election had been unwelcome to Austria. Not that he had been the First Consul's candidate; the First Consul had not had a candidate because his *coup d'état* had occurred only three weeks before the cardinals went into Conclave and he had had other things to think about. But it was welcome news at Paris that the Austrian candidate had been defeated, and still more welcome news that the new Pope had refused to go to Vienna – it is interesting to speculate what would have been Pius' position had the victor of Marengo found that he was at Vienna, engaged in making a present there of the legations to Austria.

By the time the battle was fought the clergy of northern Italy were already buzzing with conversation about the address Bonaparte had given in the duomo of Milan just nine days earlier (June 5, 1800), though all we can be sure that he said was: 'The French are of the same religion as you. Admittedly we have had our quarrels, but all will be arranged, all will be adjusted.'[2]

What exactly it was that Bonaparte had in mind had already been disclosed to one Italian cardinal. Even as he had descended from the Great Saint Bernard into the Italian plain he had found time to discuss matters with Cardinal Martiniana, Bishop of Vercelli, whom he had discovered in his diocese in the valley, the Cardinal having newly returned from the Conclave of Venice. After his victory Bonaparte passed through Vercelli again, on June 25. On this

---

[1] See Boulay de la Meurthe *Documents sur la Négociation du Concordat* (Paris, 1891), Vol. I, p. 11, for Pius VII's letter to the King. On February 18 French policy was not to recognize any Pope elected at the Conclave of Venice because it was being held *sous l'influence absolue de la maison d'Autriche* (Talleyrand to the Spanish Ambassador, *ibid.*, p. 2).

[2] Boulay, *op. cit.,* Vol. I, p. 21. But for the version of Napoleon's remarks published and believed at the time see Appendix II, p. 297.

occasion he spent more time with the Cardinal and Martiniana wrote the next day in some excitement to the Pope:

'... In an intimate talk, he told me of his ardent desire to deal with ecclesiastical affairs in France and to establish peace abroad, and he begged me to take up at once the task of negotiating between Your Holiness and himself. His wishes seemed to me truly sincere....'[1]

The letter goes on to recount how Bonaparte promised that, if the negotiations were successful, he would endeavour to see that the Pope recovered the whole of his states. His idea for the French Church was to make a clean sweep of the existing arrangements for appointing the clergy, to require the resignation both of the bishops appointed by the Bourbons and of the Constitutionals, and to start afresh, appointing the bishops himself, with the approval of the Pope, who should invest them with their Sees. The First Consul had stressed that it would be impossible to recover the Church property, now alienated, but that, if the number of Sees were reduced, he would ensure that both bishops and curés were properly paid.

Such exciting news was received by Rome with joy, but also with her habitual reserve, which was no doubt strengthened by Martiniana's reputation for poor judgement. But actually the cardinal does not seem to have misunderstood the general for we know that before he had left Paris Bonaparte had already sketched out, for his foreign minister Talleyrand, a similar plan for a settlement.[2]

Pius VII had received Martiniana's letter only a few hours after his own arrival in Rome from Venice. Whatever the reserves which Consalvi encouraged in him neither Secretary nor Pope could fail to be vastly encouraged by proposals so different from any that had been received from France in the last ten years. So Martiniana was told, on July 12, that the overtures 'give Us the greatest consolation since they tend towards the restoration of so many millions of souls to the cradle of Jesus Christ';[3] but he should realize that the matter will not be easy. Since the First Consul had chosen to confide in

[1] Mathieu Le Concordat de 1801, Paris, 1903. p. 3.

[2] Boulay, op. cit., Vol. 1, pp. 23–24.

[3] Boulay Documents, Vol. 1, p. 26.

him the Pope would agree to his acting as negotiator; but he would send him somebody to assist him in the negotiations.

He sent Mgr Spina, who had been with Pius VI not only at the Certosa but in his last hours at Valence; soon after the Pope's death Spina had actually met Bonaparte at Valence, when the general was returning from Egypt to Paris. He was acceptable to Bonaparte; indeed, soon after Spina had reached Martiniana, at Vercelli, the First Consul ordered him to come straight on to Paris for the negotiations, without bothering to invite the Cardinal at all. Possibly this rather characteristic piece of abrupt Napoleonic rudeness was due to his having formed the same opinion of Martiniana as had been formed by the Marquis Ghislieri: 'his intentions are as pure as his intelligence is limited'.[1]

Spina's position at Paris was a difficult one. It is true that the First Consul appointed as his own representative the abbé Bernier, the able negotiator of the peace in the Vendée, who understood the realities of the Church's position as well as those of his government and was as anxious not to undermine the Church as was Spina himself. But the opposition at Paris to any settlement was extremely strong. There was the foreign minister, Talleyrand, an apostate bishop, who had since married, who had himself consecrated the first bishops of the Constitutional Church, and who was inclined to befriend them and also to regularize his own position so far as might be. There was Constitutional Bishop Grégoire, acknowledged Head of the Constitutional Church, determined to safeguard his clergy and supported by the new Legislative Council and Senate who were largely hostile to the Roman position. Opposed to the constitutionals, and to the free-thinkers, but equally opposed to the idea of a new concordat, were the keen monarchists amongst the non-juring clergy many of whom – especially those still in exile – regarded their allegiance as due to the monarchy which had invested their bishops with their Sees. The exiled Louis XVIII, through Cardinal Maury, his representative at Rome, did everything in his power to prevent any accord from being reached between Pope and Consul since such an accord must go far to strengthen the usurper's new régime.

[1] Ghislieri to Thugut, *ibid.*, p. 29.

At Rome the Pope and Consalvi had the majority of the cardinals with them in their decision to negotiate on the basis of Bonaparte's proposals. But the opposition was strong, and at least five of the cardinals were absolutely opposed to any negotiations with the Revolution, whether in the person of Bonaparte or of anybody else. All were anxious about the terms of the agreement. Would the 'intruders' (the Constitutional bishops) be nominated to Sees in the new 'Church of the Concordat'? Would Bonaparte be driven by the pressure at Paris to espouse their cause, even though he had described them as a 'parcel of dishonourable brigands'? – after all, in the event of further quarrels with Rome, he could count on their support if he chose to place himself at their head in the guise of a new Henry VIII of England. Would he insist on appointing a new episcopacy altogether, prohibiting any re-emergence of the bishops of the ancien régime? Would he limit the Church to a salaried episcopacy, with curés, making no provision for seminaries, cathedral chapters, Religious Orders, property, or endowments? Would he declare France a Catholic country, with an established Catholic Church, or would Catholicism become merely one amongst many 'tolerated cults'? And would the new arrangement be 'Gallican', in the full sense of placing all contact between the French Church and Rome at the mercy of the State?

These were the issues around which discussion ranged during the winter of 1800–01 until at last, at the end of February 1801, a draft was agreed in Paris and submitted to Rome for approval.[1] Rome delayed; Holy Week and Easter had first to be observed. The First Consul, losing patience, sent an ultimatum for his ambassador François Cacault to deliver: the draft was to be agreed within five days. If it was not, Cacault was to withdraw to Florence where he would find General Murat with his army. The Roman government might draw its own conclusions as to what would follow.

Pius and Consalvi resisted. The First Consul's instructions amounted to a threat that he would eliminate the Pope's temporal

---

[1] In what follows I have followed mainly Consalvi's own account in his *Mémoires* (2nd Ed., Vol. 1, pp. 309–440). For the letters and documents see I. Rinieri, *La Diplomazia Pontificia nel Secolo XIX* (Rome, 1902, etc.), Vol. 1, and Boulay, *op. cit.*

power unless he ratified the Concordat. But the Pope and his
Secretary had sedulously avoided mixing temporal and spiritual
matters, although the opportunity to gain temporal advantages
had been great. Thus they had ignored Bonaparte's repeated hints
that he would restore the lost provinces of the Papal States in return
for a satisfactory Concordat; they had not raised the question either
of Avignon or of the legations; and they had made no difficulty
about recognizing the permanent loss of the Church's property in
France. Nobody should be able to say there had been a simoniacal
bargain over souls; in negotiating the Concordat the restoration of
the Faith in France was to be the sole consideration. But by the same
token they were not to be brow-beaten by the threat that they
might lose what remained of the temporal power.

The situation was saved by Cacault who had already, after
Tolentino, proved himself to be a humane interpreter at Rome of
the exigencies of Paris. Cacault, like the abbé Bernier at Paris, really
wanted to see the Concordat achieved, and he was convinced that
if Consalvi could only have the opportunity to explain personally
to Bonaparte why some of the demands (especially his claim for an
unlimited right of police supervision over the Church) were unacceptable, agreement could easily be secured. In this he was too
optimistic; but he saved the day in this crisis by persuading Consalvi, at the end of the five-day time limit, to go with him to Paris.
Early on the sixth morning he obeyed his instructions to the letter
(in such awe did he stand of Bonaparte) by leaving Rome and
going to join Murat at Florence. But he did so in the Papal Secretary
of State's coach, entering it with Consalvi in full view of the Roman
populace, so that their friendship and mutual esteem should be
appreciated and no Jacobin troublemaker should be tempted to
stage an 'incident' which would bring Murat's army down in
vengeance to the Tiber – a contingency feared by both if it
were supposed that the Pope had rejected the First Consul's
advances.

At Paris Consalvi found himself up against both Bonaparte and
Talleyrand. The First Consul was showing a keener appreciation of
the hostility of the French constitutional clergy to a settlement; he
had authorized them to hold a National Council. Having failed to

Cardinal Consalvi. From the portrait by Sir Thomas Lawrence at Windsor Castle. (*By gracious permission of H.M. The Queen.*)

impress the Cardinal by keeping Murat in readiness at Florence, he now harangued him on the calamity for Catholicism, not only in France but in all those European territories now once more under his control, if he should choose to follow the example of Henry VIII, adding that it would be very easy for him to do so since he was twenty times more powerful than the Tudor monarch had been. The crucial points at issue were now the terms in which Catholicism should be recognized as the official religion of France, the extent to which the government might interfere in the bishops' appointment of their curés, the provision to be made for seminaries and cathedral chapters, and above all what the French government meant by 'necessary police supervision'. There were all-night sessions, there were threats to break off negotiations if the matter were not settled the same evening, there was a calculated premature publication of agreement in the *Moniteur*. Finally, when the moment came for the signing, Consalvi was presented with a changed draft, different from the one he had agreed the day before, in the hope that he might sign it without reading it, or would be too embarrassed not to do so even if he noticed the differences. This last little deception was the work of Talleyrand's minion the apostate priest d'Hauterive; but that Bonaparte was behind it seems likely.[1] It was the kind of deception he would repeat more than once, a little later, when the Pope became his prisoner.

Yet in the end Consalvi secured most of what he wanted, and he had not been compelled to yield on any of those points which the Sacred College and the Pope had insisted, before he left Rome, were essential.[2] The quasi-official character of Catholicism in France was recognized in an introductory statement which said that it was 'the religion of the great majority of the French' and that it was professed by the Consuls of the Republic; the bishops were to appoint their curés 'with the agreement of the government' (unsatisfactory, but deliberately vague); the right of bishops to found seminaries and cathedral chapters was recognized, though no provision was made for endowing them. But the most important French concession, though it hardly leapt to the eye, was contained

---

[1] See Mathieu, *op. cit.*, p. 250.
[2] The full French text of the Concordat is given in Appendix III, p. 298.

K

in the first article which read: 'The Catholic religion, Roman and apostolic, shall be freely followed in France. Its practice shall be public, conforming itself to the police regulations which the government shall judge to be necessary for public tranquillity.' By limiting all reference to police regulation to this context Consalvi had secured that the government would only have the right to interfere with public worship (processions or public ceremonial); and this was a big concession, for it ruled out interference, for instance, with the seminaries, or with communications with Rome. Joseph Bonaparte, who signed for Napoleon, had agreed to this clause at the last moment; his brother was furious but he let it pass. Possibly he already envisaged how he would outflank the Church's position, on this as on other matters, by governmental action taken without the agreement of Rome and contrary to the terms of the Concordat.

As soon as the Concordat was signed Consalvi hurried away from Paris. Only forty days had been allowed for the governments to ratify it, which did not leave long for the Secretary to reach Rome, for the Sacred College to consider the draft, and for Paris to receive a copy signed by the Pope. Allowing himself only one day's rest – at Florence – Consalvi reached Rome in twelve days. He was given a mixed reception. Some of the cardinals were disturbed by the appearance of any reference at all to police regulations. Some were also disturbed by article 13, in which the Church renounced in perpetuity her property confiscated in France. But Pius VII and a majority of the cardinals were at one in recognizing that something of great importance had been achieved and the document was back in Paris, bearing the Pope's signature, within thirty-seven days.

On September 8 the First Consul signed it. But now a surprising delay occurred. Bonaparte, who had been anxious in July to rush the negotiations, so that he might proclaim the new settlement on the Feast of the Assumption (August 15, a date traditionally associated with the Bourbons, but which also happened to be his own birthday, and which he wished to associate in the minds of the French with his new régime) now showed no interest in proclaiming the Concordat. Rome was mystified. Not till Easter 1802 did she learn the truth. Bonaparte was not satisfied with the Concordat. It did not give him the governmental control over the Church that he wanted, and it would be unpopular with important sections of opinion in France. So he published alongside it, in the same volume and under the same title, a whole lot of regulations which would safeguard the government's position. They could not carry the signature of the Pope, as did the articles of the Concordat; but they would attract as much attention and would appear to be a part, together with the Concordat, of the new religious settlement for France.

Such were the famous 77 Organic Articles, which made their appearance as a rather lengthy appendix to the seventeen articles of the Concordat when the latter was at last published at Easter 1802. The shock at Rome was extreme. Consalvi could scarcely control his indignation when he read that all acts, briefs, bulls, etc., emanating from Rome, would require the government's *placet* before they could be received; that no nuncio, legate, or other Roman envoy could exercise jurisdiction in France save by permission of the government; that no seminaries could be established without the agreement of the First Consul, who would have to approve their regulations, including one that the professors must subscribe to the Gallican decrees of 1682 asserting the superiority of a General Council to the Pope; that there would be one catechism and one liturgy in France and no feasts other than Sunday save as might be approved by the government; that the civil contract would take precedence over the religious in marriage; and so on. By unilateral action the First Consul had calmly arrogated to the State just those powers over the Church which Consalvi and Spina had been at such pains, over a year of negotiation, not to concede.

It would seem that what had happened at Paris was that Bonaparte had decided that the Concordat, published by itself, would be given a poor reception. It was not likely to make a good impression on the Legislative Assembly, on the Senate, on the Constitutional Church, or on that wide section of public opinion, especially amongst the lawyers, which was imbued with Gallican or with Jansenist traditions, and which would perceive that the rights of Rome had been resurrected without any corresponding reaffirmation of Gallican independence or of State supremacy. Could he afford to offend, at one and the same time: the royalists (together with the bishops of the ancien régime, who would have to resign their Sees); the constitutional bishops (who would have to do likewise); the Jansenistically minded lawyers of the Assembly and Senate; the University; and the anti-clerical Jacobins? Could he, a man of thirty-two who had been in power for less than a year, afford to defy in this way almost the whole of articulate and educated France, which either supported the Church of the ancien régime, or supported the Constitutional Church, or (more commonly) was Voltairean and sceptical?

It was asking a lot. It was asking him to accept a weaker position *vis à vis* Rome than the Bourbons had occupied. There might be bitter enmity between those of the Gallican tradition and those of the Jansenist tradition, while the Voltairean sceptics laughed at both. But on one point all three were agreed: they were anti-ultramontane. What Bonaparte could not afford was to appear to be allying himself with ultramontanism. He might almost as well have recalled the Jesuits.

Nor, of course, did Bonaparte, any more than his critics, wish to be bothered by papal pretensions; he had no intention of allowing anything of the kind. He wanted Catholicism, valid Catholicism, effective Catholicism for France, and that meant recognizing the Pope as Head of the Church; it does not seem likely that he toyed very seriously with the idea of playing the part of Henry VIII. But he intended to have as much control over the Church as he could get. He had failed to secure from Consalvi any explicit recognition in the Concordat of an unlimited right of governmental interference in Church affairs. So now, after the signature of the Concordat, he would secure that control, and also appease the many potential critics of the Concordat in France, by publishing alongside it regulations which would safeguard the government's position.

At Rome it seemed that Bonaparte had been acting in bad faith, and those *zelanti* members of the Curia who had all along disliked the policy of the Concordat, and were hostile to Consalvi, were confirmed in their opinions. But in France matters appeared to the clergy in a rather different light. The Organic Articles were, after all, essentially Gallican, essentially directed against 'Roman pretensions'. They were therefore in line with the traditional views of the French episcopacy. To those returning bishops of the ancien régime who were invested with new Sees the Articles presented no particular difficulty – this was just the sort of 'independence from Rome' they had been accustomed to before the Revolution; if they were now to accept Bonaparte as Head of the State they would accord to him the same rights in respect of the Church as the Bourbons had enjoyed. As for those constitutional bishops who secured appointment to new Sees, their principle was obedience to the State, so the new regulations afforded them no difficulty.

Of the sometime constitutionals Bonaparte appointed only twelve to Sees in the new Church of the Concordat, and two of these had already made their submission to Rome. But a real difficulty arose with some of them because Pius VI had suspended all bishops and clergy who had taken the oath to the Civil Constitution, so that those who had defied him and continued to perform their priestly functions had in fact become schismatic, and Pius VI felt it necessary that they should go through some form of reconciliation. But this, for the most part, they refused to do. Believing, as they did, that the first duty of a bishop was to obey the civil government in matters of Order, they held that they had done right to accept the Civil Constitution despite the Pope's condemnation of it; indeed they believed that only by accepting it had they saved the Church in France. The most they would do now was to renounce the Constitutional Church, because the government had abolished it, and accept the Concordat, because it was now the law of the land. They would not demand pardon for having accepted the Civil Constitution at a time when that Constitution had been by law established.

But Pius VII's Legate at Paris, Cardinal Caprara, who had been sent because he was thought to be the most conciliatory envoy available, and who had lived up to his reputation, knew that he must secure something more from these bishops than a mere acceptance of the new order. What was at issue was something more than a mere piece of legalism relating to past history. With their unrepentance these bishops retained a distinct theology, recognizing divorce, and even the marriage of priests and of members of Religious Orders, because they had accepted the view that marriage was a civil contract. If they did not admit that they had been in error the whole teaching authority of the Church would be prejudiced. During the negotiations over the Concordat the Pope and Consalvi had striven, though without success, to secure that none of the ex-constitutionals should be appointed to the new Sees; when they yielded the point they did so only on the understanding that these new incumbents would confess their past fault and be absolved for it. Bonaparte thought they should not be humiliated in this way; so did Bernier, who had now been given the See of Orleans and the task of smoothing the path for the new Church. Bernier thought he could see a way out of the *impasse*. Formally and openly the ex-constitutionals should only be required to accept the new situation and renounce the Constitutional Church in terms agreeable to them, making a simple recognition of the change of fact. But in secret Bernier would receive their abjuration and reconcile them with the Holy See. In due course he told the Legate that they had all in fact given him this; but at least three of them vehemently denied it, and the two most intransigent, Saurine of Strasbourg and Le Coz of Besançon, maintained their refusal in the face of the Pope himself when he later came to Paris to crown Napoleon and Pius finally had to let the matter rest.

This devotion of the constitutional bishops to the civil power, and their suspicion of Rome, was matched on the royalist side by those bishops of the ancien régime who insisted on maintaining their allegiance to Louis XVIII and refused to recognize Pius VII's new Church of the Concordat. By no means all of them took this line; sixteen (as against the twelve constitutionals) were appointed to Sees in the new Church. Others, passed over, accepted in silence the new state of affairs when the Pope demanded it of them. But some of those in London sent a series of memorials to Rome in which they adopted the extreme Gallican position, stating that their jurisdiction, like that of all bishops, including the Bishop of Rome, was given to them directly by God, so that the Pope had no power to depose them even though they did come lower than himself in the hierarchy. These anti-ultramontane bishops of the ancien régime were not in a position to harm the restored French Church from within because they were in exile; but the more active of them, like Coucy of La Rochelle, or Thémines of Blois, by showering their some-time dioceses with exhortations, and by maintaining a correspondence with the lower clergy, sustained what was called a *petite église*, in schism with Rome, which survived long after the restoration of 1815. Even its denunciation by the restored Louis XVIII did not daunt all its members; defying the Pope, defying Napoleon, defying the restored King, they clung to what they regarded as the exclusive legitimacy of their own bishops and clergy with a tenacity that was truly remarkable and which was not forgotten by the Vatican Council, in 1870, when it pronounced that bishops received their spiritual jurisdiction not directly from God but medially through the Pope, who enjoyed the 'full plenitude' of spiritual jurisdiction and could therefore remove a bishop if he wished.

The Concordat then had many enemies. It is fair to remember this when we find the Legate Caprara behaving so compliantly at Paris and the supple Bishop Bernier going to the fullest limits of casuistry, and perhaps a bit beyond, to save the settlement. The possibilities, if it broke down, seemed too serious to bear contemplation. It seemed to those concerned that Bonaparte might yet yield to the temptation, which it suited him to advertise, to put himself at the head of the Church. There would have been many at Paris to support him if he had done so, a fact which was well known to his new 'Minister of Cults', Jean Portalis, whose devotion to Church and to State was equally strong and who strove strenuously to maintain harmony between the two legitimate authorities, that of his master and that of the Pope. Later events were to show that this fear was exaggerated, for when Napoleon was later in a stronger position to take the step, and was irritated almost beyond endurance by the Pope, he still refrained from taking it. But Consalvi believed in the reality of the danger, and the various concessions of Rome – even the final concession, when Pius VII went to Paris to crown Napoleon – were partly prompted by the fear that the new ruler might become a new Henry VIII. Thus, across the channel, and across the centuries, did the English Reformation exert its influence.

The birth of the new Church had been painful. Nor was she strong in numbers or in zeal.[1] Recruitment to the ranks of the secular clergy had virtually ceased since 1790 and if some of the regulars, turned out of their monasteries, helped to supply the deficiency, even this source of supply was drying up with the turn of the century. Despite the extraordinary efforts of the real hero of this period, M. Émery, of the seminary of Saint-Sulpice, it proved extremely difficult to build up the numbers of the clergy once more. The seminary buildings had been confiscated and were being used for other purposes; they were not returned to the Church. There was no endowment for new seminaries under the settlement. There were far too few qualified theologians left to educate a sufficient number of novices. And only those with a very strong vocation were likely to offer themselves for the priesthood since they would have to depend on charity; the 500 francs which Bonaparte was offering to the curé in the year 1804 was not a living wage.

On those who had the hardihood to accept their vocation a further delay was imposed before they could serve the Church, for they were obliged by Bonaparte to do their military service, bitterly as Rome opposed this requirement. So the shortage of priests remained serious. Although the reorganization of the Church had reduced the number of parishes, it is reckoned that in the year 1806 at least one sixth were without a priest and that a quarter of the incumbents were over sixty years old. And the position became worse before it became better for the scythe of death worked faster than did the blooming of vocations or the training of young priests.

For the whole of the twenty-five years of the revolutionary and Napoleonic era in France the Church was without even a necessary minimum of training facilities or economic support, while the sup-

---

[1] For an analysis of the evidence concerning the Church of the Concordat in France see in particular J. Leflon *La Crise Révolutionnaire*, Bloud et Gay, 1951, pp. 207–217.

pression of the monasteries and convents (only partially reopened for particularly 'useful' Orders – teachers or nurses) deprived her of the unseen support by which she lives. This situation, repeated in greater or lesser degree in western Europe generally, has to be remembered when one is considering her grave inadequacy in many directions – and especially intellectually – after the restoration of more normal conditions in 1815.

Administratively speaking, the importance of the Napoleonic Church of the Concordat in the later history of Europe and the world lay in the centralization of authority, not only in the hands of the State, but also in the hands of the bishops, and ultimately in those of the Pope, which occurred as a result of it. The numerous independent patrons who had appointed to local livings under the ancien régime just disappeared. Henceforth the curé was appointed by his bishop, and was dependent for his promotion on his bishop alone, while the *succursales* (curates), whose numbers grew greatly, were also removable by the bishop. Under these conditions the independent-mindedness of the lower clergy in the eighteenth century (which had shown itself in the National Assembly) was not likely to reappear. And another check on the authority of the bishops was removed when the new settlement, though allowing a partial restoration of cathedral chapters, deprived them (in the Organic Articles) of their traditional right of administering the diocese in the time of a vacancy, a right now transferred to the metropolitan bishop.

But if the bishops gained in authority within the Church they lost in independence outside it. For the government now paid their salaries, and not only did it appoint them but it enjoyed a right of veto over their appointment of the lesser clergy, and so acquired a control over the Church stronger than the Bourbons had enjoyed. The Church in France no longer constituted, and would never again constitute, an Estate capable of rivalling the government and acting as an effective check on it. Had it been re-endowed with a property of its own (a point for which the papal negotiators strove unsuccessfully) its position would naturally have been very much stronger than it was now that its priests were salaried by the State; but Bonaparte, too, had appreciated this point, which was one on which he was in agreement with those who had framed the Civil Constitution of the Clergy. It was indeed a fundamental concept of the Revolution that there should be no more Estates in France.

But this centralization of power, as a result of the Concordat, which operated in favour of the bishops (*vis à vis* their inferiors) and in favour of the government (*vis à vis* the Church), also operated, in the long run, in favour of the papacy. At first, and indeed throughout Napoleon's time, the Pope's powers were severely circumscribed; since for much of the time he was Napoleon's prisoner it could hardly be otherwise. But later the powers which the Concordat gave to the Pope greatly strengthened his position in relation to the Church in France. For Consalvi had secured to the Pope not merely the power of investing the bishops, which he had always enjoyed, but the right, in certain circumstances, to depose them, which was something new. It had been necessary for Bonaparte to recognize that the Pope had this deposing power, for without it Pius would have been unable to help him to wind up both the Church of the ancien régime and the Constitutional Church by requiring their bishops to resign. In this way the events of 1802 in France established *de facto* what the Vatican Council later established *de jure*, namely the plenitude of power enjoyed by the Pope in matters of spiritual jurisdiction. Consalvi and Pius VII, in collaboration with Bonaparte, had helped to pave the way for the ultramontane autocracy of Pius IX.

And in the long run – the very long run – this centralization of authority would work exclusively to the advantage of the papacy. For the State would fade out of the picture. By separating herself from the Church in 1905 she would leave the papacy as sole residuary legatee of authority. Henceforth the Pope alone would nominate, invest or remove the bishops, and they alone would appoint or remove the curés. The hierarchy of authority would then be complete, and the whole would reach its apex not in two heads but in one.

CHAPTER TEN

From the Concordat to the Coronation

Neither Consalvi nor Bonaparte could foresee that the agreement they had made would later serve as a model for treaties defining the relations between Church and State all over Europe and become, in the end, a sort of Great Charter to which rulers and the Pope would both appeal.

At the time neither side much liked it, though they were both glad that something had been agreed. Bonaparte, as we have seen, had to wrap it up in the Organic Articles before he dared display it. The Pope disliked it because it failed to make Catholicism the Established Religion of France and because it made no reference to important issues such as the family, education, and especially marriage, in which the traditional rights of the Church had been flouted by the legislation of the Revolution.

It was therefore with some reserve that, in the years immediately following its signature, Rome received the various proposals which were put to her by the smaller powers of central Europe that she should negotiate a similar treaty with them. Their affairs had all been turned upside down by the Revolution and the chaos, from an ecclesiastical point of view, was indescribable. Not only had the Ecclesiastical Electorates of the left bank of the Rhine disappeared, but more than three million Catholics had passed under Protestant (mostly Prussian) rule in this biggest change in the politico-ecclesiastical disposition of Germany since the treaty of Westphalia – a change which carried with it the suppression of monasteries and the confiscation of their lands and property.

The political changes in Germany were regulated by Bonaparte's Rescript of 1802. Though the Church had been a heavy loser one Churchman had gained substantially; Charles-Theodore de Dalberg, Archbishop of Ratisbon, had turned his brother bishops' losses to his own gain. He was given temporal rule over his See of

Ratisbon, with certain other districts, and the position of Elector-Archchancellor, which had hitherto belonged to the Archbishop-Elector of Mainz. Now that it had become evident that some new religious settlement of Germany, presumably to be modelled on that of France, would be needed, Dalberg saw in himself the man who ought evidently to be its architect. But there was the German Diet to consider, and there was also Austria. Dalberg was the protégé of Talleyrand, who had manœuvred him into his new position; if Rome negotiated with him she was accepting the view that France now controlled Germany. But the Hapsburgs, at least, had not accepted such a view, and the Emperor Francis II claimed, with some justice, that it was for him, as it had been for Joseph II, to settle the religious affairs of the Holy Roman Empire with Rome. In the end Consalvi allowed the Nuncio at Vienna to open conversations there with the Emperor, and sent another Nuncio to confer with Dalberg and with the Diet at Ratisbon. It was important to do something, and to do it soon, since the rulers of the various German states – even Maximilian-Joseph, the new Elector of Catholic Bavaria – were now pursuing extreme policies, in accordance with the most enlightened Febronian principles.

Though the position in Germany was serious Rome was more preoccupied with the position in northern Italy. The re-emergence of the Cisalpine Republic was an event calculated to reawaken every fear, religious and political, in the minds of the Curia. Once more the legations, which Rome had refused to give to Austria, were under the control of the French, and of their friends at Milan and Bologna. Complaints were soon pouring into Rome that the anti-clerical laws were being revived. Thus Bishop Giovanni of Brescia, in a letter of August 30, 1801, while admitting that Pius VII had told him to be as conciliatory as possible, insists that his conscience will not allow him to accept the government's decrees on marriage or on the election of parish priests.[1] By the end of the year the Congress of Lyons had assembled to draw up a new constitution for what was now to be called the Republic of Italy. This congress was attended by the archbishops and bishops from the Republic, though Rome was not represented; it drew up 'Organic

---

[1] Vat. Arch. *Epoc. Nap. Italia*, Busta IX, Fasc. 7.

Laws relative to Religion' to be attached to the new Constitution, and they were adopted by acclamation on January 26, 1802, the Archbishop of Ravenna stating that they satisfied the whole of the clergy of the Republic and Bonaparte stressing, in reply, how important it was that the People should remain in harmony with the maxims of its religion and the clergy with the laws of the republic.[1]

So far so good. The merit of the Lyons agreement, ecclesiastically speaking, was that it put an end to the attempt to introduce the Civil Constitution of the Clergy into the valley of the Po. But the spirit of conciliation which had prevailed at Lyons was not adopted by those in power at Milan; by the end of February Cardinal Antonelli was reporting to Consalvi that the governmental inter-ference complained of by the bishops 'makes your hair stand on end',[2] and on June 23 Melzi d'Eril imposed from Milan, in a series of decrees, a system of State control over the Church which was to be administered by a Minister of Cults, and was modelled on the Organic Articles in France. When Pius VII appealed to Bonaparte, in his capacity as President of the Italian Republic, against this viola-tion of the principles agreed at Lyons, the reply was clear and direct: if Rome did not like Melzi's decrees let her negotiate a Concordat with the government at Milan along the lines of the Concordat of 1801 with the government at Paris.[3]

So it came about that, in the summer of 1802, the Legate Caprara at Paris found himself required to negotiate a Concordat for the Italian Republic with her representative in France, Marescalchi. It took over a year to conclude, and the whole business was distasteful to the Pope, first because the Republic included the three legations, and he did not wish, by negotiating with it, to seem to recognize that it had any right over them, and second because he was in no

---

[1] *Ibid.* The proceedings at the Congress are in Fasc. 8 and Fasc. 9. Some of the documentation of the Congress, as well as some belonging to the negotiation of the Italian Concordat, was published by I. Rinieri, along with an extensive commen-tary, in his *Diplomazia Pontificia nel Secolo XIX*, Vol. 2.

[2] Vat. Arch. *ibid.*, Fasc. 3.

[3] On the negotiation of the Italian Concordat of 1803, and its sequel, see Consalvi, *op. cit.*, Vol. 2, pp. 390–91; Rinieri, *op. cit.*, Vol. 2, section 3; and A. Latreille *L'Église Catholique et la Révolution Française*, Hachette, 1950, Vol. 2, pp. 72–77.

wise disposed to settle the status of the Church in any part of Italy
on the same terms as he had settled it in France, and least of all to do
so in a region traditionally part of the Papal States and which
included his previous diocese of Imola and his birth-place, Cesena.
Nothing would induce Consalvi or his master to concede in those
places what they had been obliged to concede in France, namely the
dethronement of the Catholic Church from her position as the
Established Church of the realm, or the secularization of marriage;
even had they been willing to concede them the intense feeling of
the Sacred College on the matter would hardly have permitted
them to. Bonaparte, aware of the difference, religiously speaking,
between Italy and France, which he had recognized in his own
speeches at Milan, was helpful; in the end the Concordat, signed in
September 1803, safeguarded not only those points which were of
special concern to the Pope but also a number of other matters
which were not safeguarded in the French Concordat. It left the
Church in possession of the remnant of the endowment which
she still held, and it made suitable financial provision both for the
clergy and for the seminaries.

What gave particular pleasure at Rome was that the Italian Concordat formally abrogated all the experiments in religious legislation in which the Republics had hitherto indulged. Their satisfaction, however, was premature; they had reckoned without the
resource and determination of Vice-President Melzi. That ingenious man, who had not been the friend and companion of Bonaparte for nothing, had decided to play the same game as the First
Consul had played at the time of the concordational negotiations in
Paris. Having been unable to secure in the Concordat papal approval
for any governmental control over the Church he determined to
obtain it, as Bonaparte had obtained it in France, by attaching to the
published text a decree concerning the way in which it was to be
executed. This decree reaffirmed the validity of the Republic's
earlier religious legislation, save as specifically amended by the Concordat, and went on to assert that, since the Republic was the heir to
the Imperial Dukedom of Milan, it inherited the Hapsburgs'
powers – by which Melzi meant that it could exercise the same
control over the Church as Joseph II had exercised.

Melzi made this move on January 26, 1804. The Pope's reaction was immediate and sharp. He summoned the French ambassador at Rome, who was now none other than Bonaparte's uncle, Cardinal Fesch, and told him he would repudiate the Italian Concordat unless Melzi's decree was withdrawn. And he wrote a personal letter to Bonaparte. The First Consul, already contemplating an imperial crown, and perhaps already a papal coronation, promised to discuss the matter with Caprara. But this, the Pope replied, was not good enough. So vital a matter was the affair of the Pope himself – he did not add that he could no longer trust Caprara not to yield what was necessary to the Church.

So the year 1804 opened with a growing conviction in the mind of the Pope that he needed to have a talk with the all-powerful Bonaparte; a talk about the Organic Articles in France, about the ex-constitutional bishops there, and about Melzi's decree in Italy. To these central problems were added others: the chaos of the Church in Germany, and the distressing circumstances by which the incorporation of Piedmont into France in September 1802 had led to the introduction of the Civil Code into that country, with its secular marriage and divorce laws – something that seemed infinitely shocking in an ancient Italian kingdom, historically devoted to the Church. There were also the rather absurd claims of little Italian states like Lucca to concordats modelled on that of France, and the general disposition in the peninsula to follow the French example by secularizing Church property. The key to a settlement of ecclesiastical questions in the whole of western Europe seemed more and more to lie in reaching an understanding with her arbiter in Paris. And it was becoming less likely that it would be found at Rome because Bonaparte's new avuncular ambassador there was proving a poor substitute for his predecessor Cacault, whose understanding and goodwill had so often proved their value to Rome since the time of the treaty of Tolentino.

Such was the state of religion in the west, such was the mood of the Pope, and such was the mind of Consalvi when there arrived out of the blue the news that the French Tribunate, on May 4, 1804, had declared Napoleon to be Emperor of the French, with hereditary title, and soon after the news that the new Emperor had asked Caprara to sound the Pope as to whether he would come and crown him at Paris.

Despite his desire to have conversations with Napoleon it took the Pope some time to decide whether to accept so unexpected an invitation – too long, as it proved, for there to be any chance of his satisfying the new Emperor's hope that he would be crowned on November 9, the anniversary of the *coup d'état* of Brumaire which had made him First Consul. He could hardly hurry his reply because, at the time when the unofficial invitation was received, his relations with Paris were still clouded by the Organic Articles in France and by Melzi's decrees in Italy, besides a quantity of other outstanding issues. Napoleon was still claiming to be the heir of the Revolution, and his religious intentions for Europe were still quite obscure. Was he inviting the Pope to Paris simply to make him the Emperor's chaplain?

It was a first necessity to sift the ground of the invitation. But if the ground seemed good then, despite the serious arguments against his making the visit, he felt intuitively (and Consalvi told him) he must go. He was prompted less by the hope of striking particular bargains advantageous to the Church than by the fact that, if he crowned Napoleon in Paris, he must surely, in some sort, have a new claim upon him, perhaps even a new hold over him; he must also have unique opportunities to discuss with him the position of the Church in Europe and of pointing out to him what was necessary to her welfare, which seemed to be something he wished to promote in so far as the means proposed were consistent with his other purposes. Moreover a refusal would mean an affront to the man on whom all now seemed to depend.

Of the twenty cardinals consulted by the Pope most were inclined to agree that, under certain conditions, the invitation should be accepted, though two were for rejecting it outright on the grounds that Napoleon represented the Revolution and the Revolution, in the words of de Maistre, was satanic; the Holy Father, they said, should do nothing which could suggest that he approved of it. If only two took this extreme line all had serious misgivings.[1]

---

[1] The cardinals' attitude was summarized in a lengthy despatch from Fesch, which gives an interesting picture of the contrasting opinions at Rome at this time

Le Sacrement de Napoléon Ier. From the painting by David in the Louvre. The detail shows Napoleon crowning Josephine. Pope Pius VI is seated on the right. Madame Lucrezia Bonaparte, Napoleon's mother, is seated in the balcony on the left. *(Giraudon photograph.)*

Most serious, naturally enough, were those of cardinals who were subjects of or connected with the Hapsburgs. Nothing could disguise the affront which, by accepting, the Pope must inflict on Vienna. He had been elected under Hapsburg protection; yet he had refused a pressing invitation and an obvious opportunity to visit Vienna from Venice. By contrast with the behaviour of Austria, whose troops had made it possible to overturn the anti-clericals in Italy in 1799, France, over the past twelve years, had despoiled the Church, plundered the Papal States, and carried off a Supreme Pontiff to exile and death; there might now be a Concordat and a working understanding, but there had been neither restitution nor repentance. Whereas the French had abducted the Pope and eliminated his State, the Austrians, with however ill a grace, had restored him to Rome, even if they had not restored the legations. How could the Pope reward the behaviour of the French by going to Paris and crowning their ruler? And, on personal grounds, what sort of a view could the Emperor Francis be expected to take of the Pope's bestowing so unique a favour on his upstart rival and likely enemy, whose claim to the title of Emperor seemed to the Hapsburg to be no better than an outrage?[1]

And again, the proposed coronation might be a striking political gesture, but might it not prove to be a rash one? Was it wise to assume that the position of Napoleon, and his power over Europe, were in fact secure, that tomorrow might not be Austria's day as 1799 had so surprisingly been? Already France was again at war with Britain, and Britain was negotiating with Naples; might not French influence in the peninsula melt as suddenly as it had in the time of Cardinal Ruffo?

---

and most of which was published by Artaud in his *Histoire du Pape Pie VII*, Vol. 1, pp. 462–69.

[1] The Tsar was equally shocked. In the spring of 1804 he had broken off diplomatic relations with Rome on account of the Pope's 'excessive subservience' to Napoleon. De Maistre, ambassador of the King of Sardinia at St Petersburg, was reflecting opinion there when he wrote the notorious letter in which he said: 'The crimes of an Alexander VI are less revolting than this hideous apostasy on the part of his feeble successor'. (*Mémoires Politiques et Correspondance Diplomatique de J. de Maistre*, Paris, 1858, p. 138.) But he lived to pay his tribute to Pius VII's resistance in *Du Pape*.

Nor were such precedents as could be found very reassuring. If the Pope were thought to be going to Paris to plead for better treatment for the Church in France the effect on papal prestige was likely to be no better than had been that produced by Pius VI's journey to Vienna. If it were thought that he was going at the behest of Napoleon Europe would say that the days of the Babylonian captivity at Avignon had come again. To find an exact precedent for what was now proposed it was necessary to go back to the eighth century, when Pope Stephen II had journeyed from Rome to crown the father of Charlemagne, Pepin the Short. That was more than a millenium ago; moreover Pepin had undertaken on that occasion to meet every request of the Pope and had fulfilled his pledge by fighting the Saxons and the Lombards and making a present of Ravenna to Rome; while his son Charlemagne, whose Empire Napoleon claimed he was renewing, had made the journey to Rome to be crowned by the Pope. Carlovingian precedents were only invoked by Napoleon when it suited him to do so; he liked to be regarded at Rome as the new Charlemagne, but the relationship which he proposed between Pius VII and himself was rather different from that which had existed between the founder of the Holy Roman Empire and Pope Leo III.

To the cardinals it seemed that some concession, some *quid pro quo* for so great a service, must be demanded. The Church and the papacy would only be brought into ridicule if the French ruler continued to treat their protests with impunity while making use of their services. So long conversations were held in Rome during the summer months of the year 1804 between Consalvi and Fesch.[1] Consalvi wanted to know what Napoleon meant when he said he would take an oath, at his coronation, to respect the 'laws of the Concordat and the liberty of cults'. Did the 'laws of the Concordat' include the Organic Articles? No, said Fesch, they meant only the Concordat itself. And did the 'liberty of cults' mean parity of status for all churches and sects? No; it meant only that all churches and

---

[1] See Consalvi *Mémoires*, Vol. 2, pp. 393–412; also A. Latreille's analysis of the Fesch papers in his *Napoléon et le Saint-Siège, 1801–1808* (Paris, 1935), p. 299, etc., and J. Leflon's analysis of the diplomatic papers in the French National Archives in his *Crise Révolutionnaire*, p. 225.

sects would be protected in their different forms of worship. So far, apparently, so good. But Consalvi felt that the French government's good intentions should be demonstrated by some positive act, and especially by the removal from their Sees of those ex-constitutional bishops like Le Coz of Besançon who continued to refuse to be reconciled with the Holy See. Fesch agreed. So did Bernier, who knew how much harm Le Coz was doing. No doubt if Napoleon could have removed the offenders without seeming to weaken in the face of ultramontanism he would have done so; but on this matter, and on the matter of a modification of the Organic Articles, all that Consalvi could obtain at Rome or Caprara could obtain at Paris was a promise that, if the Pope would raise these questions when he was in Paris, Talleyrand felt sure he would receive satisfaction.

It was not very reassuring. Nor was the brusque formal invitation when it arrived from Napoleon on September 29. The Emperor, it said, would give 'new proofs' of the goodwill he had always shown towards the Church. It was a curt note, and Pius was at first so offended that he was much inclined to leave it unanswered.

Nevertheless he did answer, and with an acceptance. With misgivings, but still not without hope, he planned his departure for Paris, putting Consalvi in charge at Rome, and making it clear to the Emperor Francis II that there would be no question of his discussing at Paris a settlement of ecclesiastical affairs in Germany. This last assurance was the least he could give to appease the offended Holy Roman Emperor. He had to show that he regarded Germany as Francis' affair, though in fact Napoleon already ruled on the Rhine, and within two years the Holy Roman Empire would have been wound up.

CHAPTER ELEVEN

The Coronation of Napoleon

I t was not until November 2, 1804, that the convoy, comprising more than a hundred persons, including the Pope and six cardinals, at last emerged slowly through the Flaminian gate on the first stage of the journey to Paris. The Emperor had asked for twelve cardinals, including Consalvi. But the Pope had been anxious not to give the impression that the Sacred College as a whole was moving up to Paris. Doubtless he was right to leave the Secretary of State at Rome; on the other hand it was a pity that he did not take a stronger team with him. Of those who went the best was Borgia, and he died en route at Lyon. That left Antonelli as the leader, and he showed at Paris a lack of grasp of the essential issues which contrasted painfully with Consalvi's performance there four years earlier. Nor could he or the other cardinals speak French.

Crossing the Apennines by way of Pistoia and Modena, and the Alps by way of the Mont Cenis, the papal party had reached the forest of Fontainebleau when it met – of all people – the impatient Emperor. It was an accident contrived by Napoleon so that, meeting the Pope casually, while hunting in the forest, he was able to avoid that deferential obeisance in front of the Parisians which custom would have demanded at the gates of the capital. He could not avoid riding back to Paris in the papal coach; nor could he avoid sitting on the left side of his guest, since that was the side he was offered. But he took care that they entered Paris by night so that his humiliation was not observed. That the Pope was not only Head of the Church, but also a temporal ruler the antiquity of whose throne gave him precedence over every other European monarch, was to be ignored during the visit. The Emperor, whose own title was less than a year old, assumed the precedence over his guest on every social occasion in Paris, and seemed determined to humiliate him. Many, at the time and since, have been puzzled to account for his behaviour. Clearly, if he wanted the coronation to make the right impression on the French Church and on the French nation, if he wanted it to invest his new position with divine authority, he should have been at pains to make it as clear as he could that the rite was being administered by the highest spiritual power, the Vicar of Christ and Head of His Church, and this would necessitate his treating the Pope with the greatest deference. It seemed odd that he should summon the Bishop of Rome with a view to giving a special sanction to his new office, and then treat him with less respect than the Archbishop of Paris might hope to enjoy. The principal historian of the coronation, Frédéric Masson, who was anti-ultramontane and devoted to Napoleon, could only explain his behaviour by saying that he was a 'strange man', with an 'unconquerable aversion to being bored', who was unable to restrain himself. 'When search is made for profound reasons and thought-out designs it is often necessary to be satisfied with the workings of an impulsive temperament swayed by affection, anger, and ill-humour; one which mingles spontaneous and unguarded actions with weighed and reasoned resolutions.'[1] But the studied discourtesy of Napoleon's treatment of Pius VII, of which Consalvi made bitter complaint, which began with the meeting in the forest of Fontainebleau and only ended with the unwelcome arrangements made for the guest's return journey, was occasioned by something more than boredom and ill-humour. It was a calculated policy, possibly ill-judged, certainly ill-mannered, but intended. It was designed to show that the Emperor was master and that the Pope was little more than his chaplain.

On the other hand, in Napoleon's view it was no small distinction to be his chaplain. It never seems to have occurred to him that he was not conferring honour upon the Pope by associating him closely with himself, in however humble a capacity. Nor did he wish to humiliate him in relation to anybody except himself; it suited him, at this stage in his career, to raise the Pope above the Gallican bishops. With his authoritarian and tidy mind he liked the idea of an authoritarian Church, under a single Head, always

[1] See the introduction to his *Le sacre et le couronement de Napoléon*, Paris, 1908. There is an English translation by Frederic Cobb, Fisher Unwin, 1911.

provided that that Head were under himself. It suited him that the
Church in western Europe should be one, and that the Pope should
control it, since in that case it was only necessary that he should control the Pope in order to gain a great increase in his own authority.
By summoning the Pope to Paris to crown him he made it clear
that he fully recognized the supremacy of the See of Peter; it was an
un-Gallican act – which was why Masson, who was a Gallican, disliked it so. It showed that, though crowned 'Emperor of the
French', he did not think the Gallican Church good enough to
crown him. But having got Pius to Paris it was equally necessary, in
his view, that he should make it clear that he, Napoleon, was the
master. Hence his discourtesy on social occasions and his unsuitable
assumption of the precedence; hence, on the occasion of the coronation itself, his keeping the Pope waiting a whole hour in Notre
Dame before he himself arrived, and his refusal to let the Pope place
the crown on his head. His refusal to confess himself or to receive
Communion he claimed later were due to his still having too much
faith to wish to commit a sacrilege.

Masson asks the question: if he thus showed himself a bad
Catholic what had he to gain from the Catholic ceremonial? The
answer would seem to lie in his constantly repeated phrase that he
was 'Protector of the Catholic Church'. Without being an obedient
son of the Church, he would yet protect her; though above the
Church, he would show he had her blessing; though superior to the
Pope, he would show that the Pope would support him. It was an
advanced position, implying a very different relationship between
Emperor and Pope from that accepted by Charlemagne, of whom
Napoleon was so fond of reminding Pius. The real analogy was
much more recent, being provided by the Emperor Joseph II.
Napoleon's view of his relations with the Church was not an
original one, it was that of an enlightened despot. Like Joseph II he
was above the Church, like Joseph II he would even regard himself
as entitled to invade the sphere of the spiritual, as he would show a
little later when he introduced his Imperial Catechism, Feast of
Saint Napoleon, and similar extravagances. When Pius VI had
visited Vienna the Emperor Joseph II had treated him more cere-
moniously than Napoleon treated Pius VII but the underlying

realities of the position had been much the same. Just as Febronian Vienna (especially the university), by its anti-Roman attitude, had much strengthened Joseph's hand, enabling him to pose as a moderate so far as the claims of Rome were concerned, so Napoleon could point, at Paris, to the attitude of the philosophers, of the ex-constitutional clergy, or of the Protestants, all of whom found expression in his Council of State. In his dealings with the Pope he could remind him of what was only too true, namely that he was surrounded by men who had only swallowed the Concordat because it was coated with the Organic Articles, who disliked the Pope's visit, and who expected the Emperor to make it clear that, although he had invited the Pope, he was no ultramontane, but respected the ancient Gallican liberties. Just because he was being crowned by the Pope, who had not crowned the Bourbons, he had to demonstrate his independence, had to appear to be as good a Gallican as Louis XIV had been. Bad manners cost him nothing; they were part of his publicity.

But no doubt, too, Napoleon's feelings did have something to do with his behaviour; he was rather bored by Pius's visit and at times thoroughly irritated by his guest. The Pope, though saintly, and not without a quiet sense of humour, was not scintillating, and he had a kind of gentle, smiling obstinacy, perceptible in David's portrait of him in the Louvre, which was calculated to annoy the worldly and impatient Emperor. Moreover being determined, despite every discouragement, to raise at least some of the points on which the Curia had insisted, the Pope ended by outstaying his welcome, being still at his quarters at the Tuileries at the beginning of April 1805, by which time Napoleon had already left for Milan to be crowned there as King of Italy. All the same the Emperor respected the Pope; he called him a 'good man' and a 'good priest' and he believed he could persuade him to fill the role for which he had cast him in the new Empire. The great point, he felt sure, would be to separate the Pope from the cardinals, and especially from Consalvi; he would get what he wanted if he dealt with the Pope personally. For this reason he had already suggested that Pius would be much better advised to abandon Rome and come and live either at Avignon or – better – at Paris, where he promised to

see that the Head of the Church was suitably provided for and protected. But neither in 1804 nor later would Pius entertain this often
repeated idea. He was as determined to keep himself independent of
Napoleon as he had earlier been determined to keep himself independent of Francis II and, understanding the importance of the
Eternal City to this independence, he was as sensitive about his
position as her bishop and ruler while he was at Paris as he had
been earlier at the time of his election at Venice. The future would
show how important was his stand on this point to the rebirth of
Rome as an independent spiritual power.

Already, before the coronation had taken place, the Emperor
had been brought up sharply against the Pope's firmness when confronted by the kind of proposition which his spiritual position made
it impossible for him to accept. The Emperor had only been
through a civil form of marriage to his consort Josephine. This he
had kept dark, but the astute Josephine, aware that her husband
might one day wish for a better-born bride, especially if she proved
unable to give him an heir, thought it well to inform Cardinal Fesch
of the fact. Appalled to discover from the Cardinal that he was
being asked to crown a couple who were living in sin, the Pope insisted on a religious ceremony of marriage which was duly performed by Fesch on the afternoon before the coronation. It was the
first time Napoleon had been brought up, in a personal way,
against a fixed law of the Church and a wholly unyielding Pope,
but another occasion would arise in the following year and would
cause him much greater annoyance. This was when the Pope refused his insistent demands that he should declare the marriage of
the Emperor's younger brother Jerome to a Protestant girl,
Elizabeth Patterson, at Baltimore, to be invalid. Every political and
ecclesiastical advantage for Pius seemed to lie with making the
proposed declaration; but Canon law stood in the way.

A good man and a good priest. The Pope was both but he did
not, anyhow in the view of the cardinals, at Rome, show himself at
Paris to be a good bargainer. He allowed Cardinal Antonelli, who
took charge of the matter of the petitions which were to be put to
Napoleon, to confuse what was trivial with what was important in

a way Consalvi would never have allowed. On certain relatively minor matters the Emperor proved accommodating: he was prepared to agree to some improvement in the pay and pensions of the French clergy, to closer episcopal control over their discipline, to the return of certain secularized churches, to the restoration of some nursing Orders, and of some non-French Orders, to the encouragement of a better observance of Sunday, and to a renewal of the traditional French payments towards the maintenance of the Lateran Basilica at Rome. But these were all questions which could have been thrashed out between his Minister of Cults, Portalis, and the Papal Legate, Caprara. On the major questions which preoccupied the cardinals Pius was almost uniformly unsuccessful. Napoleon would not consider any modification of the Organic Articles, nor the establishment of Catholicism as the State or dominant religion of France, nor a modification of the divorce laws in the Civil Code. To a tentative suggestion that he should mark the occasion by restoring at least some of the territories he had taken from the Church he would only reply evasively with vague allusions to better days to come for the Temporal Sovereignty. There was a certain force in raising the matter of the legations on this occasion,[1] since Napoleon was always talking about Charlemagne, and Charlemagne had marked his own papal coronation by restoring to the papacy his father's gift of Ravenna, which was precisely one of the legations now in question. On the other hand Napoleon was about to be crowned at Milan as King of Italy, and it was hardly possible that he should mark the transformation of the Italian Republic into a Kingdom by signing away part of its territory.

On one only of the major points which concerned the cardinals did Napoleon act positively in the manner desired of him; he was prepared to tell the recalcitrant ex-constitutional bishops, and especially Le Coz of Besançon, that they should reconcile themselves with the Pope on the matter of their past adherence to the Civil Constitution of the Clergy by signing a document submitting

---

[1] But not earlier, when the *conditions* for the visit were being hammered out at Rome. A demand then for the legations would have had the appearance of simony – see A. Latreille *Napoléon et le Saint Siège*, 1801–1808 (Paris, 1935), pp. 299–300, based on the Fesch papers at Lyon. Consalvi resisted Fesch's repeated suggestions, at Rome, that he should demand the legations (Consalvi, *Mémoires*, Vol. 2, p. 401).

themselves to all the decisions of the Holy See on the ecclesiastical affairs of France. But even after this admonition Le Coz never signed, because he would not accept as valid the crucial papal decision, namely Pius VI's condemnation of the Civil Constitution; the Pope had to be content with a personal interview at which many tears were shed, and Le Coz protested his absolute loyalty, but at which the past was not discussed. The ex-constitutional bishops were all now reconciled; but this was something achieved at Paris by Pius's manifest sincerity and spirituality, which impressed them all, rather than by Napoleon's authority.

If Napoleon's behaviour towards the Pope was calculated, and not merely bad manners, and if his rudeness was partly assumed, it has yet to be admitted that his natural manners were shocking. As Talleyrand said, it was a pity that a man of his genius had been so badly brought up. Even when he intended to behave as an Emperor was expected to behave he was always failing. In the matter, for instance, of the present-giving with which etiquette demanded that such an occasion should end almost everything went wrong. It was probably as well that the gifts of money to each of the cardinals were kept relatively small, but it was a pity that Napoleon said beforehand that they would be much larger. The two state coaches, to be presented to the Pope, of which there was much talk, were never in fact presented at all. And the splendid tiara, which was Napoleon's main present, proved particularly unacceptable, for it displayed as its principal jewel the large emerald which Pius VI had been obliged to remove from the triple crown at the Vatican and hand over to the French as part of the indemnity exacted at Tolentino. Consalvi's indignation was understandable.[1]

The Pope, with his love of simplicity, disliked the present-giving and was considerably embarrassed by the pensions for his own brothers and his sister which Napoleon caused to be made payable by the French Controller-General; he managed to prevent the same thing being done for his cousins. What he liked best was to move freely about in the streets of Paris, visiting the churches, giving Communion, and blessing the crowds in the streets. Nor was he at all averse to seeing the secular sights, such as the Bois de Boulogne,

[1] Consalvi *Mémoires*, Vol. 2, p. 425.

the Invalides, the Sèvres porcelain factory, or the place where the Gobelins tapestries were woven. His companions enjoyed this too, nor did some of them see much harm in hinting that the Pope's fancy had been caught by this porcelain vase or by that piece of tapestry; it seemed to them only a fair exchange, for Paris had afforded them the sight of some rare pieces of classical sculpture which they had last seen at the Vatican labelled *ex munificentia Pii VI*.

At first, fearful that the Emperor meant to try to keep him a prisoner at Paris, Pius would demand that the conveyances be prepared for his return. Later, when it was clear that he could return when he wanted, and when Paris had proved to be a very different place from the blasphemous centre of atheism of which he had heard speak at Rome, he was more inclined to stay. It was partly that he wanted to secure some concrete concessions; but it was also that his own popularity at Paris was so evident, and the good he could do just by appearing in public, or by talking with the Emperor's entourage, so palpable, that there was some inducement for him to stay, though the Emperor was induced, by the same symptoms, to hasten his departure. When at last, early in April 1805, he felt that the time for departure had come, the roads were lined with kneeling men and women, with their rosaries, awaiting his blessing; but his movements were carefully planned for him so that he should not spend Easter either at Paris or at Lyons, where the manifestations of his popularity might have proved embarrassing to the Emperor.

The real significance, in the long run, of Pius VII's visit to Paris lay in these popular demonstrations. They represented the first flickering into flame of a new feeling about the papacy in France, a first open manifestation of a new ultramontane sentiment. The visit gave an opportunity to those who had been disillusioned by the Civil Constitution, disgusted by the anti-Christian crusade, impressed by the courage of the non-juring priests, and moved by the martyrdom of Pius VI at Valence, to show their feelings; and they found in Pius VII the kind of Pope they wanted to find, not a worldly prince, but a sensitive and spiritual person. And to the Pope his new knowledge of his hold on the French people was a joy to which he frequently returned in what he said when he was back in

Rome. That knowledge, together with the knowledge which he believed (erroneously, as it proved) he had gained of the mind and personality of the Emperor, and the chance he had had to explain the needs of the Church, provided for him the justification of his visit, outweighing the absence of practical concessions.

But it was not to be expected that all the members of the Sacred College would see matters in that light. To some it seemed that the Pope had conceded everything and gained nothing; those who had all along been opposed on principle to the visit had some sympathy with the Roman *pasquinades* which said that Pius VII had lost his faith to save his throne whereas Pius VI had lost his throne to save his faith. They resented the lack of any concessions to the Church in France, but they were at heart a great deal more concerned about the position in Italy. Were Melzi's decrees to be sustained at Milan, and thus the Church in the new Kingdom of Italy (successor to the Italian Republic and heir to the legations) to be controlled in the same way as the Church in France? Was the Civil Code, with its divorce laws, to be maintained in full force at Turin?

Unfortunately, even on Italy the Pope could say very little. One rather surprising crumb of comfort he could provide, though it did not concern Napoleon or his intentions. On the return journey from Paris, while the papal party had been at Florence, Scipione de Ricci, of all people, had presented himself and made a full and humble retraction of his Febronian errors, accepting Pius VI's Bull *Auctorem fidei*, of 1794, in which the resolutions of the Synod of Pistoia had been denounced. This act, which gave particular pleasure both to Pius and to Rome, marked the end of a movement in Tuscany which had centred itself on Ricci and on his disciples.[1]

But the legations were the prime consideration. The cardinals wanted them back. If they could not have them back they wanted to know how free the Church was going to be in the Po valley, and in particular whether Napoleon was going to support Melzi d'Eril in his religious legislation. Pius could not say much; but he could defend his behaviour at Paris and he could hold out hopes. He had

[1] Letters on Ricci's retraction in Rinieri, *Napoleone e Pio VII* (Turin, 1906), Part 2, pp. 625–34.

resisted Napoleon's pressing invitation that he should himself crown the new King with the iron crown of Lombardy, in the duomo at Milan, which would have amounted to the Pope's giving his own blessing to the loss of the legations. On the other hand he had allowed the Legate Caprara to go and perform the ceremony. This he had done becauseNapoleon had assured him that, if Caprara came, he should hear welcome things from the throne at Milan about the future regulation of the Church in Italy. But they did not prove very welcome. The new King announced from Milan at the end of May that the Italian Concordat would come into force at the end of June and he made no mention of Melzi's decrees, which it was reasonable to suppose were now dropped. But in a few days, on June 8, in characteristic Napoleonic manner, he proceeded, without consulting Rome, to reorganize both the parishes and the Religious Orders in his kingdom, suppressing some and restricting others; it was all very reminiscient of Melzi and it offended Consalvi as keenly; the Pope protested against the unilateral action, which was contrary to the Concordat. On the other hand Napoleon's re-organization was a generous one, putting the Italian Church on a better financial footing than she had enjoyed under the republics, and a much better one than that of the Church in France, and there was to be some compensation for the losses she had sustained during the period of revolution. In short, if Napoleon seemed in practice to be continuing at Milan the state-interference in ecclesiastical affairs which had been Melzi's policy (and indeed that of Joseph II and Leopold at Milan before him) there also seemed to be some grounds for hope that, after his own fashion, he would sustain the Church financially and – what seemed most important to Rome – would maintain her in the position of Religion of the State which the Italian Concordat, unlike the French, had given her and which, in the Roman view, was the essential feature of that Concordat.

But all chance that Rome would co-operate with the Napoleonic reorganization of the Church in Italy was ruined by the announce-ment that the French Civil Code would be introduced on January 1. This Code was sharply at variance with the Catholic principles of civil law in Italy, most notably in the provision which it made for divorce. Divorce in the Papal States! – for this was what divorce at

Bologna or Ravenna still meant to Rome. The scandal was un-
endurable. Pius could not believe Napoleon meant it, because he
thought it was a point he had cleared up with him at Paris. A
protest was sent at once.

But it seemed that the new King of Italy did mean it. He replied
to the Pope that the Roman view on this matter was one no longer
adapted to the century in which they were all now living.[1] To Fesch
(back at Rome now as French Ambassador) he wrote that he
intended to maintain friendly relations with the Pope but that he
could make no changes of principle in what he had decreed at
Milan.[2]

Napoleon never seemed to realize how profound was the disillusionment and anger created at Rome by his behaviour at Milan.
He would soon be noticing the change in the Pope's attitude but
would attribute it, wrongly, to the fact that his own military
position was once more endangered, this time by the armies of the
Third Coalition. Actually the change in the attitude of Rome was
due to the fact that the Pope felt himself to have been deceived, and
that some of the cardinals (notably di Pietro, who had been at Paris
for the coronation and had since become hostile to the Emperor)
felt the same thing even more strongly. And it was now that Consalvi, hitherto accused of being pro-French, became convinced that
the time had come to resist every fresh encroachment by Napoleon,
whether in the sphere of the spiritual or in that of the temporal.

Nothing, in the Roman view, so symbolized all that was repre-
hensible about the Enlightenment and the Revolution as did the
divorce laws. States which adopted them were giving legal recognition to a flat repudiation of a Catholic sacrament; for a state which
officially styled itself as Catholic to do so seemed a contradiction in
terms. How was the proclamation of the Civil Code compatible
with the proclamation of Catholicism as the Religion of the Kingdom of Italy? Already the Civil Code was operative in Piedmont,
annexed to France; it was now being introduced into Parma.
Tuscany was already encircled, with the French established in Leg-

---

[1] *Correspondance de Napoléon* (Paris, 1858–70), Vol. XI, No. 9091.
[2] *Ibid.*, No. 9092.

horn and Lucca to the west and in Bologna to the east. What Napoleon did or said at Milan would set the fashion everywhere in northern Italy; by the end of the year he would have greatly enlarged the size and influence of his new kingdom by incorporating into it Venice with her Adriatic islands.

In northern Italy then the Church, not only in her political sovereignty, in her property, in her organization, and in her administration, but also in moral matters in which Italians had always been subject to her law, saw herself threatened rather than protected by Napoleon. And the Pope, who this same summer had been trying to explain to him, in a lengthy letter, why he could not nullify his brother Jerome's valid marriage to the Protestant girl at Baltimore, was reconciling himself to the unpalatable truth that he had taught the Emperor nothing, at Paris, about what the Church held sacrosanct.

CHAPTER TWELVE

The Abduction of Pius VII

Napoleon said that Italy was a mistress he would share with nobody. But if he were to remain on terms with Pius VII it was necessary he should share her with the Pope. This he was not prepared to do; which was the immediate cause of the rupture of his relations with Rome, a rupture which came soon after the unpromising honeymoon of his coronation.

Some of the French hierarchy – and notably Cardinal Maury, who had made his peace with Napoleon – thought that the Curia was largely to blame for the conflict which followed, on the grounds that Rome was losing sight of the higher interests of the Church by allowing political questions about her temporal sovereignty in the Papal States to lead her into conflict with the Defender of Christendom, the new Charlemagne. It was nothing to them that Napoleon should occupy Ancona (October 1805), or march his armies through papal territory, in the following year, on their way to Naples, or order the Pope to blockade his ports against British shipping. They accepted the Emperor's argument that he was founding a great new Catholic Empire, whose principal opponents were the Protestant English, the schismatic Russians, and the Mohammedans he had defeated in Egypt; and they were inclined to share the Emperor's view that it was intolerable that the Pope should be so blind as to allow his miserable political preoccupations with his 'petty duchy' to stand in the way of the realizing of so great a design. No doubt their French patriotism helped them to adopt a rather rosy view of the religious complexion of Napoleon's Empire but they could point to the fact that, extending as it did over France, Belgium, the Rhineland and northern Italy it was mostly Catholic, and that to Napoleon personally had been due the restoration of the Church in France.

To the Pope however it seemed equally obvious that Napoleon's

Pius VII. From the portrait by Sir Thomas Lawrence at Windsor Castle.
(*By gracious permission of H.M. The Queen.*)

greatest victories had been won over the Catholic Empire of Austria and that his much-vaunted protection of the papacy was in fact becoming a spiritual as well as a political enslavement. If he were to be allowed to extend his political control over the Italian peninsula, and especially over the Papal States, not only would the temporal power be at an end but the secularization implicit in his Milan decrees would reach even to Rome. Nor, it seemed, would it be only a matter of political control over clergy, Religious Orders, and seminaries, or the introduction of the Civil Code. For in France, by the year 1806, matters had gone further than that. Feasts, as Holy Days of obligation, were part of the Emperor's new provisions by the year 1806. Was Rome, then, to be expected to observe the new Feast of Saint Napoléon (the obscure saint of doubtful authenticity after whom Madame Mère had named her son) which had been instituted in France for August 16, being intended to eclipse the Feast of the Assumption on August 15, and for which Bernier had been induced to write a suitable liturgy? Or would Italian children have to learn the new catechism, devised by Napoleon for universal use in French Sunday schools, which included the following questions and answers:

QUESTION: What are the duties of Christians towards the princes who govern them, and what, in particular, are our duties towards Napoleon I, our Emperor?
ANSWER: Christians owe to the princes who govern them, and we, in particular, owe to Napoleon I, our Emperor, love, respect, obedience, loyalty, military service and the taxes ordered for the preservation of his Empire and his throne. . . .
QUESTION: Why are we bound in all these duties towards our Emperor?
ANSWER: First, because God, who creates Empires and apportions them according to His will, by heaping upon him His gifts, has set him up as our sovereign and made him the agent of His power, and His image on earth. So to honour and serve our Emperor is to honour and serve God himself . . .

Such a catechism might secure the approval, as it did, of the compliant Legate Caprara at Paris, and so be accepted by the French hierarchy, who were told that it had the approval of Rome. But in

M

fact the Congregation charged with its examination had rejected it, as did the Pope. If he could not defend France from this sort of Caesaro-Papism Pius would yet strive to defend Italy.

The French occupation of Ancona on October 18, 1805, by Gouvion Saint-Cyr, on Napoleon's orders, had sound military reasons behind it. The Third Coalition against the Emperor was already in being, and he himself was engaged in his campaign against the Austrians in Bavaria, leaving his Viceroy of Italy, Eugène, to confront them in Lombardy. The British navy was sailing into the harbour of Naples and a Russian force was being landed. Once more Napoleon was in serious military danger, for behind the Austrian army with which he was engaged in Bavaria lay a large Russian army. What if, while Eugène was preoccupied in opposing the ablest of the Austrian generals, the Archduke Charles, the events of 1799 were to be repeated in Italy? This danger Napoleon had foreseen, and he had laid his plans in advance; an important part of those plans was the occupation of Ancona. Saint-Cyr's troops were there to discourage the Neapolitan army from marching north, and to prevent the British navy from occupying it and opening up communications through the Adriatic with the Austrians.

But the Pope saw the occupation as a clear sign that his sovereignty over what remained of the Papal States was no longer to be respected and that the whole Italian peninsula would fall under French control. He therefore wrote to the Emperor on November 13, 1805, threatening to break off diplomatic relations if the force were not withdrawn:

'... We will speak frankly; ever since Our return from Paris We have experienced nothing but bitterness and disillusionment whereas the personal knowledge which We had acquired of Your Majesty, and Our own invariable conduct, had promised, by contrast, something quite different. In a word, We have not found in Your Majesty that return of Our goodwill which we had the right to expect.

'We feel this keenly, and, in regard to the present invasion, We say sincerely that what We owe to Ourselves, and the obligations which We have contracted towards Our subjects, force Us to demand from

Your Majesty the evacuation of Ancona; and We do not see how it would be possible to reconcile a refusal to do this with the continuance of relations with Your Majesty's minister at Rome. . . .'[1]

Napoleon never forgot or forgave this letter. Even on Saint Helena he spoke of Pius VII having taken up the pen of Gregory VII; a turning-point had been reached in the relations between the Emperor and Rome. Disillusioned by Napoleon's attitude at Milan and threatened by his action at Ancona, the cardinals showed a new unanimity in deciding to resist. On this the Pope, Consalvi and the Sacred College were now at one.

On January 7, 1806, having imposed onerous terms on the defeated Austrians at Pressburg and acquired Venice and her dependencies (to be added to the Kingdom of Italy) Napoleon replied to the Pope. He told Pius he had felt it keenly that 'when all the powers in English pay were in coalition to make an unjust war on him' the Pope should have sent so ill-considered a letter. The occupation of Ancona had been necessitated by its lack of military preparedness; it was in the Pope's interest that it should be in the Emperor's hands rather than in those of the English and Turks. Like his Bourbon predecessors he was the Eldest Son of the Church, and he would go on defending her from Greeks (i.e. Russians – of the Orthodox Church) and from Moslems, despite the ingratitude of those who thought he was lost. His Holiness could dismiss his minister and welcome instead the English, or the Caliph of Constantinople; but he would not expose Cardinal Fesch to such insults. He would replace him by a layman. Fesch, the Emperor said, had met with nothing but hatred from Consalvi, who had refused to see him, while receiving the Emperor's enemies.[2] And in another letter of the same date, Napoleon told Fesch to tell Consalvi that he must either do as the Emperor wished or else resign from the Secretaryship of State.[3]

In the crisis which now developed rapidly there were personal factors and religious factors; but Napoleon's immediate and press-

[1] Artaud, Vol. 2, p. 103.

[2] Nap. *Corr.*, Vol. XI, No. 9655. Napoleon particularly resented Consalvi's friendliness towards the Emperor's disobedient brother Lucien who was at Rome.

[3] *Ibid.*, No. 9656.

ing needs were military, and Rome's immediate aim was to save
the Papal States. The personal factor was the antipathy between
Cardinal Fesch and Consalvi, which dated from the mistrust Consalvi had shown during his negotiations with the ambassador about
the Pope's visit to Paris.[1] This antipathy was at least partly due to
Consalvi's professional dislike of the very unprofessional Fesch,
who irritated him by fussing over every scuffle in the streets of
Rome, and by getting over-excited. The religious factor was
Rome's grave disillusionment over Napoleon's behaviour at Milan.
Napoleon's religious plan for Italy had become the Italian Concordat, as interpreted by Melzi, coupled with the Civil Code; and
with every fresh acquisition – Venice, Lucca and Guastalla, Naples,
Tuscany – this unacceptable state and secular control were advanced. Were they to be advanced as far as Rome herself? The
prospect lent some religious colour to Consalvi's obstinacy in
defending temporalities.

All the same, the struggle which opened with the year 1806 was
essentially directed, on Napoleon's side, towards bringing Italy
into his political system, and preventing her from becoming again
the potential source of danger to him which she still had been in the
autumn of 1805, while the Pope's immediate aim was to preserve
the independence of his states. It was awkward for both sides that
those states lay in the middle of the peninsula. As Elliott, British
Minister at Naples, drily observed to Cardinal Benvenuti, who was
urging that England, too, should observe Roman neutrality, the
geographical position of those states was 'unfortunate'.[2]

In a long reply to Napoleon on January 29, 1806,[3] the Pope was
at first conciliatory. He had never thought of giving Fesch his passports, only of breaking off public relations with him, so as to show
the Russian ambassador at Rome that the French occupation of
Ancona had not been undertaken at the Pope's instigation. And so
far from supposing the Emperor 'lost', he reminded him that at the
time when he had written to him, on November 13, his armies had
already been at the gates of Vienna, and the 'glorious success of his
great genius' had decided the issue of the war. (This was partly true.

[1] Consalvi Mémoires, 2, 402–403.   [2] Vat. Arch., Loc. Sit., Busta VIII, Fasc. 12.
[3] Printed in Artaud, Vol. 2, pp. 108–112.

Ulm had been won; but Austerlitz was yet to come.) Consalvi, the Pope went on, had been very distressed to hear that he was thought to be hostile to Fesch; he could call to mind no instance of this hostility. Indeed the Secretary of State was begging the Pope to let him resign, rather than be an obstacle to understanding, but he (Pius) could not let him do that. The Pope's letter, however, ends in a less conciliatory vein. Now that Napoleon holds Venice, Pius begs him to 'preserve intact the religion which is dominant there, and not to make innovations in regard to the regular or secular clergy'. And further, in view of his other gains, will he not think the time opportune to hand back the legations? And again, now that the danger is past, could not life at Ancona return to normal? The letter ends with a request for immediate payment to meet the Pope's expenses in provisioning the French troops at the port.

But life at Ancona could not return to normal because it was a base for the French invasion of Naples, begun on February 8, 1806. By the 15th French troops were in the capital, and Joseph Bonaparte, amidst scenes of enthusiasm, was attending Mass at Saint Januarius.

On February 13 Napoleon replied to the Pope. Now that he had invaded Naples his claims were doubled. 'All Italy will be under my law. I shall not interfere with the independence of the Holy See. I shall even pay the expenses which the movements of my troops will occasion. But the conditions must be that Your Holiness has the same respect for me in the temporal sphere that I have for him in the spiritual, and that he abandons useless intrigues with the heretic enemies of the Church, and with powers which can do him no good. Your Holiness is Sovereign of Rome, but I am the Emperor. All my enemies must be his.' The Pope must banish all enemy nationals, and exclude their ships from his harbours. 'Most Holy Father, I know that Your Holiness means well, but he is surrounded by men who do not.' Such men are causing unreasonable delays in investing his bishops, making it impossible for him to administer the Church in France or in Germany, trying to oblige him to see his family accept Protestant marriages. While thinking about 'worldly interests, and the vain prerogatives of the Tiara, they are allowing souls to perish, souls which are the true foundation of religion.'[1]

[1] Nap. *Corr.*, Vol. XII, No. 9805.

The Pope's reply of March 21 provides the classic statement of the papal position in regard to the temporal power. He formally rejects the Emperor's claims. The Emperor is menacing the dignity of the Holy See and the most unalterable and respected rights of its free sovereignty. The Emperor's demands conflict with the Pope's defending his trust, namely 'the patrimony of the Roman Church which has been transmitted to us over so long a series of centuries, by our predecessors, and which we have promised, in face of the All Powerful, at the foot of the altar, and by the most sacred oaths, to pass on intact to those who will succeed us'. He cannot exclude the allied nationals, or their ships, not because of his temporal interests, but because it would be an act of war, and 'We are the Vicar of a God of peace, which means peace towards all, without distinction between Catholics and Heretics, or between those living near at hand and those living far away, or between those from whom we hope for benefits and those from whom we expect evil . . . only the necessity of withstanding hostile aggression, or defending religion in danger, has given our predecessors a just reason for abandoning a pacific policy. If any of them, by human weakness, departed from these Principles his conduct, we say it frankly, can never serve as an example for ours.' Besides, hostile action would cut him off from Catholics in the countries offended. 'The Catholics living in those lands are not small in number; there are millions in the Russian Empire, many millions in the lands ruled by the King of England; they enjoy freedom in the practice of their religion, they are protected. We cannot foresee what would happen if the rulers of those states found themselves provoked by us, by so hostile an act as the expulsion of their subjects or the closing of our ports. Resentment against us would be all the stronger in that, to all appearances, it would be just, since we should have received no injury from them.' What the Emperor was proposing would mean that the temporal power of the Church would be reduced to a condition of servility and vassalage, and the sovereignty and independence of the Holy See would be destroyed. 'We reply with apostolic freedom that the Sovereign Pontiff, who has been such over so great a number of centuries that no reigning prince can compare with him in seniority, this Pontiff, become sovereign of Rome, does not recognize and has never recognized in his states a power higher than his own. You are immensely great; but you have been elected, crowned, recognized Emperor of the French and not of Rome. There exists no Emperor of Rome. . . . There exists, indeed, an Emperor of the Romans; but this title is recognized throughout Europe, and by Your Majesty himself, as belonging to the Emperor of Germany . . . it is only a title of dignity and honour and in no way diminishes the real or apparent independence of the Holy See.'[1]

After a brief excursion into the question of Pope Leo III's relations with Charlemagne, designed to refute Napoleon's contention that the Pope had held his lands in some sort of fief from the Holy Roman Emperor, Pius proceeds to the more cogent argument: 'But, indeed, ten successive centuries since the time of Charlemagne have made it futile to enquire any further back. A pacific possession for a thousand years is the most evident title to possession that can exist between sovereigns . . . the extension of the states acquired by Your Majesty cannot give him any new right over our temporal domains. Your acquisitions find the Holy See in possession of an absolute and independent sovereignty. . . .'

Napoleon's only reply was to send a short line on April 18 announcing the replacement of Cardinal Fesch, as ambassador at Rome, by the ex-Jacobin and regicide Charles Alquier. Events were overtaking diplomatic correspondence. First Città Vecchia, then other points on the Tyrrhenian coast were occupied by the French. Yet with punctilious insistence Rome went on contesting every point, even arguing that the Pope's traditional right of investing the Neapolitan sovereign with his throne meant that Joseph Bonaparte could not legitimately be crowned without papal approval. On May 17 Fesch visited the Quirinal to present Alquier, and there was a stormy scene when the Pope told him that, if the Emperor used force against him, he would protest in the face of Europe, and would use the spiritual as well as the temporal means which God had put into his hands. Fesch replied that he had no right to use his spiritual powers in the present quarrel, which was about temporalities; at this the Pope's voice rose to a shout as he asked the

[1] Artaud, Vol. 2, p. 126.

Cardinal where he got that idea from, and Alquier thought it better to leave the room rather than become involved.[1]

With Joseph King of Naples, and Eugène Viceroy in northern Italy, it was evident to Napoleon that Rome lay geographically within the Bonapartist 'sphere of influence' and would be a source of weakness to his new Empire if she lay politically outside it. The Pope's position seemed to him the same, in principle, as that of an Ecclesiastical Elector within the confederation he was forming on the Rhine; he was to be an Italian Dalberg, enjoying a wider religious authority than the Elector-Archchancellor at Ratisbon, but the same temporal status – that of a prince within the new Empire. There was no room now for an independent sovereignty within Italy or western Germany. The significance, for Italy, of the Confederation of the Rhine (July 12, 1806) and of Francis II's renunciation of the Holy Roman Empire (August 6) were profoundly felt at Rome, where it was considered lamentable that the Hapsburg Emperor should have dissolved a temporal sovereignty in some respects analogous to that of Rome, and closely associated with her history. The pressure upon Pius to adopt Grand-Electoral status became intense during the summer. In May Cardinal Maury abandoned his See of Montefiascone to go to Paris and become the 'Emperor's man'. At the beginning of June Napoleon brought such pressure to bear on Caprara and Spina, at Paris, to try to compel them to persuade the Pope to accept the new status provided for him, that they both yielded and joined their voices with him. On June 17 Pius himself yielded so far as to sacrifice Consalvi;[2] but this only made the chances of agreement more remote, for the influence Consalvi had enjoyed over Pius was now replaced by that of the more intransigent Antonelli and di Pietro who, with the Pope, directed the moves made by the aged new Secretary of State, Cardinal Casoni. On July 15, having consulted the Pope and the Sacred College, Casoni rejected Alquier's formal request for the closing of the ports, and early in September Pius secured the

---

[1] Alquier to Talleyrand (Artaud, Vol. 2, p. 135).

[2] 'Go and see the Pope', Napoleon wrote to Fesch on May 16, and 'tell him that (Consalvi) . . . through folly, or through treason, means to lose the temporal states of the Holy See, and that he will succeed.' Nap. *Corr.*, Vol. XII, No. 10239.

cardinals' approval to a draft Papal Allocution rejecting the idea of
Rome entering any Italian federation: 'Our nature as Common
Father of the Faithful and our character as Minister of Peace forbid
us to put ourselves into any political relationship which would progressively lead us to take a permanent part in the wars which
desolate Europe'.[1] His policy settled, but expecting the worst, Pius
wrote to Caprara on August 31:

> 'We are in God's hands; who knows whether the persecution
> with which His Majesty menaces Us has not been decided by the
> decrees of Heaven in order to bring about the revival of faith and
> to reawaken religion in the hearts of Christians?'[2]

By the summer then of the year 1806 the elimination of the temporal power seemed to be at hand. Yet it was another two and a half
years before its collapse was finally consummated. The length of
this interval was due partly to the Emperor's preoccupations with
Prussia (Jena was fought in October 1806) and with Russia (the
treaty of Tilsit was signed in July 1807) and partly to the real reluctance of Napoleon, despite his contemptuous references to 'that
little Italian duchy', to treat the Papal States quite as though they
were on an equal footing with the other states of Italy. His system of
defence required that there should be no *enclave* of neutrality in
central Italy but he still hoped that he could compel the Pope to
recognize that he had no choice but to enter into his own military
camp, and thus to avoid the scandal of a military occupation of
Rome and a forcible confiscation of the donations of those Carlovingian kings whose names he so liked to invoke.

At the end of July 1807, immediately after Tilsit, the Emperor
proposed, through his Viceroy of Italy Eugène (he had ceased himself to write to the Pope), that Caprara should be empowered to
open discussions in Paris. But the Pope would have none of Caprara, and Napoleon would have no other Italian cardinal. In the end
they both agreed to accept the French Cardinal Bayane. But un-

---

[1] Vat. Arch., *Ep. Nap. It.*, Busta VIII, Fasc. 12. For Alquier's note, and also for
Roman reactions to Napoleon's new plans for Europe in 1806, see *ibid.*, Busta VI,
Fasc. 8.

[2] J. Schmidlin, *Histoire des Papes*, Vol. I, Part I, p. 108.

fortunately, while the extent of Bayane's powers was still being discussed, the French general Lemarois was sent to take over a wide strip of territory in the Papal States, comprising much of Umbria and the Marches, and intended to safeguard and improve French communications with Naples. Pius promptly withdrew Bayane's powers; when the French proposals arrived in Rome, and were found to include the demand that a number of French cardinals should be created, he broke off the negotiations altogether.

These were the events which led to Napoleon's despatch of General Miollis, at the beginning of January 1808, to occupy Rome; he entered the city on February 2. It was still in theory only a military occupation designed to protect French interests;[1] the new French Foreign Minister Champagny (who had recently succeeded Talleyrand) insisted that it was not intended to eliminate the temporal power but only to secure the Pope's adherence to an Italian confederation within the imperial system. To Alquier, who brought the proposals, the Pope replied in phrases perhaps more vivid than he would have employed had Consalvi still been his guide: 'You may tell them at Paris that they may hack me in pieces, that they may skin me alive, but that always I shall say NO to any suggestion that I should adhere to a system of confederation.'[2]

It was now Napoleon's plan to transfer sovereignty over the Papal States so gradually that, when the Pope's temporal power had ceased to exist, its disappearance would hardly be noticed. He wanted to avoid any violent seizure of the Pope's person, such as had occurred in 1798, because of the effect this would have on the parish priests throughout his empire. Most of Umbria and the

---

[1] There is an interesting account of Miollis' entry in the Vatican Archives (*Ep. Nap. It.*, Busta VI, Fasc. 12) by Colonel Colli, Commander of the Sant' Angelo, who had instructions not to resist. He was given an hour to clear up and clear out, after which he was to take his troops to the Piazza Barberini for demobilization and dispersal. The Papal government was to carry on but, apart from the Swiss guards inside the Quirinal, only those enlisted with the French were to remain under arms in Rome. On April 7 a French officer secured entrance to the Quirinal by a ruse and, with his men, effected the capture and disarming of the Swiss Guards. (Gabrielli's account in *ibid.*, Busta IX, Fasc. 21.) Yet the position of the French remained very difficult. General Radet, in his report in the following year (see below p. 198 and note 3), wrote: '*Le Pape gouvernait du bout du doigt beaucoup plus que nous avec nos bayonettes*'. [2] Schmidlin, *op. cit.*, Vol. 1, Part 1, p. 115.

Marches he added to the Kingdom of Italy by an edict of April 2, 1808,[1] but the Patrimony of Saint Peter remained nominally under papal rule, and the papal flag still flew over the Sant' Angelo, although Miollis had been sitting in the fortress since February. The Quirinal remained the headquarters of the papal administration; but since Napoleon, in his edict of April 2, had ordered the removal from Rome of all cardinals who were his subjects (which by now meant most of them) the Curia in fact could no longer assemble. One after another Consalvi's successors as Secretaries of State succumbed; Casoni became too ill to continue; Doria, then Gabrielli was banished by the French. All that remained to Pius, after June 1808, were his latest Secretary of State, Cardinal Pacca (a man of courage and resource, who had served as Legate in Germany and in Spain), some half dozen cardinals, and the obstinate support of the Roman people, who boycotted and insulted the French and even went so far as to abstain from their favourite festivity, the carnival.

His choice of the intransigent Pacca was a sign that the Pope would not yield. The new Secretary fell foul of the French by issuing instructions to the bishops not to take an oath of loyalty to the new order and by placarding the papal protests, by night, on the walls of Rome. At the beginning of September 1808 Miollis sent two officers round to the Quirinal to arrest him. Pacca told them he could only accept orders from the Pope; but he was not allowed to leave his room to go and obtain them. Told of what was happening, the Pope appeared in Pacca's room his hair (according to Pacca's account)[2] literally standing on end with his indignation.

[1] Edict in Vat. Arch. *Ep. Nap. It.*, Busta VII, Fasc. 3. But already, on March 3, Miollis had compelled Cardinal Doria (Secretary of State) to give fourteen cardinals three days' notice to quit Rome (*ibid.*, Fasc. 37).

[2] The Cardinal published his account of these events in his *Memorie Storiche del Ministero* . . . Rome, 1830, chapter 2. On the day following the attempt to arrest him he issued a notification to the ministers of the allied governments telling them what had occurred, and on the next day he sent them another, telling them of the arrest of Cardinal Antonelli and of Mgr Arezzo, the pro-Governor of Rome. These two documents can be seen in the manuscript room of the British Museum, being no.s 157 and 158 of an interesting collection entitled *Papers Relating to the Papal States, 1808–1811. Italy* (18.288). These papers provide a record of the numerous kidnappings, confiscations, and other French irregularities at Rome in this period, which were faithfully recorded by Pacca, and by Gabrielli before him, in their numerous protests to Miollis.

He ordered the Cardinal to follow him to his own apartments, and
as they passed through each of the doorways the doors were locked
behind them. Soon a series of locked doors stood between the two
officers and the man they had come to arrest; and since the Pope
now made him take up his quarters permanently in the papal apartments it became evident to Miollis that nothing less than a small-
scale military operation would be needed to separate the Pope from
his Secretary of State. He would require a clearer indication of
Napoleon's wishes before he undertook that.

About a week before this attempt to arrest Pacca there had been
a plot, apparently first hatched by his predecessor Gabrielli, to rescue the Pope by night, get him on board an English frigate, and take
him to Sicily. Pacca himself didn't know about it (Gabrielli had
been removed at short notice and, not surprisingly, had left
nothing in writing), and was rather startled one dark night to find a
fearful looking fellow lurking in the Quirinal, whom he took for a
Sicilian bandit, but who assured him he was a Franciscan friar in
disguise, and that he had come off a British frigate. This frigate, he
said, had sailed from Sicily in accordance with an arrangement
made by the British Cardinal Erskine with Gabrielli and with King
Ferdinand, and it was even then lying off Fiumicino; it could only
lie there for three more nights. Pacca made enquiry of Erskine and
of the Pope, both of whom confirmed the truth of the story,
though the Pope claimed that the plot was not one to which he had
ever consented and the Franciscan's offer to take him on board was
not accepted. Although various plans were made to rescue the Pope
and take him to Sicily or Spain, Pius VII always refused to go and
Pacca sustained him in his refusal, arguing that it would be as wrong
for the Pope to place himself under British protection as it would be
for him to place himself under Napoleon; and that if he did so
voluntarily he would make it much easier for the Emperor to declare
him an enemy of his Empire and possibly to bring about a schism.[1]

[1] Pacca, *Memorie*, chapter 3 and Note 10. Later on, in June 1812, when the Pope
was imprisoned at Savona, the British Admiralty had a plan to rescue him, which
was forestalled by Napoleon's removal of his prisoner to Fontainebleau. The
evidence for this plan, which is convincing, is given on p. 18 of J. T. Ellis's *Cardinal
Consalvi and Anglo-Papal Relations*, Catholic University of America Press, 1942.
But we do not know that the Pope would have agreed to go.

So in the face of eight French cannon mounted outside in the piazza and pointing their barrels at his windows the Pope remained at the Quirinal with Pacca during the winter of 1808–9. There was nothing much that he or Pacca could do, whether for the government of Church or of State; not only were they prisoners, separated from the ordinary machinery of government, but the French had taken over the papal printing presses. Before this happened, however, the Pope had managed to secure the printing of a formal sentence of excommunication, drawn up by di Pietro, and directed against all those in any way responsible for the sacrilegious seizure of the city; it only remained for him to date it, to sign it, and to publish it when he judged that the moment had come.

Napoleon knew of the existence of this document and feigned indifference. But he was not indifferent, as he showed later when it came to be published. And it is not without significance that throughout the winter, and still through the spring of 1809, he refrained from giving the signal for the elimination of the temporal power. During much of the year 1808 he was in Spain and trying to gain the support of the Spaniards for the new king he had given them, his brother Joseph, and the strength of Spanish Catholic feeling gave him no encouragement to press to a conclusion his quarrel with the Head of the Church. In the following spring he was once more in the field against Austria, and it was in the month of May, during his campaign on the Danube, and some six weeks before the battle of Wagram, that he decided to take the final step. His purposes were military. Faced once more with the possibility of Russian intervention in support of Austria, and knowing the British navy was ready to make trouble around the coasts of Italy, he felt the need to obtain fuller control over the centre of the peninsula, where many refugees and friends of the coalition were still harboured, and plots were still hatched against his various puppet régimes. So he issued his decree on May 17: the Papal States were to become part of his Empire; Rome was to become a 'Free Imperial City'; the Pope was to be allowed to remain Bishop of Rome, in possession of his palaces and of a suitable revenue, but holding no temporal power.[1]

[1] Napoleon's decree (Vat. Arch., *Ep. Nap. It.*, Busta VII, Fasc. 20) expresses his

In obedience to these orders Miollis on June 10 lowered the papal flag from the Sant' Angelo and raised the tricolour in its place. After the Pope and Pacca had listened, from the windows of the Quirinal, to the proclamation of this new order for the Eternal City, the Pope signed the Bull of Excommunication against the authors of the sacrilege, and Pacca secured that it was pasted to the walls of the great basilicas of the city.

Once more news of the Pope's defiance reached Napoleon at a bad moment; he was now in the most critical phase of his campaign, two weeks before the battle of Wagram. He ridiculed the Pope's action, calling him a *fou insensé*: 'He is a raving madman who must be shut up. Arrest Cardinal Pacca and the Pope's other adherents.'[1] His difficulty was that he could not now hope to hide the fact of the excommunication from the Italians or from the Spaniards, though by setting his apologists to work he proved fairly successful in disguising its significance in France.

Napoleon's letters to his commanders in Italy show that, even before he received news of the excommunication, he was quite prepared to see Pius VII removed from the Quirinal and placed under constraint, in order to prevent him from damaging the imperial authority. General Miollis, at Rome, was now under the immediate authority of Murat, who had succeeded Joseph as King of Naples; it was therefore to Murat that Napoleon had outlined most clearly what was to be the policy. On June 19 he had written to him: '. . . matters at Rome must be dealt with brusquely; no resistance can be tolerated. . . . If, contrary to the spirit of the Gospel, the Pope preaches revolt, and uses the immunity of the Quirinal to print cir-

---

now fully developed thesis rejecting the temporal sovereignty of the Popes. Charlemagne only gave them their lands in fief; Rome remained part of his Empire. But, in any case, 'this mixing of a spiritual with a temporal authority has been, and remains, a source of confusion, leading the pontiffs too often to use the influence of the one to support the pretensions of the other; and likewise spiritual interests, and the affairs of Heaven, which are changeless, have become mixed up with earthly affairs which, by their nature, change according to circumstances, and the politics of the time.'
[1] Letter of June 20, to Murat, *Lettres inédites de Napoléon* (Plon, 1897), Vol. 1, p. 317.

culars, he must be arrested. There is no more time for discussion. Philip the Fair arrested Boniface, and Charles V kept Clement VII for long in prison; and they had done much less to deserve it.'[1] And to Miollis on the same day: 'You should arrest, even in the Pope's establishment, all those who plot against public order and the safety of the army'.[2]

These letters go far to implicate the Emperor in responsibility for the distressing events that followed – perhaps as far as King Henry II of England had been implicated, on an earlier occasion, in a sacrilegious murder at Canterbury. And just as Henry's famous outburst had implied that the King looked to his companions to rid him of a nuisance, so Napoleon's generals in Italy might be excused for supposing that what the Emperor meant was that it was up to them to deal with the Pope.

If something were to be done the immediate responsibility rested with General Miollis. But he was a civilized and sensible man and he was also aware that Napoleon's considered policy, over the last two years, was to treat the Pope with respect, but to remove those cardinals who were giving him bad advice. In Miollis's view it was evidently time that Cardinal Pacca, who had caused the excommunication to be published, should be removed. But since the Pope was now keeping him by his side it would not be easy to secure him; it might mean placing the Pope himself under restraint, at least for a time.

While Miollis was hesitating his second-in-command General Radet, whom Napoleon had ordered, with a troop of horse, from Tuscany to Rome, was showing his readiness to play the hand more dangerously. Radet believed that what the Emperor really wanted was to see the Pope removed from Rome, with the minimum of fuss, and taken to some safe spot, away from any important centre of Catholic popular feeling. So he prevailed on Miollis to let him organize the seizure of both Pope and Secretary and their removal to the Certosa, outside Florence, where they could await further instructions from the Emperor. Miollis appears to have agreed, but he was too cautious to give any written order, except for the arrest

[1] Letter of June 19, to Murat, *Nap. Corr.*, Vol. XIX, No. 15384.
[2] Letter of June 19, to Miollis, *ibid.*, No. 15383.

of Pacca. In writing the day after the arrest to Napoleon and to
Fouché to explain what had happened he insisted that he had given
orders only for the arrest of the Cardinal; but that when the Pope
refused the demand that he should renounce the temporal
sovereignty, and when he made himself the centre of resistance at
the Quirinal, Radet had found it necessary to arrest him as well as
the Cardinal.[1]

Radet was very pleased with the way in which he executed his
plan, sending in to his government a report which suggested that
he had successfully planned and carried out a difficult military
operation.[2] Dividing his force between shock-troops, who had
to perform the dangerous task of ascending the outside walls of
the Quirinal with scaling-ladders before descending through the
roof, and a reserve which surrounded the walls of the palace, his
advanced troops finally came in contact with the enemy who was
sitting behind a table, fully robed, with five cardinals (including Pacca) and other prelates. To the General's demand that he
should renounce the temporal sovereignty Pius is reported by
Pacca to have replied: 'We cannot renounce what does not belong
to us; the temporal power belongs to the Roman Church, and we
are only its administrators. . . . So this is what I receive in return for
all that I have done for your Emperor! This is the recompense for
my great condescension towards himself and the Gallican Church!
But perhaps, before God, I am guilty for what I did for him and He
wishes to punish me; I submit myself humbly and I pardon your
Emperor.'[3]

We may guess that Pacca was here expressing his own views
rather than reporting the Pope's words; the Cardinal thought that
in the past the Pope had gone a great deal too far in trying to come
to terms with Napoleon and he blamed Consalvi for it. On the
other hand Pius's own viewpoint had greatly changed since the

[1] Miollis's letter in Mayol de Lupé, La Captivité de Pie VII (Paris, 1916), Vol. 1,
p. 185.
[2] See below, p. 198, note 3.
[3] Pacca's Relazione della scalata . . . in Vat. Arch., Busta VII, Fasc. 17. Rinieri
published it in Part 2 of his Napoléone e Pio VII, pp. 542–56. The account in Pacca's
Memorie del Ministero (Part 1, chapter 6) is briefer. For General Radet's two accounts
of the kidnapping see below, pp. 198, note 3, and 199, note 1.

hopeful days of the Concordat and Coronation, and the words attributed to him are in keeping with that tendency towards scrupulosity which was several times, during the next five years, to lead him into agonies of doubt as to whether, on the various critical occasions of his difficult pontificate, he had acted as God wished him to act.

Radet now gave his prisoner half an hour to prepare himself; at the end of that time he was bundled, still in his ceremonial surplice and cape, alongside Pacca in his cardinal's robes, into a coach which had been waiting at the main entrance on Monte Cavallo. It was still only four o'clock and dawn had not yet broken when the doors of the coach were locked, Radet mounted in front, and they moved rapidly away. The prisoners understood they were being taken to General Miollis's headquarters in the Palazzo Doria. But no; the coach went rumbling up the *via Pia* (the modern *via Venti Settembre*) until, bearing left, it ran out of the city through the *Porta Salaria*. Here, however, it turned sharp left and ran round the outside of the great Aurelian wall, past the Pincian gate, and down the Pincian hill, until it reached the *Porta del Popolo*. Post-horses were then quickly attached and the coach headed out along the main road for Florence by way of Viterbo and Siena.

It was little more than eleven years since Pius VI had been bundled out of Rome as unceremoniously by the French. Pius VII assumed that a similar fate awaited him.

N

CHAPTER THIRTEEN

Pius VII at Savona

While the post-horses were being harnessed to the carriage outside the *Porta del Popolo* the Pope reproached General Radet for his lie in telling him he was being taken to General Miollis and for depriving him of any counsellors, of any servants, or even of the chance to pack a change of linen. When they were under way again he and Pacca found, on emptying their purses, that they had less than twenty *sous* between them; they saw the funny side of this and both burst out laughing. But a grim journey lay ahead, in the hottest of the Italian weather, with the windows closed to prevent the Pope from being recognized, and the local inns at which they put up for the night and ate their hasty meals quite unprepared for their reception. Pius was in his sixty-seventh year; he developed dysentry.

Late on the first night they reached a small inn at Radicofani; Pacca had to make the Pope's bed and Pius had to be left in it most of the following day because the cold mountain air, following the intense heat in the plain, had given him a chill with fever. But the next day Radet insisted on pushing on as fast as possible in a desperate attempt to reach the Florentine Certosa before the peasants, already beginning to hear what was happening, should have the chance to try to organize a rescue operation. Through the night they drove, as fast as Radet dare; at Poggibonsi the coach overturned on a curve but the General, who was thrown off the driving seat into the dust, was a worse sufferer than Pope or Cardinal. During the last stages, beyond Siena, when the secret was known, Radet hit on the device of lowering the coach windows and encouraging the Pope in his desire to bless the crowds; this brought them to their knees, which made it easier for the coach to drive past them.

The Certosa was reached on the evening of July 8. Too exhausted to make more than a few signs in response to the welcome given him by the monks, the Pope went straight to his bed, with the request that he might be undisturbed for the night and throughout the following day. But at 4.0 a.m. messengers arrived from the sovereign in whose territory he now found himself, the new Grand Duchess of Tuscany, who was none other than Napoleon's sister Elisa. In her estimation the Pope was altogether too embarrassing a guest; he must be moved on as quickly as possible. So he was roused from his bed while it was still dark and bundled back into the coach; though it was Sunday he was not allowed the time either to say or to hear Mass. To avoid the crowds he was taken by a circuitous and hilly route in the direction of Genoa and – worst of all – he was separated from Cardinal Pacca, who was taken in the opposite direction over the Apennines to Bologna. Pacca noted that the Pope's face, from fatigue and sickness, had assumed a greenish colour; Pius told him he was convinced that the intention was to bring about his death by making his journey insupportable.

Yet actually Pius VII was not in the grip of so ruthless an enemy as the men who had ordered that his predecessor be brought over the Alps 'dead or alive'. He was in the hands of embarrassed and frightened subordinate rulers who did not know how their peoples would react to the Pope's presence amongst them as a prisoner and who did not know the Emperor's intentions in the matter. Elisa had despatched the prisoner promptly, and with due regard for what she believed would be her brother's wishes, namely that the Pope's identity be kept as secret as possible and that he be separated from the intransigent Pacca. Now it was the turn of her brother-in-law, the Prince Camillo Borghese, a revolutionary member of the great Roman family, who had married Pauline Bonaparte and had become 'Governor General of the Departments beyond the Alps'. In this capacity Borghese ruled over what had, until recently, been the Kingdom of Piedmont and the Republic of Genoa, regions at least as devoutly Catholic as Tuscany. The Prince was as embarrassed by the approach of the Pope as the Grand Duchess had been and he too acted promptly. The Pope was not to be allowed to appear either at Genoa or at Turin. He was to be met on the Ligurian coast, short of Genoa; he was to cross the bay of Genoa by boat and by night; a coach was to be ready to meet him at San Pier d'Arena, west of Genoa, to transport him over the Mont Cenis to Grenoble.

When Pius reached Alessandria Cardinal Pacca, by an odd chance, was in the town; he had reached it by way of Bologna and Parma and was being given a brief rest. But the Cardinal was not allowed to rejoin the Pope. That reunion only occurred when both coaches (having carefully avoided Turin) had reached the top of the Mont Cenis. During the last miles into Grenoble, which was reached on July 21, the efforts hitherto made to avoid the crowds by taking bye-roads and travelling by night were abandoned; the excitement in Savoy had become too great to be contained and the journey became a triumphal procession. Nor was it easy, once they had arrived in the French city, to prevent the crowds from thronging around the Prefecture where the Pope was lodged or from pressing forward to receive his blessing through the railings of the garden. The Prefect of Grenoble being (conveniently) in Paris it had fallen to a certain M. Girard, one of Fouché's secret police, to make the arrangements, and he had judged it best to see that the Pope and the two or three companions who had followed him were given every comfort, as also Cardinal Pacca whose nephew and two servants were now with him. But he had received instructions from Turin to ensure that the two dignitaries of the Church neither corresponded with the outside world nor met each other; and these he followed faithfully.

Borghese had chosen Grenoble as the place to keep the Pope because it was a strong place, being well fortified and an army divisional headquarters. More important it was in France, and so outside his own jurisdiction. The Prince and Elisa had passed the Pope on as quickly and as quietly as they could. Now, like everybody else – Fouché at Paris, Miollis at Rome, Murat at Naples – they waited in some trepidation to see what the Emperor would think of what they had done and what his orders would be.

The Emperor was angry.

No doubt the knowledge that he was largely to blame for what had occurred only made him the angrier. At the time when these events had been in progress he had been winning the battle of Wagram and forcing the Austrians to sign an armistice. His immediate anxieties were now over; it was the more annoying to learn that his lieutenants in Italy had acted precipitately on the strength of letters he had written when his anxieties had been greater.

On July 18 he had just received from Miollis the news of Radet's operation at the Quirinal and he wrote at once to Fouché:

'... I am angry that the Pope has been arrested; *it is a piece of utter folly.* Cardinal Pacca should have been arrested and the Pope left peacefully at Rome. However, there is no way of remedying the matter; what is done is done. I do not know what the Prince Borghese will have done by now, but I do not want the Pope brought into France. If he is still on the riviera around Genoa the best place to put him would be Savona. There is a large house there where he could suitably stay until it is possible to see what will happen. If he stops being so foolish I should not be opposed to his being taken back to Rome. If he has already been brought into France, have him taken back towards Savona and San Remo. Keep a close eye on his correspondence.

'As for Cardinal Pacca, have him shut up in the Fenestrelle, and let him know that, if a single Frenchman is assassinated as a result of his instigation, he will be the first to pay for it with his head.'[1]

By July 23 he had heard that Borghese had sent the Pope into France. He wrote to the Imperial Arch-Chancellor, Cambacérès: '*It is without my orders and against my will that the Pope has been removed from Rome;* it is again without orders from me and against my will that he has been brought into France.'[2]

By August 6 he had heard that the Pope had arrived at Grenoble. He now told Fouché: '*I would have preferred that only Cardinal Pacca had been arrested at Rome and that the Pope had been left there.* I would have preferred that, since the Pope was not left at Genoa, he had been taken to Savona; but, since he is at Grenoble, I shall be angry if you have already removed him, to take him to Savona; it will be better to keep him at Grenoble since he is there; otherwise we should seem to be playing about with the old man. ... But understand that, if you have already had him removed to go to Savona, you must on no account have him brought back.'[3]

This letter was too late. In the small hours of the morning of

[1] *Nap. Corr.*, Vol. XIX, No. 15,555.
[2] *Ibid.*, No. 15578.   [3] *Ibid.*, No. 15615.

August 2 those at Grenoble had put into operation the orders which
Napoleon had first sent to Fouché. The Pope had been carried back
again over the Alps towards Savona and Pacca had been taken
off to the fortress of the Fenestrelle high in the mountains of
Savoy.

Now, on August 10, the Emperor vented his feelings on Miollis:
'... *I am angry that the Pope was removed from Rome. I had ordered that
Cardinal Pacca should be arrested and not the Pope.* An operation of such
importance ought not to have been carried out *without my being
warned in advance and without my naming the place to which he should
be taken. . . .*'[1]

Napoleon more than once harked back, on later occasions, both
before and after his abdication, to this mistake about the Pope's abduction, and to his own freedom from responsibility for it. But
these later reflections are of less importance than what he said at the
time. It is in the light of what he wrote unguardedly in June, and of
what he wrote in July and August when he was trying to lessen the
damage the deed might do, that he must be judged. Those letters
lend colour to the view that his subordinates had exceeded their
instructions and that the primary responsibility for the abduction
rests with General Radet. Whether some responsibility also rests
with General Miollis depends upon whether or no he gave Radet
verbal instructions to arrest the Pope if necessary.[2] The initiative
rested with Radet, who thought his action would be pleasing to the
Emperor and wrote up an account of it immediately afterwards[3] in
which he stressed his own initiative and implied the reluctance of

---

[1] *Ibid.*, No. 15634.

[2] This is one of the few points on which I find myself in disagreement with the
late Mr J. M. Thompson, whose *Napoleon Bonaparte* (Blackwell, 1951), chapter 10,
is the best short account in English of the conflict between Emperor and Pope. To
Mr Thompson (p. 263) Napoleon's letter to Murat of June 19 was both a reply to
the excommunication and 'a sufficient answer' to his subsequent protestations that
he was not responsible for ordering the abduction. But Napoleon did not receive
the news of the excommunication until June 20, when he wrote again to Murat
saying he had 'just received' it and ordering the arrest of Pacca and of the Pope's
'other adherents'. There is no clear order in either letter to anybody to abduct the
Pope. In the second letter he is to be 'shut up'. See the convincing analysis of the
evidence in Mayol de Lupé *La Captivité de Pie VII*, Vol. 1, pp. 195–96.

[3] Printed, in part, by the Abbé Feret, in his *La France et le Saint-Siège* (Paris, 1911),
Vol. 1, p. 202, from the copy in the Paris National Archives.

Miollis. It is true that in 1814 he wrote another account,[1] in which he portrayed himself as the reluctant executant of orders given him by his superior; but by then the Emperor was on Elba and the Pope was back in the Quirinal and Radet was trying to avert the opprobrium which was being cast upon him. Radet was clearly a rather unpleasing kind of opportunist; perhaps the real criticism of Napoleon is that he had created an atmosphere in Italy in which generals like Radet felt encouraged to initiate their own *coups*.

The Pope's lengthy journey from Grenoble to Savona, by way of Provence, provided opportunities for just those demonstrations of devotion on the part of the people of France which the Emperor was most anxious to avoid. At Romans the Pope's escort, Colonel Boissard, was manhandled by the crowd. At the ancient Papal city of Avignon – most surprisingly included in the itinerary – the populace turned out to greet its 'sovereign' and there were demonstrations against his 'oppressors'. At Nice the streets were strewn with flowers and the night brightened with illuminations. Avoiding the populous riviera coast Boissard now took a roundabout inland route. It was on August 17 that the prisoner at last reached Savona and came under the control of the Prefect of the Department of Montenotte, M de Chabrol. He was now lodged honourably in the episcopal palace and Chabrol did his best to make him comfortable. But although he had a beautiful writing desk inlaid with gold he had no secretary; and although he had two or three personal servants he had nobody whom he could consult on the affairs of the Church nor a confessor of his choice whom he could consult on those of his own soul. From now on he would quietly insist that he could not discuss seriously the affairs of the Church with anybody sent by Napoleon until he was enabled to perform his functions as Pope, which meant until he had proper means of consultation and the necessary machinery for administration. Failing these – and they continued to be lacking for nearly five years – he would become once more a simple Benedictine, the 'poor monk Chiaramonti', and spend his time in spiritual reading, meditation, and the

[1] In Vat. Arch., *Ep. Nap. It.*, Busta VII, Fasc. 17, and printed in Pacca *Memorie del Ministero*, p. 447.

performance of such practical tasks as lay to hand, like mending his soutane. For a time he would write a few letters, using his valet to smuggle them out of the palace; but at the end of eighteen months Napoleon gave orders to Chabrol to take away even his paper, pen, and ink.

When he returned from Wagram the Emperor was in no great hurry to reach a settlement with the Pope; he was 'waiting for him to ripen' under the influence of kindly treatment at Savona and isolation from pernicious cardinals like di Pietro, Pacca and Consalvi. But it was necessary for him to settle the affairs of Rome, and make it clear that there was to be no restoration of the Temporal Power. By the end of January 1810 he had removed all the cardinals to France, save for the aged and infirm Casoni. Even di Pietro, whom Pius had left as 'Delegate' in charge of the government of the Church, had been evacuated to France. So had the heads of the Religious Orders and the chief officers of the Congregations and Departments of State. The archives had been taken to Paris. The Pontifical Seal had been confiscated. The famous Fisherman's ring had fallen into the hands of that intrepid adventurer General Radet, now Chief of Police. Never at a loss to assume new responsibilities, the General had made known his willingness to use the ring to endorse bulls and rescripts, a facility of which the Minister of Bavaria hastened to avail himself, on behalf of his prince, until the irregularity became known.[1]

This wholesale clearing out of the Papal government was the necessary preliminary to the incorporation (February 17, 1810) of Rome (no longer a 'free imperial city') into the French Empire, with the accompanying declaration that she was now the 'Second City of the Empire'. Napoleon's intention was to transfer the papacy to France; preferably to Paris ('It would be an advantage to have the Head of the Church at Paris, where he could not be a nuisance') or possibly to Avignon. But the Pope never proved willing to consider either city.

Whatever different titles or institutions Rome might be given she

[1] Mayol, *op. cit.*, Vol. 1, p. 441, quoting the letters of the unofficial French agent at Rome, Ortoli.

remained in practice under the rule of General Miollis. It was a more effective rule than had been provided at the time of the Republic of 1798, and although nothing could disguise the fact that it was both French and military it made some show of giving the Romans a voice in their own affairs by setting up a *Consulta*, where leading citizens of the Empire's second city could express their opinions, and appointing as Mayor none other than Duke Braschi, that nephew of Pius VI whom his uncle had so ill-advisedly loved to honour. But these concessions were of small importance when set against the struggle which followed with the Church. A large proportion of the clergy refused to take the required oath of allegiance to the new régime, a course of action in which the Pope encouraged them with letters smuggled out of Savona. These non-jurors were normally deprived of their livings and banished; the Sees of nonjuring bishops were abolished.[1] The Religious Congregations suffered similar treatment unless they accepted the new order. There was a general destruction of papal emblems, a huge confiscation of works of art, and a cancellation of the public debt. The Holy Office of the Inquisition was closed; Jews and Freemasons were surprised to find themselves not merely relieved of disabilities but receiving preferential treatment; the French Civil Code was introduced.

Meanwhile at Paris, if Napoleon got no nearer to establishing a Parisian Papacy than to effect some extensions to the archbishop's palace, designed to make it look more like the Quirinal, he set in motion a considerable propaganda drive throughout France and her dependencies designed to justify his liquidation of the political power of the Popes. Thus the Comte d'Hauterive was put to work to write a treatise which should show that, ever since the days of Gregory VII (characterized by the author as a brigand), the Popes had been peculiarly animated by hostility to France; Boniface VIII, Julius II, and Innocent XI came in for special attention. It was not very difficult to persuade the French, or even very many Italians, that the liquidation of the temporal power was an overdue reform which might be expected to redound to the advantage of the Church. It was more difficult to persuade some of them to reconcile

[1] See Appendix 4, p. 300.

themselves to the excommunication. The royalist adherents of the *Petite Église* naturally made much of it, since it weakened the position of the usurper of the Bourbon throne, while some of the Religious Orders – often now existing only in secret – were suspected of depicting the Emperor as anti-Christ, and a wholesale suppression of such Orders as still survived, or had been reconstituted since the Concordat, was undertaken in 1809–10. But the hierarchy as a whole accepted the stirring events with a notable docility. Even the cardinals now at Paris (with exceptions, such as Consalvi and di Pietro) were prepared to pray publicly for the Emperor's welfare and to take part in his religious and secular ceremonies, which caused the Emperor some amusement as well as satisfaction. The official line in France was that the excommunication was invalid because the offence complained of was temporal in character; but many ecclesiastics, who could not accept this view, were able to take advantage of the fact that it did not name the Emperor personally, as had been usual on comparable occasions. Such was the ruling of the Emperor's Minister of Cults, M. Bigot, although the Bull of Excommunication, *Quam Memoranda*,[1] anathematized 'all those who had ordered, favoured, advised' the attacks on the Holy See 'of whatever position, rank, order, preeminence or dignity they might be, even if they were worthy of specific and individual mention and designation'. Only in Spain (where King Joseph suppressed the Religious Orders, and the French army carried off parish priests by the hundred into France), and to a lesser extent in Belgium, and in the Rhineland, does the excommunication seem seriously to have affected the outward forms of religion and thus the political hold of the Emperor.

The most serious difficulty which was beginning to confront Napoleon by the end of the year 1809 was how to keep the ordinary machinery of the Church running because the Pope, having been deprived of the means of running it, had retaliated by passive resistance, refusing to institute to their Sees the bishops nominated by

[1] Latin and French texts in *Correspondance officielle de la Cour de Rome* (Rome, 1814), pp. 306–349.

the Emperor. This inaction on the part of Pius was more effective than his action in launching the excommunication. It was not easy to circumvent it because not even the advanced Gallicans had argued that a bishop could lawfully be invested with his full episcopal authority save by the Pope. Any alternative means of investiture, not authorized by him, meant schism, and after the experience of the Civil Constitution of the Clergy schism was what the French Church was anxious, above all things, to avoid.

In November 1809 Napoleon began to give his attention seriously to achieving a settlement. To a select committee, which included his uncle Cardinal Fesch, Cardinal Maury (now very much the Emperor's man) and the courageous Head of the seminary of Saint-Sulpice M. Émery, he put several questions. The most important were: 'Was the excommunication valid?' and 'How should he provide for the service of the Church if the Pope persisted in refusing to invest with their spiritual powers the bishops he had nominated?' To the first question he obtained the answer he wanted; by Gallican theory the excommunication was unacceptable in France. But the committee went on to point out that, although the Emperor had done so much for the Church, and although in their view the Organic Articles were not incompatible with the Concordat, the existing position of the Pope was very shocking; he should be given his 'entire liberty' and be surrounded by his 'natural counsellors', otherwise he could not 'communicate with the Churches confined to his care, nor settle any serious matter, nor provide for the needs of Catholicism'. And this they wrote in their report although the more papal members of the committee, including M. Émery, had withdrawn because they felt the others were too subservient to the Emperor.[1] The line taken by the committee was essentially that of Cardinal Fesch, who was now making some amends for his unfortunate tenure of the French Embassy at Rome by standing up to his despotic nephew both in the matter of what was essential to the papacy and in the matter of the missionary Religious Orders, of which he was a great patron in his diocese at Lyons.

But the second question, the investiture question, was the more

[1] Evidence in Leflon, *op. cit.*, p. 256, etc.

critical one. The committee took the line that if the Pope continued
to refuse to institute bishops to their Sees then it might be necessary
to settle what should be done in a National Council. If the National
Council felt itself incompetent then it might be necessary to summon a General Council of the Church. But nothing was said about
the role of the Pope at such Councils. The Emperor had failed to get
what he wanted because he had failed to exclude the Pope from the
question. He also had no appetite for any Councils. So he ignored
his committee.

He was encouraged at this time to take his own line in Church
matters by his success in this same winter (1809–10) in side-stepping
the Pope in another matter which was evidently Pius's concern,
namely his divorce from Josephine and marriage to Marie-Louise,
daughter of the Emperor Francis I of Austria.[1] That he did not
refer this matter to Pius is understandable. It was the Pope who had
insisted on the Church marriage of the royal couple before their
coronation in 1804; it was the Pope who had refused a divorce for
Napoleon's brother Jerome; it would certainly be useless to approach him with such a project as this. Yet Napoleon had to handle
the matter with a proper regard for forms, if only because Francis
would not give away his daughter unless they were observed.
Already the Tsar Alexander had shown his unwillingness to see his
young sister (whom Napoleon would perhaps have preferred)
unite herself to so incorrect a man as the upstart Emperor.

So the useful Fesch, who had been the only clerical witness of the
marriage he himself had performed, was persuaded to explain that
there had been irregularities on that occasion, and that Napoleon
had been pushed into it unwillingly, being pressed by Josephine;
and this, indeed, was true. The lack of witnesses, lack of consent,
and later lack of children sufficed to satisfy the Parisian Ecclesiastical Court, and the annulment which it pronounced sufficed to satisfy
the Hapsburg Emperor. So the conventional Marie-Louise was
handed over to the adventurer who had just defeated her father's
armed forces for the fourth time, and who had been excommunicated by the Pope. But she was quite happy to do what was
expected of her; and in less than a year she had borne to her hus-

[1] Until 1806 he had been the Holy Roman Emperor, Francis II.

band the needed heir, who was styled King of Rome, thus having a
present made to him of the Papal city.

It now occurred to Napoleon that, where he himself had failed so
signally, namely in his dealings with the Pope, his new father-in-
law, His Catholic Majesty, might succeed; nor could Francis very
well refuse his good offices. So on Metternich's advice the Austrian
diplomat Count Lebzeltern was sent in May 1810 to Savona, with
the excuse that he wanted to discuss matters affecting the Church in
Austria, but really to discuss the possibility of settling those of continental Christendom, now so happily united by the recent wedding, and by the birth of an heir to the Emperor. Pius received the
envoy cordially, and seemed to entertain real hopes of reaching a
settlement through the talks. But he insisted that Francis would
have to guarantee any settlement; that he himself should return to
Rome (but not necessarily as temporal ruler); that he should have
his counsellors restored to him; and that Napoleon should give
clear evidence of a change of heart. Given these conditions he said
he might even lift the excommunication, which would not necessarily be maintained solely on account of Napoleon's infringement
of the temporal sovereignty. Such terms were satisfactory enough
to Metternich, whose chief desire was to avoid a schism in Europe
and to prevent the establishment of the papacy at Paris or at Avignon. But they did not satisfy Napoleon, who was not prepared
either to see the Pope return to Rome, or to give him back, as his
advisers, cardinals of the stamp of Consalvi, Pacca, or di Pietro.

He was the less likely to give him back his advisers because only a
few weeks earlier Consalvi and di Pietro (Pacca was still in prison),
together with eleven others of the twenty-nine Cardinals resident
in Paris, had mortally offended him by failing to appear at his
wedding to Marie-Louise. On that occasion, losing his temper, the
bridegroom had rounded, at the reception, on the cardinals who
had turned up and had sent them flying through the corridors of the
Tuileries. Then he had deprived those who were absent of their
purple (after which they were called the Black Cardinals) of their

---

[1] *Mémoires et papiers de Lebzeltern*, publ. by E. de Lévis-Mirepoix in *Un collaborateur de Metternich* (Plon, 1949). The envoy's account of the Savona conversations
is on pp. 157–86.

pensions (which the prouder of them had never accepted) and of their rooms (mostly in left-bank hotels) and had banished them to remote places in the provinces of France, where they were kept under surveillance.[1]

Clearly it was no time for anybody to try to tell Napoleon that he should allow the Pope to have back the advisers of his choice. But he paid enough attention to Lebzeltern's report to send two cardinals, whom he supposed the Pope would find congenial, to discuss matters with him at Savona in July 1810. Of these one was Caselli, who had been involved in the negotiation of the Concordat, but who had since accepted the position of Senator at Paris; him the Pope treated with the most icy politeness. The other was Spina, who had been the principal negotiator of the Concordat before Consalvi's arrival in Paris. He was rather more acceptable to the Pope; but no Italian cardinal who had since become one of the 'Emperor's men' could expect a welcome at Savona, such as Pius had given to Lebzeltern. The two cardinals brought no real offers of restitution and they returned equally empty-handed.[2]

As the number of vacant Sees mounted all over western Europe at the end of the year 1810 Napoleon determined to have resource to an expedient once used by King Louis XIV, in his analogous dispute with Innocent XI over the *Regale*; he would have his episcopal nominees elected by the cathedral chapters as 'Administrators Capitular', thus enabling them to perform their functions, even if they could not take their titles. The most obvious and important case was the archiepiscopal See of Paris itself, where the venerable Archbishop Belloy, who could remember Louis XIV, had died in June 1808 at the age of ninety-nine, and had not yet been replaced. Napoleon offered the position to Cardinal Fesch; but the cardinal, impressed by what he thought his own indispensability, and by his lofty title, 'Primate of the Gauls', overplayed his hand by making a spirited attempt to combine the proferred See of Paris with the See he held of Lyons. This Napoleon would not allow; so Fesch stayed at Lyons and Paris was offered to Cardinal Maury, who hastened to

[1] Consalvi *Mémoires*, Vol. 1, pp. 440–91.
[2] The Prefect Chabrol sent an account of these conversations to the Minister of Cults which was published by Feret in *La France et le Saint-Siège*, Vol. 1, pp. 408–413.

accept. Pius VII not only reproved Maury for his acceptance, and refused to institute him, but he wrote (being still possessed of pen and ink) to the Vicar Capitular at Paris, D'Astros, who was opposed to Maury's appointment, to say that it would be entirely irregular for the Canons of Notre Dame to confer upon Maury the proposed administrative powers; so far as the Pope was concerned Maury remained Bishop of Montefiascone in Italy. While the canons were hesitating as to what they should do, Napoleon's police discovered one of Pius VII's letters, and promptly imprisoned D'Astros, whereupon the canons complied with the Emperor's wishes. A parallel case at Florence, where Grand Duchess Elisa overbore the canons and imposed her brother's nominee upon them, as Administrator of the Diocese, against the orders of the Pope, set a precedent as useful to Napoleon in Italy as the Parisian precedent proved to be in France. For other cathedral chapters soon followed suit and General Savary (the new Minister of Police who had replaced Fouché) felt strong enough to launch an energetic and effective campaign which led to the rounding up and imprisonment of a 'League' which was supposed – not without reason – to be implementing the instructions which the Pope managed to smuggle out of Savona. The most important victim of this crusade was the stalwart Cardinal di Pietro, who was put in the Vincennes.[1]

The beginning of the year 1811 marked the nadir of Papal hopes, as it marked the zenith of Napoleon's power. He was now determined to solve his relations with the Church by a course which would reduce the Pope's authority to that of a mere *primus inter pares*. First he deprived Pius of all means of correspondence; this was the time when his pen, paper, ink and desk of inlaid gold were all taken away from him. Then his gaoler, the Prefect Chabrol, was ordered to cease to treat him with so much respect; in particular he was not to imply that the Emperor was anxious for an accommodation with him; he was to make it clear that the Pope had little significance for the Emperor, because 'people were too enlightened, to-day, not to be able to distinguish between the doctrine of Jesus

<hr/>

[1] Latreille *L'Église Catholique et la Révolution Française*, Vol. 2, pp. 195–201.

Christ and that of Gregory VII'.[1] It only remained to find a regular
and proper way of instituting bishops without recourse to the Pope,
so that they should be no mere 'administrators of dioceses', but
bishops in the full sense; the Church would then be able to carry on
quite smoothly until the 'imbecile old man' came to his senses.

So a new Ecclesiastical Committee, with Fesch and Maury as its
leading members, was called in February 1811; and although
M. Émery was a member, and although he bravely defended the
Papal prerogatives in a two-hour speech (to which Napoleon paid
him the compliment of attending) the committee recommended
that, failing an accommodation with the Pope, a solution to the
investiture problem should be reached by a National Council. The
lines along which the Council should reach this solution should be
that, failing investiture by the Pope, after six months bishops
nominated by the Emperor should be instituted to their Sees by the
Metropolitan of the province.

Napoleon was still not sufficiently sure that he had the episcopacy
of France fully behind him to feel much enthusiasm for a National
Council. So he sent three bishops, of unimpeachable piety, and
likely to be acceptable to the Pope, to plead with him at Savona
that he should agree to the 'six months' proposal. They carried
with them letters signed by ten cardinals, two archbishops, and
seven bishops – Italian and Spanish, as well as French – pleading
with him to make 'all possible sacrifices' for the sake of the peace
of the Church.

It seemed that he would do so.

By May 18 he had agreed, in principle, to the 'six months'
proposal; this was then embodied in a draft and carried off very
promptly by the little delegation before the Pope could change his
mind, but also before he had signed it. As he meditated upon the
copy they had left with him the Pope came to see the situation more
as Consalvi, or Pacca, or di Pietro would have seen it, and as later on
they did see it. He realized that, deprived of his counsellors, abducted, imprisoned, spied upon, and rendered powerless, he should
have discussed nothing until his own position was rectified. Yet he
had orally and provisionally agreed to yield an important part of

[1] *Idem*, p. 201.

the traditional authority of the papacy, namely the investiture of the bishops of the Church.

In despair at what he had done, the day after the bishops' departure he told the Prefect, Chabrol, to send word immediately to the returning delegation to warn them that he had promised nothing, and that he repented, as a folly, having even considered, as a basis for discussion, the document they had drawn up.[1] Naturally the Emperor took no notice of this disclaimer, and at the National Council, which opened in Paris in June, he blandly stated that he had the Pope's agreement on the vital issue which they were called to discuss.

Always subject to extremes of mood, Pius had never shown them more markedly than at the time of this strange interview. At first he had been affable, conciliatory, inclined to try to reach an agreement. But on hearing of the departure of the delegation he had been beside himself with remorse, thankful only that he had signed nothing. Chabrol thought him near to madness, and Napoleon assumed he was mad. Others have supposed that his doctor, Porta, administered some drug on this occasion which accounted for his early complacency and for his subsequent reaction. There is no proof of this, nor is there need to look further than to the character of Chiaramonti and the inhuman isolation he had endured since January, an isolation broken only by the arrival of copies of the *Moniteur*, carefully selected by Chabrol, in which the Pope was invited to read the statement of the many bishops and cathedral canons – especially in Italy – who seemed to be taking the Emperor's side against himself. He had always been a Pope who needed good guidance and when he had been free he had chosen good guides. His lasting glory is that when he was not free, when he had no guides, and when he was subjected to every sort of seduction he hesitated, but did not finally yield.

The National Council which assembled on June 17, 1811, in Notre Dame was an imposing affair. There were no less than ninety-five bishops present (forty-two of them from Italy) including six cardinals. The Emperor, with his Minister of Cults, Bigot, was now

[1] *Idem*, pp. 208–210.

attempting to settle a major matter of the discipline of the Church in the west without the active assistance of the Pope; in effect, he was falling back on the Gallican theory that a Council was superior to the Pope. Misled by the comparative ease with which he had succeeded in securing the election of his nominees to the administration of the vacant Sees, he supposed that he could now secure from this Council a resolution which would enable the full canonical investiture of bishops to be effected in future without the Pope. Had he been able to do that he would, indeed, have achieved a victory over the papacy such as to match the dreams of a Febronius, a Joseph II of Austria, or a Scipione de Ricci, and the subsequent development of ultramontanism would have been impossible. But, in fact, he was out of date. What many French clergy had accepted at the time of the Civil Constitution hardly any French bishop would accept now that they had all experienced schism and had succeeded in healing it. When the Emperor, through the mouth of his minister Bigot, invited the assembled Fathers, on June 20, to consider the iniquities of Pius VII, how he had shown 'nothing but indifference for the true interests of religion', they looked askance, and many of them wanted to march to Saint-Cloud to appeal to the Emperor to release the Pope and be reconciled with him. When he sought to flatter their self-esteem, and to arouse their patriotic sentiment, by assuring them that he could find 'no better guarantee for the tranquillity of his peoples against the abuses of the spiritual power perpetrated by the Popes, of which the pages of history were filled, than in the mission and authority of those bishops who, attached to the soil by all the ties of blood, had been at pains to reject the aggressions of a Gregory or a Boniface . . .' they remained mute. Who was this master to tell them what they ought to do? Instead of setting themselves up as judges of the papacy the Council began its proceedings by listening to a sermon from the Bishop of Troyes, Mgr de Boulogne, in which, following Bossuet's famous *Discourse on the Unity of the Church*, of 1682, he declared they would 'never detach themselves from that first link in the chain, without which all the others would fall away and would leave nothing to be seen save confusion, anarchy, and ruin'. And afterwards each bishop in turn swore before Cardinal Fesch (chosen by the Emperor as President) the oath customary at the inauguration of Councils: 'I recognize the Holy Church, Catholic and Roman, Apostolic and Roman, as mother and mistress of all the Churches. I promise and I swear true obedience to the supreme Roman Pontiff, successor of Saint Peter, prince of the apostles and Vicar of Jesus Christ.'[1] In a frightful scene with his uncle, the Emperor denounced the bishops as traitors for having taken an oath to two sovereigns who were at enmity with each other.

It was the Emperor's contention at the Council – in whose affairs he intervened constantly – that there was nothing to prevent the Fathers from speedily settling the main issue since he already held the Pope's approval to the investiture of bishops by Metropolitans after a six months' delay. But the bishops, not without reason, doubted whether this was true and insisted that the Council could register no valid decree without the consent of the Pope, obtained from him by a deputation from the Council, and bearing his signature. This was the Council's final decision, reached on July 10, and the same night Napoleon, in his rage, dissolved the Council and threw the three bishops whom he regarded as the ring-leaders, those of Troyes, Gand and Tournai, into the Vincennes.

Napoleon now hit upon the expedient of securing from each of the bishops still in Paris a personal agreement to his proposed new procedure on investiture. Frightened by the imprisonments, and hood-winked into supposing that a personal agreement would carry no responsibility for committing the Church over the head of the Pope, the bishops, who had been brave in the Council, showed themselves very much weaker outside its walls; by the beginning of August his minister Bigot had secured for the Emperor no less than eighty-five signatures. Delighted with this unexpected success Napoleon now announced that the Council was not, after all, dissolved; a last session was accordingly called on August 5 which re-affirmed, collectively, what the large majority had already agreed privately. The bishops did however strive to satisfy their consciences by saying that their agreement must be approved by the Pope. In the outcome honours were about even; the bishops had failed to win their point that the investiture question could not even be dis-

[1] Leflon, *op. cit.*, p. 266. For what follows see Latreille, *op. cit.*, Vol. 2, pp. 211-25.

cussed without the prior written agreement of the Pope; Napoleon had failed to win his point that they should accept his word for it that the Pope had already agreed.

After the vote of August 5 the Council met no more and another deputation was hurried off to Savona. The Emperor had gained all he needed from the Council just so long as he could secure the Pope's approval to what had been done. And the Pope now gave it to him. Impressed by the weight of episcopal opinion, flattered by the messages of respect and goodwill brought to him from Paris, believing that Napoleon sincerely wanted a just settlement, he agreed to metropolitan investiture in the event of a six months' delay. But he insisted that the Council was no valid Council, he re-wrote the decree as one which emanated from himself, as Supreme Pontiff, and he couched it in terms which could be taken to exclude the bishops of the Papal States from being reckoned amongst those who could be invested by Metropolitans. The deputation was both surprised and delighted by his compliance and even the minister Bigot recommended the Emperor to accept his Brief.

Incredibly, the Emperor refused. The deputation was told that it must insist upon the inclusion of the Papal States within the terri-tories where the new investiture procedure would apply and that the Pope must immediately show his goodwill by instituting to their Sees those whom the Emperor had already nominated. He had over-reached himself. Pius would not budge from his Brief. At the climax of his career, a few months before he crossed the river Niemen to begin the invasion of Russia, Napoleon had thrown away the opportunity of a religious settlement which might have done much to strengthen his hold upon the Mediterranean coun-tries. Despite the protestations of even many of the French bishops he had decided to assert his authority, in matters of spiritual as well as of secular discipline, over the papacy. Not even over the hier-archy of the Patrimony of Saint Peter would he allow the Pope to have final authority.

Pius had been saved from his own surrender.

Though he had forgotten the true reason, the necessary reason, why he should continue to refuse to negotiate any new religious settlement with Napoleon, namely that he was a prisoner, and deprived of the counsellors of his choice, Pius had yet been saved from the consequences of his mistake by his concern about something much less important, namely his special relation with the Papal States. Just as the Papal States had been the occasion of his falling foul of the Emperor, in the year 1809, so now, in 1811, his refusal to let the Emperor reorganize religion in Rome and central Italy had prevented him from issuing a brief which would have surrendered the papal position on a point of fundamental importance every-where, namely papal investiture of bishops with their spiritual authority.

Popes had been accused before this of sacrificing the true interests of the Church to those of the Papal States, and a successor and protégé of Pius VII, Pius IX, following in his predecessor's foot-steps, would expose himself peculiarly widely to the accusation. But paradoxically on this occasion the Pope's concern for the Papal States helped to save the liberty of the whole Church.

CHAPTER FOURTEEN

Pius VII at Fontainebleau

The last discouraged delegates left Savona in February 1812 but Napoleon was not discouraged. Pius, he reckoned, was now ripe to be handled by none other than himself; but for that it would be necessary to have him nearer at hand. Fontainebleau would be a better place, near enough to Paris, but not so near that the Pope would attract large demonstrations of affection from the Parisian crowd. He had lodged him before at Fontainebleau, in the imperial suite, when his guest was on his way to perform the coronation; and in August 1809 he had had the idea of bringing him there again, and receiving him in state.

Now it would be rather different. He would not be present himself to receive the Pope because he would be engaged in invading Russia. But that campaign, he reckoned, should not take him more than three months; he would be back by the end of August and able to settle matters by means of that combination of flattery and bullying which was his chosen technique and which should not fail to prevail over a Pope who, in spite of the treatment he had received, still held in special regard the Emperor who had restored Catholicism in France.

The journey would also have to be rather different. It would not do to have any more of those demonstrations which had taken place in Provence, or at Nice. 'Take care', he wrote to the Prince Borghese, 'to see that he passes through Turin at night, that he stops only at the hospice on the Mont Cenis, that he passes through Chambéry and Lyons by night, and that in the same way he is brought to Fontainebleau, where orders have been given to receive him.'[1] In point of fact no such orders had been given at Fontainebleau, and when the Pope arrived it was a complete surprise, as the Emperor intended it should be. If the secret were to be kept it was clearly

[1] Mayol, Vol. 2, p. 373.

necessary not to make ready for the Pope at Fontainebleau; only the Minister of Cults, Bigot, the Minister of Police, General Savary, and the Prince Borghese at Turin were in fact let into the secret. But Borghese had to make the necessary arrangements at Savona, so he had soon to enter into confabulation with the Prefect Chabrol, and with Captain Lagorse, who commanded the Pope's 'Guard of Honour' and was to be his escort.

The removal from Savona was effected with great skill at midnight on June 9.[1] The first the Pope heard about it was at 5.30 p.m. on the same day, but he made no difficulty, allowing himself to be disguised in black, as a simple priest, with his white satin slippers inked in to complete the picture. After the coach doors had been locked upon himself and his doctor, Porta, and the equipage had slid silently away on wheels which had been covered with cloth and were drawn by unshod horses, the Prefect Chabrol returned to the Palace to perfect the details of a carefully contrived deception: the servants, on pain of imprisonment for life in the Fenestrelle, were to continue to carry the meals to and from the Pope's room, the guards were to go through their customary routines, and the Prefect himself was to contrive to call, as usual, on his state visits. It was more than ten days before Savona knew that her royal guest had gone.

He had been carried off quietly, but he had been carried much too fast. It is more than 130 miles from Savona to Mont Cenis, by way of Genoa, Alessandria and Turin, and much of the route lies in Alpine passes and round hairpin bends. Yet this journey was accomplished in less than two and a half days, without more than an hour's stop anywhere. In the last stages of the climb into the Alps it was necessary to stop every ten minutes to relieve the Pope, who was suffering from a complaint of the urinary system to which he was subject when travelling, and which was made much worse if he was compelled to travel without suitable rests. By the time they arrived at the Mont Cenis, where at last the Pope could be laid in a bed, in the care of the Benedictines, he had a fever and it was evident he could go no farther. Lagorse wrote off at once to Prince Borghese in Turin:

[1] The documentation of the Pope's removal to Fontainebleau is given in Mayol, Vol. 2, pp. 372–424.

'*Chaque fois que le Saint-Père voyage, il éprouve de fortes retentions d'urine, et, dans cette circonstance, l'accès a été plus violent, parce que la corse a été plus rapide. Nous étions obligés d'arrêter toutes les dix minutes, et le Pape epanchait alors avec des efforts très douloureux quelques gouttes. Les souffrances étaient telles que nous craignions de le voir s'évanouir, et lui-même, malgré tout son courage, se croyait incapable d'une plus longue résistance. Son médecin vient de me faire des observations judicieuses. . . . Il est possible que trois ou quatre jours de repos et des remèdes convenables amélioreront la santé du Saint-Père, et que, sous quatre jours, je pourrai me remettre en route. . . .*'[1]

The Prince (whose legitimate sovereign was still the Pope) got word back to Lagorse the next day to say that he had been infinitely distressed by his message. But he had been distressed not, as might be supposed, at hearing of the Pope's suffering, which he ignored, but at hearing that it had not been found possible to continue the journey. If the journey were not continued immediately the secrecy, he insisted, upon which the Emperor set such store, would be lost. Lagorse was to go on. If it proved absolutely impossible to do so he was to send back a courier straight away to Turin, and he himself would telegraph Savary, the Minister of Police, at Paris.

But Lagorse could only reply, on the 13th, that the Pope was worse. He could not stand, and he was in great pain. Unable to cope with the ailment, his physician, Porta, was demanding the help of a competent consultant, equipped with syringes and other necessities; Lagorse begged the Prince to send one from Turin.

Borghese telegraphed Paris on the morning of the 13th. At 2.0 p.m. on the afternoon of the 14th he received this reply from Savary: 'The captain cannot, in any circumstances, stay at Mont Cenis. Consequently he must make up a bed in the coach. . . .' Borghese sent it straight to Lagorse, adding that he must find a doctor locally. But Lagorse, to his eternal credit, had just written off bravely to Borghese: 'Whatever orders come from Paris it is impossible to dream of resuming the journey. The Pope has not slept; his bladder is inflamed; the journey would give him gangrene and, without being a doctor, it is easy to foresee that a disastrous accident would occur. Further, it would be useless to put the traveller into

[1] *Idem*, p. 400.

the coach; it would be impossible for him to endure its move-ment. . . .' And he repeated his pressing demand for a properly equipped doctor.

But Borghese would not send him one; to Savary he made a virtue of this, explaining that he did not wish to be a party to any action which might tend to cause the Pope to be kept at Mont Cenis. Lagorse had to bring in the local doctor from Lans-le-Bourg. Meanwhile the Pope, supposing that his end was come, received the last sacrament from the Abbot of the Monastery. At 10.0 p.m. on the evening of June 15 he was carried into the coach and laid on the improvised bed. The journey was resumed.

That Pius VII survived, and reached Fontainebleau four days later, still alive, was probably due to the fortunate chance that the doctor from Lans-le-Bourg, whose name was Claraz, was a com-petent man, and a valiant one, remaining by the side of the Pope for almost the whole journey, and nursing him with great devotion. Lagorse, too, as we have just seen, had some of the qualities of mercy, but his fear of the government, and his genuine devotion to his Emperor combined to make him a ruthless escort. The coach only stopped occasionally, and at remote houses, for perhaps an hour, to enable the passengers to have a hasty meal. When it came to Lyons, the biggest city on the route, the cobbled streets were taken at the gallop, to avoid curious crowds, and the doctor had to hold the Pope's head, and his stomach, to alleviate his pain. There was a brief stop after they had passed through the city, and the Pope was heard to be offering up a prayer that God would forgive the Emperor.

For whole weeks after his arrival at Fontainebleau Pius remained in his bed, too ill to be moved. Fortunately there had been no hurry after all. The Emperor was still engaged in Russia; he seemed likely to be there for longer than he had expected. Bigot paid a courtesy call at Fontainebleau, but left without the Pope's being able to see him. The Red Cardinals (those who were compliant to Napoleon, and were still allowed to live in Paris) also called; some of them came to stay in the castle. Gradually the Pope became well enough to hold conversations with them. But they had nothing new to say. They only went over the old arguments, counselling the Pope to be conciliatory for the sake of the Church, to restore her normal life and to prevent a schism. Only Maury, who had disobediently assumed the duties of Archbishop of Paris, was shown the door and not allowed to return. To most of them the Pope listened quietly; but it was clear he would do nothing until he had talked with Napoleon.

And at last Napoleon came. He came in January 1813 ready, indeed determined to reach a settlement; prepared to make sacrifices for it. But how was the Pope, still closely guarded from all but the Emperor's friends, to know how great a change had come over the situation, how possible it had at last become for him to insist upon reasonable terms? How was he to appreciate the extent of the disaster to the *Grande Armée*, left struggling in the Russian snows? How was he to know the extent of the opposition to the Emperor, and of the support for himself which had been growing amongst the clergy in France and Italy, throughout the year 1812? Or of the Emperor's violent treatment of the more obdurate bishops, of the disgrace of even his uncle, Cardinal Fesch, of the closure of the great seminary of Saint-Sulpice, of the purging of the professors of the other great seminaries? How was he to know that many of the younger clergy were becoming passionately anti-Gallican, or that cathedral chapters would no longer passively elect the Emperor's episcopal nominees as their administrators?

Of all these things he was ignorant, and it is against the background of his isolation both from accurate news and from adequate advisers that one has to consider his conversations with Napoleon in January of the year 1813. When Cardinal Pacca, in his fortress of the Fenestrelle, where he had endured a hard imprisonment of three and a half years, heard startling news that the Emperor and the Pope were closeted together in conference at Fontainebleau he saw immediately the great danger in which the papacy and the Church stood: 'Knowing as I did the quiet and gentle disposition of the Pope, and that he was battered and brought low by illness, suffering, and the hardship of a long imprisonment, and knowing him to be surrounded by people who had either sold themselves altogether to the Emperor or were miserably timid and behaved like courtiers, I realized at once that the struggle between Gregory Barnabas

Chiaramonti and Napoleon Bonaparte would be conducted with forces too unequal in strength, and I saw which side would gain the victory.'[1]

Pacca little supposed that the first result of these conversations would be his own release. Soon (February 5, 1813) he was travelling over the Mont Cenis by the same route on which the Pope had suffered so. At Rivoli he met the Marchese D'Azeglio (father of Massimo, of Risorgimento fame) and learnt from him that the Pope and the Emperor had agreed together on a new Concordat, and that it sounded like a bad Concordat for the Church. At Susa he attended Sunday Mass at the parish church and heard the priest tell the congregation that a Te Deum would be sung at the High Mass in gratitude for the Concordat concluded between the Pope and the Emperor. He spent that night at the Benedictine Hospice at Mont Cenis, where they told him about the Pope's stay. At Lansle-Bourg he had to wait all day while they mended a wheel on his coach; but the stop enabled him to hear, from the local doctor, Claraz, the whole story of the Pope's journey to Fontainebleau. Grimly foreboding, he pursued his way towards Fontainebleau. What kind of Concordat, he asked himself, could a Pope in that condition have wrested from Napoleon? At Lyons the rumoured provisions of the agreement alarmed him still more; by the time he reached La Charité, on the Loire, he was able to read its details in the *Gazette de France*. By February 18 he had reached the palace of Fontainebleau, which he found deserted and gloomy, more like a prison than a palace. He had some difficulty in finding the Pope, and when at last he reached his room he found him 'bent, pale, emaciated, with his eyes sunk deep into his head, and motionless as though he were dazed. He greeted me, and said, very distantly, that he had not expected me so soon; when I told him that I had made haste so as to have the joy of placing myself at his feet and bearing witness to my admiration for the heroic constancy with which he had suffered so long and grievous an imprisonment, he was filled with distress and replied in these precise words: "But, in the end, I was defiled. Those cardinals . . . they dragged me to the table and made me sign." '[2]

[1] Pacca, *Memorie del Ministero*, pp. 222–23.   [2] *Idem*, Part 2, ch. 5.

It was a strange tale that the Pope had to tell: how Napoleon had begun by sending four cardinals and four bishops with some impossible demands, including the nomination of two-thirds of the Sacred College by the 'Catholic Sovereigns', the condemnation by the Pope of the 'Black cardinals' who had not attended the Emperor's marriage, the establishment of the papacy at Paris; how he had declined to consider these, only to find the Emperor himself on his doorstep (January 19); how the Emperor, cordial and threatening by turns, had remained six days with the Pope, endeavouring to explain to him that the times had changed, that the Church had to be reconciled with the Revolution and a New Order in Europe, embodied in the Emperor, that she had everything to gain from the ruin of both the Bourbons and the Holy Roman Empire if she would only give up all idea of political power, and if 'so powerful a conqueror and so virtuous a priest were to walk hand in hand'.[1]

To the powerful persuasions of the Emperor had been added those of the Red cardinals and the French prelates by whom the Pope was surrounded. These were the men who 'dragged him to the table and made him sign'. And this was the agreement he had signed: full recognition of the Pope as a sovereign, but not as a sovereign over Rome; the seat of the papacy to be left undecided. Investiture of bishops by Metropolitans, after a six months' interval, with nomination and investiture of bishops in the Patrimony of Saint Peter reserved to the Pope; release of the Black cardinals, bishops, and others in prison on account of the quarrel, and their restoration to the Emperor's favour.

The shock to ultramontanes, whose hopes had been raised by the retreat from Moscow, was stupefying. Many refused to believe that the Pope could, by implication, have signed away the temporal power, or have yielded over the investiture of bishops; many never did believe that the alleged signature really came from the Pope's own hand. In this they allowed their wishes to father their thoughts. But they were correct in their belief that the Pope had not signed a Concordat. He had signed certain Heads of Proposals, to

[1] The fullest consideration of the evidence about these conversations is in Mayol, Vol. 2, pp. 436–42.

serve as the basis for an understanding, proposals whose preamble specifically stated their provisional character, and which the signatories had agreed together should be confidential. In publishing them as a Concordat, and ordering the singing of Te Deums, the Emperor had been guilty, as ever, of some sharp practice. 'He has betrayed me,' exclaimed the Pope.

For the Emperor it was nothing short of a triumph. At this dangerous time, when he had to raise new armies from France and her satellites, he could point to a settlement with the Church, publicly demonstrated by the release of cardinals and bishops who were now free to join the Pope; and all this without yielding any of the positions upon which he had taken his stand. He had removed a grievance which had come to be felt as keenly, in some parts of Europe, as his conscription or his taxation. He had put the ultramontane opposition, for the time being, out of countenance, embarrassing the zealous, now organized in bodies like the *Chevaliers de la Foi*. He had rallied those who understood little of the issue at stake but who did know that they wanted to see the Pope free, and the Church in harmony once more with the Emperor. The 'Concordat' was a sensation; for those who understood it seemed a disaster, but for many it was a real relief, and that many would include parish priests like the one Cardinal Pacca heard announcing a Te Deum at Susa, and their flocks who followed them. To some the Pope's only real sacrifice seemed to have been the temporal power, and it was not easy to excite many people about that.

This was the reasoning not merely of parish priests or Gallican bishops but of the majority of the cardinals now assembled at Paris or Fontainebleau. They numbered no less than twenty-five, a respectable proportion of the thirty-three members of the Sacred College who still remained alive. But the three of greatest courage and ability Consalvi, di Pietro, and Pacca, who had, at different times, been Pius's principal advisers, now resumed their natural position close to the Pope; by his own choice they, together with Gabrielli (Secretary of State before Pacca), Mattei and Della Somaglia took up their chambers in the palace of Fontainebleau with him; the others made do with lodgings in the town. Consalvi became once more the Pope's Secretary of State.

These were the men who, with the Pope's full support, pushed through the difficult policy of cancelling the 'Concordat of Fontainebleau', against the advice of the majority of the cardinals, and in face of the certainty of the Emperor's wrath. It was done by a letter which the Pope wrote painfully with his own hand, in which he expressed his surprise that provisional proposals for an agreement should have been published as a Concordat, declared that his conscience had revolted against these proposals, that he had only signed them out of 'human frailty, being only dust and ashes', that he was willing to negotiate a definite settlement. When he had written this letter, which was carried to Napoleon on March 24 by Lagorse, the Pope's whole mood changed; he became cheerful, even jovial, and recovered his appetite.

Napoleon kept this letter secret. He realized that the Pope had been helped to change his mind and therefore gave orders that he was to be isolated once more, as strictly as he had been isolated at Savona; no cardinal was to be allowed to discuss any business with him; di Pietro, whom Napoleon evidently regarded – with some reason – as the ringleader amongst the ultramontanes, was to be removed to Auxonne. The rest of the cardinals were to be allowed to stay at Fontainebleau. He would settle the business on his return from his campaign in Germany.

But in October came the Battle of the Nations, at Leipzig, and that was the beginning of the end for the Emperor. Too late, he now sent envoys to the Pope offering even the return of his temporal sovereignty. But Consalvi had been at work, was in touch with Metternich and the Allies, knew that it would now be a mistake to do any deal with the falling Emperor. So Pius replied that he could only enter into any negotiations after he had returned to Rome, and had been restored there to his full liberty, surrounded by the Sacred College. By January 22, 1814, Lagorse had received instructions from the Emperor to remove the Pope from Fontainebleau (lest he be rescued by the advance of the Allies) and to lead him southwards, towards Rome, but by a circuitous route through central France. Once more he was separated from the cardinals, who were despatched in groups of four, under different escorts, to different addresses. Fortunately this time there was no great hurrying or secrecy about the Pope's journey, so that he maintained his health and everywhere received immense ovations.[1]

By February 16, 1814, he had reached Savona once more. In the next month the Allies, at Châtillon, made it a part of their peace proposals to demand the full liberty and independence of the Sovereign Pontiff; but Napoleon outbid them by ordering that the Pope be restored forthwith to Rome and to the full sovereignty over his states. So the Pope's triumphal progress proceeded. At Imola, his former bishopric, he stayed two weeks; at Cesena he rejoined Consalvi. At Cesena, too, he met the actual occupant of Rome, none other than King Murat of Naples, who had deserted his Emperor, joined the allies, driven Miollis out of the Eternal City, and embarked upon a grandiose project for possessing himself of most of Italy. He asked the Pope whither he was travelling and the Pope, in a tone of surprise, replied: 'but surely you know? – to Rome'. At that the king presented him with a memorial, signed by his own friends at Rome, in which they demanded a temporal ruler. After glancing at it the Pope quickly threw it on the fire. 'Now there remains no obstacle to our returning to Rome' he said to the king, and so ended the interview. Such, according to Artaud,[2] was Murat's own account of his meeting with the sovereign whose kidnapping from Rome, in 1809, he had facilitated by sending troops from Naples.

If Murat was received coolly members of the Bonaparte family, now seeking refuge in Italy, were greeted very cordially. Near Loretto the Pope met Laetitia, Napoleon's formidable mother, and Cardinal Fesch; both were promised a refuge at Rome. Already the Pope had received a letter from Lucien, from England, saying he was leaving with his wife and children, whom he would be bringing to Rome. At the Villa Giustiniana, near Rome, he found King Joseph, who had been driven from Spain, and Elisa, Grand Duchess of Tuscany, who had been driven from Florence. Both brother and sister were granted asylum; one wonders whether the

---

[1] Mayol, Vol. 2, pp. 425–77; Pacca, *op. cit.*, pp. 243–385.

[2] Vol. 2, p. 372. Artaud's account of this interview is, however, unconfirmed. For Lebzeltern's account of how he persuaded Murat to evacuate Rome and procured a troop of Austrian cavalry to escort the Pope thither see Lévis-Mirepoix, *Un collaborateur de Metternich*, pp. 313–19.

sister had the grace to recollect with some shame a night in July 1809 when she had denied the Pope some badly needed sleep at the Florentine Certosa.

Meanwhile various communications had been received from Talleyrand, now Foreign Minister to the Provisional Government at Paris, but still styled Prince of Benevento. The egregious ex-constitutional bishop had sent instructions that the Pope's journey was to be facilitated in every way possible, and that full honours were to be accorded him, and had then written to Consalvi to assure him that it would be his special care to recommend the virtues and concerns of the Holy Father to his king (Louis XVIII) and that it was peculiarly pleasant, in these happier times, to renew correspondence with the Secretary of State.

A hard tussle between these two lay ahead; in the meantime, as he journeyed with the Pope towards Rome, Consalvi became increasingly aware that the destinies of Europe would be decided amongst the Allies, now meeting together in Paris, and he was not satisfied that the Nuncio Extraordinary, Mgr della Genga, already sent there by Pius, on May 7, to look after the interests of the papacy, would be equal to the task. So on May 20, four days before the papal party reached Rome, Consalvi, having heard that the Allies were already negotiating a treaty with the restored Louis XVIII, persuaded the Pope to let him go to Paris himself.[1] Travelling night and day, at top speed, he arrived to find that he was just too late; the treaty had been signed. Della Genga, taking his time over his journey, had only himself arrived two days before the Cardinal-Secretary, and had had no influence upon the treaty. For his dilatoriness he was so castigated by the Cardinal that he returned to Rome a shattered man. It was unfortunate for Consalvi that nine years later della Genga was elected Pope. As Leo XII he showed that he had not forgotten the humiliation to which he had been put by the Secretary of State.

[1] His instructions, which he had no doubt drafted himself, were to demand a restitution of all the lands in Italy held by the Pope before the French revolution, including the *enclaves* of Benevento and Pontecorvo within the Kingdom of Naples, and also Avignon and the Comtat Venaissin. Della Genga's mission was cancelled. The Nuncio was to take his orders from Consalvi (Rinieri, *Diplomazia*, Vol. 4, p. 663).

Consalvi supposed that, had he been present, he might have prevented the recognition at the treaty of Paris of French sovereignty over Avignon and the Comtat Venaissin; but it seems unlikely, and in any case the papacy was well rid of an embarrassing and untenable *enclave*, whatever its pecuniary value. He was justified in his journey, which gave him an opportunity for talks with the principal sovereigns and ministers, who would shortly be meeting at the Congress of Vienna, where the business that most interested him, the redrawing of the map of Italy, would be undertaken. Already he had persuaded the Pope to write a brief denouncing the treaty of Tolentino, with its renunciation by Pius VI of the legations. He now made it clear, to all alike, that he was claiming the full restoration of the Papal States. He was even able to fit in a short visit to London where he listened to the Prince Regent extolling the virtues of Pius VII and seized himself of the essentials of the Irish question and the possibilities of Catholic Emancipation.[1]

So Pius VII had to ride into Rome without Consalvi, but he had Pacca, who had joined him on the last stage of his journey. Down the Corso the coach was drawn by the youthful patricians of Rome, while their sisters, in white, waved palms, and their fathers hurriedly retracted the document they had signed to please Murat. As in 1800, on his arrival from Venice, so now he drove not to the Quirinal but to St Peter's, to give thanks for his deliverance, and to pray for further protection. Later, at the Quirinal, he was

---

[1] An interesting account of his private audience with the Prince Regent of July 1, 1814, is given in his letter to Pacca of July 5 (Rinieri, *Diplomazia Pontificia*, Vol. 4, pp. 131–41). In the Vatican Archives (*Sgr. di Stato*, Anno 1820, Rub. 242, Busta 391) is a copy of the letter he addressed from London on June 14 to the ministers of the other governments. Here, while still smarting under the disappointment of the Treaty of Paris, he spoke very candidly of the Pope's needing to have his states fully restored to him to enable him to 'sustain his dignity with decency'; complained that whereas Clement VI had paid hard cash for Avignon and the Comtat no financial compensation was now being offered for their loss; argued that France herself had torn up the treaty of Tolentino when she occupied the whole of the Papal States in the following year; and pointed out that the other sovereigns would weaken their own claims to the territories now being restored to them if they denied to the Pope *la plus belle partie de ses États* – the legations. In the following October, at the Congress of Vienna, he made the same points, expressing them rather more urbanely, in the document which he handed to the Powers (Vat. Arch., *ref. cit.*). Rinieri printed this latter document (*ibid.*, p. 665).

P

greeted by those whom he had had to leave so abruptly, now nearly five years ago.

By the time he entered Rome, on May 24, 1814, the Pope had been travelling almost continuously for four months since he had left Fontainebleau, and it had mostly been a triumphal procession. The contrast with earlier journeys was continually coming to his mind – improvised journeys, in disguise, mostly at night, and under guard. Such journeys, for him, were over now. But as he progressed through Provence another ruler, on a parallel road, not far away, was making the kind of journey that he himself had been compelled to make in the past. The ex-Emperor, in fear of the mob, was heading with speed and secrecy for Fréjus; and he was preferring to travel by night.

CHAPTER FIFTEEN

The Congress of Vienna and the Congress System

Th hat the years following the fall of Napoleon were a period of Catholic revival – indeed of religious revival generally – in Europe has often been noticed. What is less certain, though often claimed, is that it was a period of widespread ultramontane revival.

That the Holy See emerged with a new prestige within the Church will not be denied; nor will the connection between the ultramontane movement and Pius's long resistance to Napoleon. We may accept Dr A. R. Vidler's estimate of the effect of this resistance on the greatest of the ultramontanes, Lamennais, namely that it was paramount: '. . . it is fair to say that in the end he (Pius) alone consistently withstood the Emperor's will to dominate the Church. It is this fact more than anything else that accounts for the complete conversion of Lamennais to ultramontanism.'[1] Another sign was the revival of the older Religious Orders – always dependent on the protection of the papacy – and the growth of new ones. The number of these in France, and their geographical spread, were impressive, extending from Brittany, where Lamennais's brother Jean founded the *Frères de l'Instruction Chrétienne*, to Provence, where de Mazenod founded the *Missionaires oblats de Marie Immaculée*. The older, and especially the contemplative Orders, made their return more slowly in western Europe; Napoleon had disliked contemplatives and it is estimated that the number of their houses had fallen from some 1,500 before the revolution to thirty at the time of his abdication.[2] The general restoration of the Benedictines took time, and the Benedictine Pope, Pius VII, was able to do little to effect it.

[1] *Prophecy and Papacy*, S.C.M. press, 1954, p. 54.   [2] Leflon, p. 370.

The most obvious sign of the current of ultramontanism was the pressure put on the Pope to re-establish the Society of Jesus. With this demand Pius was strongly sympathetic. In 1801, at the beginning of his reign, he had hoped to achieve it; but in the face of opposition from Madrid he had only secured the regularization of the position of the Jesuits in Russia and three years later their return (at Ferdinand's request) to Naples. In 1814, however, the Spanish King, Ferdinand VII, joined the chorus which demanded the restoration of the Society and Pius felt able, in a bull published on the feast of Saint Ignatius (August 7, 1814) 'expressly and specially to repeal' Clement XIV's *Dominus ac Redemptor Noster*. There were a few aged and impoverished members of the Society still alive around Rome – some of them men whose spirits had been kept alive by the faith and devotion of Saint Joseph Pignatelli – who were able now to take the opportunity afforded them to shuffle their way into the *Gesù* for the ceremony of restoration and to kiss the feet of the Supreme Pontiff; but in Russia there was a flourishing province, and its leader Brzozowski became General of the restored Society.

The numbers of the Jesuits grew rapidly in most countries after 1814, but the damage done by Clement XIV was not easily to be undone. A great educational tradition had been broken and its repair was not seriously taken in hand until the generalship of Father Roothaan (1829–53). Moreover the governments of the great states were still very suspicious. The Austrian Emperor refused to readmit the Jesuits, and in France they soon became a casualty of the revolution of 1830. Even in Russia, where they had been protected, they ran into trouble soon after 1815. De Maistre reminded the Tsar Alexander that the French clergy of 1762 had warned their king: 'defend the Jesuits as you defend the Catholic Church . . . and it will be as impossible to upset the State as to remove the Alps' and he drew his attention to the Protestant Saint-Étienne's remark 'had the Jesuits not first been abolished the French revolution would have been impossible.'[1] But Alexander, in 1820, expelled the

---

[1] De Maistre *Mémoire sur la liberté de l'enseignement public.* The *Mémoire* was printed by A. de Margerie in *Le Comte Joseph de Maistre* (Paris, 1882), pp. 44–53, and the words quoted are on p. 47.

Society from Russia because he found it was converting too many of the Orthodox.

The rulers north of the Alps were, indeed, by no means convinced after the restoration that they stood in need either of the Jesuits or of closer contact with Rome. They realized that there was a religious revival amongst their peoples and they saw the practical value of an alliance between throne and altar. But they were still impenitently Gallican or Josephist and Consalvi discovered at the Congress of Vienna that the Pope's restoration of the Society was a liability to him in his diplomacy. The de Maistre thesis of a natural alliance between Pope, Jesuits and monarchs against liberals and revolutionaries proved unacceptable because the monarchs still thought they could 'go it alone', with the help of a Church under their own control. Nor is it demonstrable that they did need the Jesuits for their own purposes. The fault of Clement XIV in suppressing them had not been to knock away a prop from underneath the thrones; it had been to weaken the papacy and the Church, spiritually speaking, at the behest of the rulers.

Just how suspicious of Rome the restored governments were was quickly shown during the negotiations undertaken by Consalvi to conclude concordats with them. In France it proved impossible to secure more generous terms for the Church than Napoleon had been willing to grant, and in the end the Concordat of 1801 was reaffirmed. But it was in Germany that the need for a settlement was most obvious, on account of the chaos inherited from Napoleonic times and the political rearrangement of the German states to which the Congress of Vienna gave effect. Consalvi protested against the secularization, without compensation, of the ecclesiastical electorates; against the immense loss of Church property and revenues of all kinds; against the encroachments of temporal sovereigns on spiritual rights; against the failure to resurrect the Holy Roman Empire. He hoped to secure a concordat which would cover the confederation as a whole; and so (with a very different kind of concordat in view) did Metternich. But Pacca (an expert on Germany), acting as pro-Secretary at Rome, opposed this, and in the end separate agreements were made with the different states. Perhaps Pacca was right. The dangers, from the Roman standpoint, of trying to negotiate a general agreement were evidently great. It would have put the Austrian Emperor Francis and also that rather equivocal figure Dalberg, Napoleon's Prince Primate of Germany, who was still Archbishop of Ratisbon and was possessed of his own envoy at Vienna, into a very strong position. By negotiating with the states separately Rome was more likely to avoid the emergence of a separatist Church of Germany. Sometimes (notably in Catholic Bavaria) not only were the points Consalvi had insisted on in 1801 at Paris secured but rights, too, in the sphere of censorship and education. On the other hand the most important agreement, a 'convention' with Prussia, which was not concluded until March 1821, made scanty provision for the maintenance of the clergy or of the seminaries in Rhenish or Polish territories where the Catholic population was large; and although it avoided nomination of the bishops by a Protestant King it allowed him a veto over episcopal elections by the cathedral chapters and it left him with unlimited control over communications with Rome and over the publication of episcopal instructions even within a bishop's own diocese.[1]

In short, the attitude of the great rulers in 1815, while appreciative of the Pope, was very far from friendly to Rome; they were soon to discover, however, that she was about to support their thrones with a fervour which left them little room for complaint.

Consalvi's chief concern at the Congress of Vienna lay with the interests of his own sovereign, regarded as a temporal ruler. When he arrived in the city at the beginning of September 1814 the cards were stacked against his achieving his aim of a full restitution of the former possessions of the Holy See. He held only one ace – the respect felt for his sovereign, Pius VII. The rest were held by his opponents, for King Murat still occupied the Marches, with his Neapolitan troops, the Austrians and Murat occupied the legations, and the papal treasury was empty. Amongst the Great Powers the most kindly disposed was England. Already Lord Bentinck had made the journey from Sicily to Modena to greet the returning

[1] For the German negotiations see the detailed analysis in Schmidlin, Vol. 1, Part 1, pp. 273–329.

Pope, to persuade him to resist the pretensions of Murat to Rome, and to give him some much needed ready cash.[1] And of all the rulers Consalvi had talked with the most eloquent on the subject of the Pope's heroism had been the Prince Regent in London.[2] Consalvi knew enough to know that neither Bentinck nor the Prince, both of whom promised to support a full restitution of the papal possessions, could in fact commit the British government; but Lord Castlereagh had promised the same thing, and had added that in this matter the sentiments of all England were Catholic.[3]

In the summer of 1814 the political talk was of hereditary right and legitimacy; there was to be a restoration of the order upset by the revolution and the usurper. If this was to be the principle governing the resettlement of the continent then the Pope seemed to be strongly placed for, as Consalvi was able to show, in his note to the assembled rulers and representatives, no sovereignty had more manifestly been usurped than that of his master. On the ground of traditional principle there was no answer to the Secretary of State. But would the decisions of the Congress in fact be determined by principle?

It soon became evident that that was unlikely, that in fact a bargain would be struck between the Great Powers, each obtaining what it could with a view to increasing its territories or increasing its security. Was Consalvi to enter into the bargaining? An opportunity to do so was afforded to him when the committee constituted by the Big Four (Russia, Prussia, Austria and Britain) was enlarged to include France, Spain, Portugal and Switzerland. Talleyrand, looking for support against Metternich, even wanted him to enter this committee and to assume the presidency of it.[4] But he preferred to cling to his principles and remain outside.

No doubt it was more dignified for him to do so; as the bargaining became bolder and the pressures more powerful so it became easier, in the end, for the governments concerned to save face in Italy by making a virtue of handing back the disputed territories,

[1] Rinieri, *Diplomazia Pontificia* . . . , Vol. IV, pp. 88–89.
[2] *Idem*, pp. 131–41.
[3] To the Nuncio at Lucerne, April 13, 1814 (Schmidlin, Vol. 1, Part 1, p. 167).
[4] 'To ensure decency and justice'. See Consalvi's letter to Pacca of November 1, 1814, in Rinieri, *op. cit.*, Vol. 3, p. 51.

as a matter of 'right and principle', to the obstinately neutral papacy. But Consalvi had, all the same, an Achilles' heel, which handicapped him in adopting his virtuous posture, for Metternich was not slow to remind him that Pius VI had signed away the legations at the Treaty of Tolentino in 1797. Nor was the point wholly met when Consalvi protested that the Pope had only signed under duress, and that in any case the Treaty of Tolentino had been nullified by Napoleon's subsequent war on the Pope.[1] It remained true that the Pope had renounced his rule, in a formal treaty, in order to preserve the rest of his states, and this was never quite forgotten in those later storms of the Risorgimento which centred around the separation of the legations, or when Pius IX talked about the 'seamless robe of Jesus Christ', which no Pope had the power to rend.

The continental big powers considered that the legations were disposable. Metternich did not propose that they should be annexed by Austria, only that she should retain the land north of the river Po and occupy such fortresses across the river as seemed militarily worth holding. The rest of the rich territories could be given to a suitable and deserving candidate, such as the Hapsburg princess Marie-Louise, who had lost her position as Empress of France. When Consalvi replied that this would make her liable to excommunication for usurping papal territory her father thought he was being unreasonable. It had been all very well, indeed very helpful to the Hapsburgs, that the Pope should excommunicate Napoleon for seizing Rome; but to excommunicate a new ruler of the legations would be an abuse of the spiritual power.

There was no lack of candidates for this sovereignty over Bologna, Ravenna, and Ferrara. There was the ex-King of Italy, Eugène Beauharnais; there was Napoleon's infant son, the King of Rome; there was the displaced Spanish Bourbon Queen of Etruria, Maria-Louisa. The territory might even be given as compensation to the King of Saxony, whose lands the King of Prussia wanted. More original, and more significant in its politico-religious implications, was the offer of the Tsar Alexander. He would see that the Pope received back his legations, but only on

---

[1] Consalvi to Pacca, February 15, 1815, *idem*, p. 276.

condition that he should confer upon the disloyal and dangerous Archbishop Siestrezencewiez of Mohilev (who was willing to help the Tsar to gain control over the Catholic Church in Russia) the dignity of Papal Legate, and Principal Bishop. This suggestion caused Consalvi acute embarrassment;[1] but he did not fail to explain to Alexander (as he had always made clear to Napoleon) that, however anxious the Pope might be to recover his temporal dominion, he was Pope before he was Prince and could not sacrifice religious principle to gain a temporal advantage; to do that would be to commit the sin of simony.

On one point the Allies found themselves strangely agreed: whoever should hold rule over the legations it should not be the ruler who in fact held them, namely King Murat of Naples. Yet Murat's troops were there by arrangement with Metternich, and Metternich had offered Murat, as a reward for his treachery to Napoleon, substantial gains at the expense of the Papal States. Now that Napoleon was defeated the General-King was nothing but a nuisance to Metternich; indeed, with his wild dreams of uniting the whole of Italy under himself, he was a potential source of danger to the Austrian position in Lombardy, the more so since he was stirring up the secret societies in his own support. It had been partly in order to checkmate Murat's plans that Metternich had facilitated Pius VII's return to Rome. Nobody now wanted Murat; Talleyrand and Castlereagh were agreed in working for the return of King Ferdinand to Naples. But Murat had one card up his sleeve which the Allies did not know about. He was in touch once again with Napoleon, on Elba, and was planning to raise Italy on behalf of the ex-Emperor when the latter should be able to make his escape to France. As soon as Napoleon had sailed, at the end of February 1815, Murat marched north once more, the Pope withdrew from Rome to Genoa, and the citizens not merely of Rome, the Marches, and the legations, but of Turin, Milan, and Venice were invited by their would-be liberator to prepare a constitution for an independent Italy. The episode has its interest, historically, because it anticipates Mazzini's appeal for a United Italy, and it anticipates Mazzini's method, for in 1834 the Founder of Young Italy would stake

[1] *Idem*, p. 56.

his chances on the military leadership of an ex-Bonapartist military adventurer, General Ramorino. But the response from the Italians was as negative in 1815 as it would be later, and the Austrians made short work of the adventurer; while the Pope was being fêted at Modena, Florence, Siena and Viterbo, on his return in May from Genoa to Rome, the unfortunate Murat, routed at Tolentino, was taking refuge in France.

The episode of Napoleon's Hundred Days, though it had caused Pius VII to leave Rome once again, had brought nothing but gain to his cause. It had demonstrated his popularity in Italy, and the ineffectiveness of the revolutionary secret societies; it had removed the menace of Murat; it had compelled the Congress to delay no longer in settling the affairs of Italy. On June 9, 1815, less than a week before Waterloo, the Final Act of the Congress of Vienna restored the temporal power of the Popes as far as the right bank of the river Po; and on June 12 Consalvi recovered the *enclaves* of Benevento and Pontecorvo, though only after paying a monetary compensation to the 'Prince of Benevento', Talleyrand.

Consalvi's achievement at Vienna was as remarkable as it would later prove to have been disastrous. It was remarkable because the settlement of Vienna was one in which the claims of the small principalities generally, and of the ecclesiastical principalities always, were ignored; he succeeded, on behalf of the Bishop of Rome, at a time when archiepiscopal electorates were dismissed as out-of-date and when the fate of the smaller states was to find themselves eliminated (as in Germany) or amalgamated for strategic purposes (as on the borders of France) or parcelled out amongst the Hapsburgs (as in Italy). Consalvi himself insisted, with sincerity, that his success was due to the veneration felt for Pius VII;[1] but even his many enemies amongst the cardinals at Rome were willing to allow him personally a large share of the credit.

[1] Consalvi to Pacca, June 12, 1815, in *idem*, p. 704. Consalvi expressed the view with unusual warmth: 'Without the immense personal reputation of the Holy Father, and the view that is held about his sanctity and his character, it would have been useless (and God knows I do not lie or flatter in saying so) I repeat useless to have made claims, and negotiated, and cajoled; or at least we should have gained very little' (p. 705).

That his success was also disastrous was due to the fact that the legations had become untenable. To the historic causes of their dislike of rule from Rome (causes rooted in their inaccessibility, across the Apennines, in the independent and proud cultural tradition of Bologna, and in the economic interests which made them look to the plain of Lombardy rather than southwards) there were now added some seventeen years of separation from the papacy, of union with Lombardy, and of French political, judicial, and administrative institutions. The French had been hard taskmasters; they had taxed, conscripted, and exploited; but they had brought into power, of a sort, Italian laymen at Bologna and Ferrara, at Ravenna and Rimini, at Forlì and Imola and Cesena, who had never enjoyed any share in government before, and who would not now find it easy to hand it back to the clergy. The troubles of the next forty years in the Papal States mostly had their roots in that region; Cavour and Napoleon III, however interested their motives, were right, later on, when they warned Pius IX he would be better off without the legations.

There was, however, a practical difficulty about the Pope's abandoning them, of which Pius VI and Pius VII had not failed to remind the French government in the years following the Treaty of Tolentino (1797), for the legations were the only profitable part of the Papal States. Governments do not readily yield their richest provinces to others, and where the rest of the territories become economically unviable by such separation it is suicidal for them to do so. Consalvi knew that it might be difficult to hold the legations in the future; but he also knew that if they were lost the rest, too, would be lost. And there was a further consideration of which the names Imola and Cesena will have served as a reminder. Pius VII and Pius VI both came from Cesena, and their immediate predecessors, as we have already seen, came from the same region. And Pius VII had been Bishop of Imola – as the later Pius IX was. The roots of the papacy as well as the roots of a revolutionary liberalism lay, in the first half of the nineteenth century, in that fertile region of the valley of the Po.

If, then, Consalvi had abandoned the legations at Vienna he would have abandoned the territories (outside Rome herself) in which the papacy, from every point of view, was most particularly interested, and he would have opened the way to the loss of the rest of the temporal power. It was not in the nature of the papacy, as then constituted, that her chief servant should be empowered to serve her in such a way; yet his victory proved, in the event, to be too great, serving only to postpone and to prolong the death agonies of a temporal order that was moribund.

Having resettled Europe on the ostensible basis of legitimacy, but on the actual basis of the security of the governments of the great powers, the Bourbons and Hapsburgs, together with the Tsar Alexander, sought to secure the blessing of the Pope for the new arrangements. Such a blessing seemed the least that might be expected from him, now that he had been given back his states. It also seemed as though it would be wholly in harmony with the principles and teaching of the restored Church, which by now had become almost everywhere opposed to liberal revolutions. Yet, guided by Consalvi, Pius VII refused to oblige his protectors and patrons in this way, or to give an over-all spiritual sanction to their new order for Europe. He would commit the papacy to no particular political order. During the Hundred Days he had refused to fulminate a 'personalized'[1] excommunication against Napoleon, for which Talleyrand had pleaded with Consalvi. And now he refused to give a spiritual blessing to the position of the Hapsburgs and the Tsar.

In the light of what was to follow, in the ensuing decades, when Rome did not hesitate to employ spiritual censures in condemning the teachings of revolutionary liberals, and always sought to restrain potential revolutionaries, even when they were fighting for the freedom of the Church; in the light, too, of previous centuries, when Rome had not hesitated to give her moral support to princes, such as Philip II of Spain, with whose efforts the fortunes of the Church seemed to be involved, it is surprising and significant to find her refusing to bless the work of the Congress of Vienna, with which both her spiritual and her temporal fortunes seemed so closely interwoven.

[1] The 'omnibus' excommunication of 1809 still stood, however.

But it was not evident in 1815 that the times of disturbance were over. During the disturbance Rome had taken her stand on neutrality, Pius VII refusing, on the one hand, to be lured by Napoleon into his continental system, and on the other hand to seek refuge in Malta, or under British protection elsewhere, because he wished to put his political neutrality beyond question. At least in the earlier stages of the Congress the Big Four looked to Rome merely like a continuance of the military coalition, and Consalvi was no more inclined to commit Papal policy wholly to their keeping than he had been while the war lasted. So we find that when Metternich proposed, in January 1815, that the papal government should closely co-ordinate its policies with those of Vienna, with a view to keeping order in the Marches, and to restraining potential revolutionaries, Consalvi remained silent.[1] His government had refused to enter Napoleon's system; it would not now enter Metternich's. Though Consalvi clearly understood the reality of the revolutionary danger, his determination to enter into nobody's 'political bloc' remained strong; later events were to prove, however, that he was hardly realistic in his isolationism.

The Congress of Vienna became something more than a treaty conference; under the influence of Metternich it laid the basis for the Congress System, designed to put out the fire of revolution wherever it might appear; under the influence of Tsar Alexander it invoked spiritual sanctions, in forming the Holy Alliance. With Metternich's Congress System Consalvi would not directly co-operate, refusing the Chancellor's proposed Italian League because he would not prejudice the neutrality of the Papal States. And with the Holy Alliance, likewise, he would have nothing to do, because it did not seem to him to be Holy, as he understood the word. Paradoxically, he shared Castlereagh's view that it was 'sublime mysticism and nonsense', though he would not have brought the word 'mysticism' into contempt by using it in this context. So far as the Tsar's religious conception was susceptible of logical analysis it was a form of the 'Divine Right of Kings' theory; when it was supported by the Emperor Francis and Metternich the spectre of Josephism seemed at Rome to become luminous once more. The

[1] Consalvi to Pacca, January 18, 1815, in *idem*, p. 223.

Pope, therefore, would not give his spiritual blessing to an alliance which had sought its religious inspiration in Erastian rather than in Catholic teaching, and which seemed very unlikely to maintain the essential distinction between those things which were Caesar's and those which were God's.

Consalvi's objections to the Holy Alliance and to the Congress System make an interesting contrast with the objections entertained by the English and continental liberals of his own day. Both talked about these things as though they constituted a tyranny; but whereas the liberal revolutionaries saw in them an instrument for shackling the peoples of Europe, to prevent them from being emancipated by the principles of 1789, and so being enabled to enjoy the benefits of Liberty, Equality, and Fraternity, Consalvi saw them as a clumsy and crude attempt to patch up the leaky structure of European society, an attempt doomed to failure because it failed to perceive and to remove the real cause of the rot. Surveying the scene with the eye of a cool and intelligent conservative, who believed in the universality of his principle, he saw the opposite side of the coin to that which, for instance, Mazzini, with an equal belief in the universality of his own revolutionary principle, saw; and he condemned the Congress of Vienna for exactly the opposite reason to that which led Mazzini to condemn it. To Mazzini it was an immoral tyranny, resting on censorship; to Consalvi it was a futile military system which failed to take into account the need to guide men's minds – through censorship. Writing during the Congress, in scattered notes which were later published by Crétineau-Joly, he tells how:

'In the frequent audiences which King Louis XVIII at the Tuileries, and the Prince Regent at London or at Windsor were good enough to grant me. . . . I dared to say that the freedom of the Press, as it was established in France by the Royal Charter, is the most dangerous weapon ever put into the hands of the opponents of religion and the monarchy. The liberty of the Press is no mere passing or limited evil, it will be permanent and will develop, so to speak, with each public crisis and with each social upheaval. The perils to which it gives rise are palpable and incalculable; its advantages and benefits will be nullified by criminal influences. King Louis XVIII, in my view, makes the great mistake of seeing this balancing of powers as wise and necessary. He believes in his work; is tied to it by the tenderness of a father; but the Prince Regent, who for long has experienced this despotism of the mind exerted by unknown men, or by men unfortunately only too well known, came to share my apprehensions much more readily than he did the liberal theories of the Bourbon. The Prince Regent gave me an historical picture of the Press in his country; he portrayed very clearly for me its advantages and disadvantages in that altogether exceptional kingdom; but he is alarmed by this new danger on the continent, where this freedom is even being offered to peoples who have not thought of asking for it.

'Without doubt, it is with this hidden power, brought into play the whole time and playing simultaneously on the different passions, that it will be necessary to reckon one day. Europe has experienced long years of discord and of war; but amidst all the calamities she has endured she has never been menaced with a more startling spectre. Anonymity will soon be the arbiter of the public conscience, and it will be necessary to bend the brow beneath the pen or beneath the whip of masters without name from whom our subservience will have earned us our alms. Some see the peril and smilingly ignore it, others accept it as an experiment; nobody will understand that it amounts to infecting whole populations with a fever unrelenting and timeless.'[1]

Meanwhile the members of the Congress

'apply themselves to drawing the frontiers of this or that State, to guaranteeing it against the invasion of a neighbour; Europe provides for her internal security and for her external defence; then, by a folly of which she does not dare to calculate the consequences, she commits all the peoples, in advance, to revolutions without end and to errors which will give birth to inevitable crimes and to passions ceaselessly reborn which nothing can assuage. The struggle between the good and evil principle will never be equally matched. Talent, even genius, cannot triumph in these daily combats in which pens venal and filled with hatred take issue with the men of goodwill, distorting their characters and behaviour, and putting themselves forward as the sole defenders of the people and of liberty.'[2]

Consalvi claimed to have persuaded the Prince Regent of the

---

[1] Consalvi *Mémoires* (1866), Vol. 1, Introduction, p. 25.
[2] *Idem*, p. 27.

truth of his views; it is possible also that he had some influence on Metternich, whose principles at Vienna he did not regard as altogether 'sound'. At all events, Metternich tried to hold secure the political position in Germany and Italy, after 1815, by a system of political censorship of the kind Consalvi had in mind. The French revolutions of the nineteenth century would show that both the Chancellor and the Cardinal were right in anticipating that the journalists would play an important part in making the revolutions. But the Cardinal's distinction between the 'good principle' and the 'men of bad faith' would be shown to be as over-simplified as Mazzini's analogous classification by which all Europeans were either *buoni* (the liberals) or *mali* (the existing ruling classes). Moreover when Consalvi went on, in the same document, to say that it would be 'against the See of Peter, as being the foundation of all truth and of all stability, that the journals, once masters of the ground, would direct their most terrible blows', he seemed to be treating the papacy as though it must always be allied with the monarchs and must make their cause its own. Consalvi's ideal was a Europe of absolute monarchies, but of monarchies obedient to the Pope in matters concerning the Church. Their own unruly members they were to keep quiet by means of the censorship. It is very difficult to reconcile his views with those, say, of Cardinal Chiaramonti in 1797; but it becomes easier to appreciate them when it is remembered that his aim was to recover and to hold the Papal States for the Pope, and that, being a theocracy, the Papal States, by their very nature, could never embrace fully the principles of political liberalism.

If Metternich stood in debt to Consalvi for advice about the Press, he repaid it in 1846 by warning the young Pio Nono, then embarking on his liberal reforms in the Papal States, of the danger he was piling up for himself by allowing the indiscriminate proliferation of newspapers and clubs. Indeed, from the time of his Carlsbad Decrees of 1819, and the Congress of Troppau in the following year, a strict censorship of the press, in the German and Italian States, designed to prevent the publishing of liberal revolutionary sentiments, became an essential part of his famous 'system.'

With this side of Metternich's work Consalvi naturally had no quarrel; he may have helped to inspire it. When, at the Congress of Verona, in 1822, Metternich required the Italian rulers to say what they were doing to prevent a recurrence of the revolutionary movements which had put Vienna to the trouble of intervening in Naples and Piedmont, Consalvi's envoy, Cardinal Spina, was able to assure the conference that the pontifical government 'would always be ahead of the desires of the Allied Powers and of the Italian Governments whenever there was any need to work for that purpose'.[1] But when it came to a question of collective military action, designed to suppress a revolutionary movement which might 'infect' a neighbouring state (action of the kind agreed upon by Metternich and Hardenberg at Teplitz in August 1819, and adopted by the Congress of Troppau, in 1820, in its famous Protocol, as of universal application) the papal government made difficulties. Just as at the Congress of Vienna Consalvi had rejected the idea of an Italian League, so to the Congress of Troppau he sent a protest against the proposed passage of Austrian troops across Papal territory, on their way to suppress revolution in Naples; and he refused to contribute a contingent of papal troops to help in this 'police' action although the Papal States were those most likely to catch the new infection. At the Congress of Laibach in January 1821 the Papal envoy, Cardinal Spina, was instructed to have nothing to do with the Austrian intervention, and to insist that peaceful mediation in Naples was the right policy. And at the Congress of Verona, at the end of the following year, Consalvi caused Spina to join with the representatives of the other Italian States in encouraging the Austrians to withdraw from the Italian peninsula as soon as possible after their interventions in Naples and Piedmont. Evidently, while he wanted to see 'law and order' kept in Europe (he was quite in favour of France being given a free hand to intervene against the revolutionary movement in Spain), he did not want to see the Austrians cross the river Po. Too easily that could mean Austrian domination of the peninsula, and the end of effective neutrality for the Papal States, for which he had striven for

---

[1] Vat. Arch. *Segr. di Stato.*, Rub. 242, Busta 392, Spina's declaration of December 13, 1822.

so long against the French and for which he had stood against the
Austrians themselves at Venice in 1800 and at Vienna in 1815.

In the Secretary of State's correspondence with Metternich in
1820 we see him attempting to maintain his two inconsistent principles: first the suppression of the secret societies and revolutionary
movements; and second an absolute neutrality for the Papal States.
He is offended because Metternich has come to doubt the adequacy
of his measures against the societies; yet he insists on treating it as a
domestic problem and is determined to make clear that the Pope
must remain neutral and never be drawn into interventions outside
his own territories. On August 23, 1820, he wrote to the Chancellor about the revolutionary societies:

'The Holy See flatters herself on being the first government to
understand the malign intentions of the secret societies and to expose them before the whole of Europe. The bulls and edicts of the
supreme pontiffs Clement XII, Benedict XIV, Pius VI, and Pius
VII bear luminous testimony of this to the whole world'. If only the
other governments had realized how right the Holy See was about
this 'the evil would have been suffocated at birth'. Metternich need
not fear that there will be any failure to meet the menace in the
Papal States, as the suppression of the revolt at Macerata, in 1817,
proves. 'No other government could be more diligent than that of
the Pope in suppressing the sects and in refusing to allow any
changes incompatible with the institutions which characterize his
polity'. It is good of Metternich to offer to intervene in case of
trouble, but Consalvi does not expect trouble. So long as Austria
maintains an army in Lombardy all will be well.[1]

By the same post, however, Consalvi sent the Chancellor another
letter, marked 'Confidential and Reserved', in which he sought to
explain to him why, despite the hatred of secret societies and revolution which he shared with Metternich, he could not co-operate
with him in intervening to suppress the revolution in Naples.

'If the Holy Father was unable (though his refusal cost him his
political existence) to enter into hostilities against non-Catholic
nations, so as to avoid damaging his relations with their Catholic

[1] C. van Duerm *Correspondance du Cardinal Hercule Consalvi avec le Prince
Clément de Metternich, 1815-1823* (Louvain, 1899), p. 396.

subjects, how much less can he do so now against a state entirely
Catholic . . . the religious relations . . . which the Holy See must
maintain with all governments, relations whose maintenance is
intimately bound up with the nature and duties of the Holy See,
forbid his taking up a hostile attitude against any government and
demand that he avoid even the slightest appearance of doing so. . . .'
This is so important a principle that 'he can never forget it, nor give
preference over it to any temporal advantage.'[1]

Of the two principles, then, that of isolationism was regarded as
the more important, because rooted more fundamentally in the
Pope's spiritual position. Rather than violate it he would refrain
from co-operating with Metternich, or entering his system, even
though he knew that the secret societies were an international problem. He could feel comfortably sure that, even though the Papal
States were not playing their part in a collective effort, Austria
would be sure to play hers, if the situation at Bologna or at Rome
should demand it.

Consalvi's principle of isolationism would be maintained in the
face of any ideological sympathies entertained by Rome, of whatever complexion. When it was applied at the time of the Austrian
intervention in Naples, in 1821, the Curia had much sympathy with
Austrian motives; but it would be applied again, in 1848, when Pio
Nono had much sympathy with the anti-Austrian motives of the
Piedmontese armies and of the Italian volunteers. But unfortunately, however 'fitting', religiously speaking, such a principle of
neutrality might be, it could not be successfully maintained, because the Papal States were not capable of that isolation which had
become increasingly difficult for any small state. Only when the
power of France and the power of Austria were nicely balanced in
Italy was there any chance at all of Rome retaining her independence; every time that that balance became upset she became subject
to the pressure of the preponderant power. Nor was she, in fact,
able to withstand within her own borders that liberal revolutionary
'infection' which Consalvi feared so greatly, but which he would
not enter into collective action to meet. When the Revolution

[1] *Ibid.*, p. 262.

struck, in her own territories, in 1831-32, she had to call in the Austrians; when it struck in 1848 the French came to the rescue in the following year. It is easy to see why Metternich became irritated, as Napoleon had before him. Was Austria to maintain a large army in Lombardy (as Rome expected) to be used only when the Pope requested? Since the Papal States depended wholly upon what happened outside, it seemed reasonable to expect that they should enter into some sort of collective system. In such a case, it is true, papal troops would be liable to find themselves fighting on foreign soil, in other peoples' quarrels, and that would create an awkward predicament for a prince in the Pope's peculiar dual position. But so long as he was possessed of a state, in temporal matters analogous to other states, and situate in the middle of the Italian peninsula, that was a predicament he could not avoid. In a Europe of big powers, alliances, and spheres of interest, total independence for a small state, almost unarmed, was unattainable. The only hope of safeguarding the frontiers so laboriously re-covered lay in the collective security system demanded by Metternich. Any estimate of Consalvi's genius must take into account the awkward fact that he set himself a goal which could not be achieved. The desperate expedients to which his successors had resort (the arming of civilians, or the calling in of 'emergency' foreign help) were made necessary by the endeavour to maintain political abso-lutism alongside of territorial integrity and political neutrality, all of which had been insisted upon by the Great Cardinal, though they proved to be both inconsistent and impracticable. Without con-scription (which the Popes would not countenance) and without more than a token army expedients of a desperate kind became inevitable for subsequent secretaries of state. The hope was enter-tained at Rome that both alliances and armaments could be avoided by a constant repetition of the doctrine that it was sacrilegious for lay rulers or revolutionaries to lay hands on papal territory. Unfortunately that doctrine, for all Consalvi's eloquence, failed to carry conviction in the nineteenth century.

CHAPTER SIXTEEN

The Restoration in the Papal States

In June of the year 1815 Consalvi returned in triumph from Vienna, bringing his sheaves with him in the form of restored papal rule over the whole of Rome's traditional dominions.[1] It seemed a great moment. His many enemies amongst the cardinals joined in the chorus of applause and a picture was commissioned, to be executed in the classical style of the Empire, representing the 'great Cardinal' offering the cities of Rome, Ravenna, Bologna, and Ferrara (depicted by kneeling female figures) to the 'good Pope', who was surrounded by allegorical figures of Strength, Mercy and Glory. Much was said about the liberation of these cities from the Jacobin tyranny.

It was confidently hoped that the Temporal Power was secure at last. It seemed only necessary that the great Cardinal and the good Pope should use the years that remained to them (there proved to be as many as eight) to reorder the affairs of their territories so that there should be no doubt in men's minds (especially at Bologna) that they had, indeed, been liberated from tyranny, and so that there should be no temptation to revolutionaries from outside to fasten upon the Papal States as a good breeding ground for insurrectionary movements.

Though implacably opposed to the kind of liberties which advanced European liberals were now beginning to demand, Consalvi understood better than most of those at Rome what was needed to make the papal government more efficient and more acceptable in the legations. And since Pius VII's confidence in him

[1] Strictly, the legations were not 'restored' but 'given back', the text of the final act of Vienna reading *remises*, not *rendues* (Rinieri, Vol. 3, p. 709). Thus did Metternich, who had been obliged to surrender his chosen word *données*, still manage to avoid using the word which implied that the papal rule in that region was of inalienable traditional right. He also secured for Austria, for defence reasons, the part of Ferrara lying north of the river Po.

was unshakeable, and the disposition of the Pope's own mind remained, as it always had been, sympathetic towards measures of reform, it is not self-evident why, by the time of the Pope's death in August 1823, the glories of the restoration had already begun to look tarnished and the prospects of the papal government were arousing the anxieties of her friends and the hopes of her enemies.

Consalvi's relative lack of success, during the eight years of uninterrupted power which he enjoyed at Rome before the Pope's death, is generally attributed to the jealousy and hostility of reactionary *zelanti* cardinals who thwarted his attempts at reform and tried to put the clock back to 1792.

Their responsibility is certainly great. They held a useful advantage, at the outset, over the Secretary of State in that, for more than a year, while he was negotiating at Paris, at London, and at Vienna, they were on the spot; and in that year they managed to do much of the damage. It was begun by Mgr Agostino Rivarola – not yet a cardinal – whom the Pope, on his own initiative, sent ahead of him from Cesena, on May 4, 1814, to prepare for his own arrival. Rivarola instituted the policy, against which Consalvi protested from London, of expropriating from their positions, both in Church and in State, those who had supported the French régime. Some reallocation of offices was obviously to be expected; nor was it unreasonable, for example, that those clergy who had consistently refused to take the oath of loyalty demanded by Napoleon, and who had suffered for their devotion, should be recompensed. Yet the wholesale eviction from their benefices of those clergy who had taken the oath was harsh,[1] while such measures as the dismissal of distinguished professors from the universities, or the driving back of the Jews into their ghetto, made a bad impression, especially in London, and were not to be excused by saying that the same sort of thing was being done elsewhere in Europe. Consalvi, embarrassed in his diplomacy by the complaints, protested about what was going on, and the Pope found it necessary to send a distinguished lawyer, Giovanni Vera, to England, to give the Secretary of State first-hand information on how matters stood. But after the congress had opened at Vienna the complaints continued, tending

---

[1] For papal policy towards these jurors see Appendix IV, p. 300.

always to weaken Consalvi's lofty moral stand amongst the plenipotentiaries, so that he was compelled to protest further in letters
to Cardinal Pacca.

For Pacca was in control of policy. In Consalvi's absence the Pope
had made him pro-Secretary of State, a move which his record
during the year before Pius's abduction, his fortitude at the Fenestrelle, and the part he had played at Fontainebleau made natural
enough. Only di Pietro, who had held a skeleton Church government together as Delegate at Rome in 1798–99, and again in 1809–
10, could point to service in support of the papacy, during the years
of tribulation, to compare with Pacca's. But Pacca was not the
right man to superintend the difficult transition from the rule of the
French to the rule of the priests. He saw matters in black and white;
and the Revolution, Napoleon, and any Italian 'patriots' who had
collaborated with them seemed to him to be very black indeed.
Nor was he prepared to believe that anything that the French had
done at Rome could be worth preserving. He therefore supported
Rivarola in his proscriptions, cancelled the various Napoleonic legal
codes which had tidied up civil and criminal procedure, and set up
an ecclesiastical commission to supervise the return of the secularized religious property.[1]

It was 1799 once again. Those who had then been called Jacobin
or patriot friends of the French were now beginning to be called
liberals, but their essential character was the same: they were
against the clerical government. The most important difference in
1814 was that the French-patriot rule at Rome had this time lasted
for nearly five years and had therefore had the chance to effect certain changes – some of them salutary. The Napoleonic codes were
thought offensive in some respects – for instance in their provision
for divorce – but technically speaking they were a great improvement on the multitude of different codes and different courts
existing previously and now restored. And although aspects of the
French administration, especially the military conscription, and the
many confiscations, had been odious to Romans of all classes, while

[1] For a general account of these events see, in particular, Schmidlin, Vol. 1,
pp. 179–84, and F. Hayward Le Dernier Siècle de la Rome Pontificale, Vol. 2, Pie VII
(la Restauration).

others, such as the suppression of begging, had betrayed a type of moral outlook quite un-Roman, yet some of the changes that had been introduced, such as uniformity in the weights and measures, street lighting, or vaccination, had had their evident advantages, and their abolition seemed to many to be merely a bigoted *revanche*. Similarly, on the personal side, the comparatively long duration of the French rule on this occasion had meant that a substantial pro-portion of the lay nobility had become 'infected' with the French ideas. The document which Murat had brandished in front of the returning Pope at Cesena, demanding a lay government for Rome, had probably not been wholly spurious. It had been signed by mem-bers of distinguished Roman families which had followed the lead of the late Pope's nephew, Duke Braschi, who had gone to Paris, with other lay patricians, in November 1809 and made obsequious speeches there, telling Napoleon his 'Third Rome' would be greater than the Rome of Augustus or Leo, and inviting him to 'ascend the steps of the Campodoglio'.[1] As Mayor of Rome, under the military governorship of Miollis, Braschi had had his party, men whose support of the secular government arose naturally from their in-clinations and ambitions, and not merely from compulsion. If the number of those who wanted to replace the Pope as Head of the State was restricted by the fact that only substantial laymen were likely to benefit by the change, this number was likely to grow as more laymen acquired property and position.

The Roman restoration went through several phases, during each of which it had to have regard to what was happening outside Rome, both in Italy and abroad. In the first phase the presence of Murat confused the situation. It was to Murat that Miollis was com-pelled to surrender the Sant' Angelo in January 1814; and it was under his military and secularist régime, and not under the rule of the priests, that the most violent acts of revenge against the French and their supporters, and especially against those who had been in-volved in Radet's assault on the Quirinal, were perpetrated. In trying to establish his own position at Rome Murat was bound to look for support amongst the anti-clerical patriots, yet they were

[1] *Gazzetta Universale* of Florence for November 25, 1809 (Vat. Arch. *Ep. Nap. It.*, Busta VI, Fasc. 16).

the people whose régime he was replacing. Having ruined that régime, and being unable to turn to the clericals, who were demanding the return of the Pope, Murat had only his army to rely on, so that when he was obliged by the allied diplomacy to withdraw his troops he left a vacuum in authority at Rome which the Pope and Pacca, entering in May, were strongly placed to fill. The opposition was disorganized and confused, which would seem to have provided a good reason for trying to win over some of it to the support of the restored Pope. Pacca insisted, in his letters to Consalvi, that he was showing the utmost moderation and was thereby giving scandal to many. No doubt he was; but it might have been the better part of wisdom for him to ignore the scandalized and try harder to reconcile the leading laymen. In fairness, however, to Pacca, it should be noticed that Consalvi himself conceded that, while he hoped restraint would be used in punishing past offences, it was important to deal firmly with present plots. And these were soon very much in evidence, for Murat's agents were known to be in correspondence with the isle of Elba, and by March of the year 1815 that remarkable adventurer was marching north again, brandishing every kind of proclamation designed to unite the Romans as well as other Italians behind himself, so that the Pope – having no military force at all at his disposal at this time – was obliged, as we saw, to withdraw for some weeks to Genoa. In short, in the early part of the year 1815 Pacca was trying to carry out the Roman restoration against the background of a highly explosive Italian situation.

With the return of Consalvi from Vienna in June 1815 an entirely new problem arose, namely what was to be the character of the restored régime in the legations, where the Austrians were in possession, and in the Marches, which the Neapolitans were in course of evacuating. The legations, except for a year between the summer of 1799 and the summer of 1800, had been under French-patriot rule since 1797. They were also, as has been emphasized, the part of the papal dominion least enamoured of Rome or of clerical rule. It would be impossible merely to restore the pre-revolutionary régime there in the way that it was being restored at Rome. In any case Metternich was interested in them, having taken them over from the French, and being concerned by their close economic and cultural connection with Austrian-ruled Lombardy. It would be particularly inconvenient to Vienna to have them become a centre of disturbance, so the Chancellor told Consalvi he would not hand them over at all unless the existing secular administration were maintained, unless a general amnesty were extended to those who had supported the Napoleonic kingdom, unless responsibility for the public debts of the previous régime were accepted, and unless a guarantee were given to existing possessors of secularized ecclesiastical property that their title to it would be protected. Consalvi was not pleased;[1] but he understood Metternich's standpoint better than it was understood at Rome.

Back once more at Rome, Consalvi worked on his project for a reconstruction of the papal system of government and it was ready for publication in a *motu proprio* on July 6, 1816.[2] Under the supreme authority of the Secretary of State there were to be four legations (Ravenna, Bologna, Ferrara, and Forlì), to be ruled by cardinal-legates, and thirteen delegations, to be ruled by bishop-delegates. There was nothing new about this, except the demarcation of the jurisdictional boundaries. What was new was the plan that each legate or delegate be assisted by a congregation of four laymen; but since these were to be nominated by the government, and to act in a consultative capacity only, while Rome herself was provided for separately, the importance of this particular reform was limited. The most significant changes envisaged in the *motu proprio* were the suppression of all independent local rights and authorities, whether feudal or municipal, and the clear separation of administration from civil or criminal justice. Judicial powers were not to be held by legates or delegates, nor were they to be exercised by priests, although the clergy were to retain their own ecclesiastical courts for

---

[1] Consalvi to Pacca, Memorandum of June 12, 1815, in Rinieri, Vol. 3, pp. 711–40.

[2] For an analysis of the *motu proprio* see M. Petrocchi *La Restaurazione, il Cardinale Consalvi, e la Riforma del 1816* (*Le Monnier*, 1941). Petrocchi has here published the Consalvi-Severoli correspondence of 1816–17, in which the Secretary of State was justifying his handiwork in the face of the criticisms of Severoli, who was then Nuncio at Vienna.

their own persons and for cases deemed to belong to the canon law.

The changes envisaged by the *motu proprio* all lay in the direction of centralization and of secularization, both of them qualities which it took over from the French administration. In that it confirmed the French abolition of the innumerable feudal rights it might be called democratic; but in that it failed to restore the local liberties of the municipalities (their councillors and officers were now to be chosen by the legates and delegates) it was more generally regarded, with justice, as aiming at strengthening the hand of the central government. It was the work of a man seeking to establish some degree of centralization and order into a state which had enjoyed little enough of either, and who also saw the absolute necessity of allowing the lay element to enter effectively into the administration of government and justice. Consalvi's own preference would have been to secularize the administration throughout, with lay administrators in charge of departments.[1] But the *motu proprio* in fact kept all the political power that mattered in the hands of the cardinals and bishops.

The Consalvi programme was given a chilly reception. It was regarded as French and Jacobin by those many who wanted to see the old ways restored, while it did nothing at all to open the path to political power for the substantial laymen of the legations, who had begun to enjoy a little lately and were bitter about the return to Roman rule. On the other hand it did something to calm opinion in Vienna, in Paris, and in London; and no doubt it would have done more had it been more fully carried out. In particular, the advisory lay councils, to be nominated by the government, in the legations, delegations, and municipalities, seldom materialized; while the vast tangle of criminal jurisdiction was not sorted out. Against strong opposition Consalvi succeeded in introducing a new code of civil procedure, new measures for regulating the roads and water supplies, and a reorganization of the institutions of higher education. Metternich, influenced perhaps by the fact that the points he had insisted on in regard to the legations had been observed, apparently believed that it was only the enlightened character of Con-

[1] Rinieri, Vol. 4, p. 636.

salvi's administration in the legations that prevented the Papal States from imitating the example of Naples and Piedmont and rising in revolt in 1820 and 1821.[1]

The Secretary of State was at first served, in the legations, by cardinals of some capacity who did not shut their eyes altogether to the need for changes. Perhaps the most enlightened was his own pupil Spina, of the Napoleonic Concordat, who was Legate at Bologna. But Malvasia at Ravenna, and Arezzo at Ferrara were not blind reactionaries.[2] At Forlì, however, he had to put up with a legate very much of the old school, in the shape of the intransigent *zelante* Sanseverino, Neapolitan confidant of King Ferdinand's restored court. Sanseverino made no secret of his hostility to Consalvi's plans so that his appointment at Forlì can only mean either that Consalvi himself was not too serious about them or – more likely – that the Secretary was simply unable to find cardinals of the stature needed for the position of legate who also belonged to his way of thinking. Sanseverino was a good legate, with a strong sense of duty, and he came to be greatly loved at Forlì for his open-handed generosity; but he saw no need to change the system.

If the opposition to Consalvi grew always stronger amongst his colleagues of the Curia, so that he had to act more and more on his own, a wider circle within the city of Rome could forgive him much for what he did for her improvement. Of all the administrative reorganizations which he undertook the most permanently successful were those by which he persuaded the Pope to issue edicts in 1818 and 1819, first reassessing the rates of Rome, so that the better-class properties paid more towards the maintenance of her roads, fountains, and ancient monuments, and then to centralising the city's planning authority. Consalvi had been in Paris and Vienna; he knew how far Rome had fallen behind contemporary standards in the servicing and maintenance of a great capital. He was not content to reflect complacently, with Pacca,[3] that the great

---

[1] Schmidlin, Vol. 1, Part 1, p. 190.
[2] Cf. L. C. Farini's opinion in *Lo Stato Romano* (Florence, 1850), Vol. 1, pp.16–18.
[3] *Memorie del Ministero*, Part 2, chapter 6.

buildings of Rome were finer than those of Paris (though this was true) nor to add, as Pius VI had added, to the artistic effects of the capital by setting up obelisks at focal centres, embellishing and enlarging the churches, or extending the collections of sculpture. Not that he neglected these traditional ways of giving splendour; no visitor to the Chiaramonti wing of the Vatican gallery will be likely to feel that he was niggardly in the acreage which he added to that palace. But his distinctive contribution was rather to the replanning of the city. Thanks to Consalvi the visitor to Rome, entering by the Flaminian gate, is confronted by the grand perspectives of the widened *Piazza del Popolo*, with the newly buttressed Pincian hill on the left, and the twin churches ahead, with the three straight streets, the Corso in the centre leading straight into the heart of the city. And when he penetrates farther he finds the fountain of the *Trevi*, as well as lesser outpourings, flowing with a vigour unknown in the eighteenth century on account of the stimulus the cardinal gave to the work of the *fontanieri*.

The reassessment of the rates of Rome, designed to pay for all this, was based on the sensible principle that the responsibility of property holders was to the city as a whole and not merely towards their own street. In the same way the administrative reorganization of the State carried with it a reassessment for purposes of taxation, intended to relieve the burden on some of the poorer communes, especially the cis-Apennine ones, and to secure more money from the better-off places, which generally meant the trans-Apennine towns of the legations and the Marches. But this reassessment, which worked to the disadvantage of the privileged, whether clerical or lay, did nothing to improve the Cardinal's position with those who were already calling him a dictator and a Jacobin. Nor was he helped by the fact that he was obliged to increase taxation. The French administration had paid its way by its seizure of property; but if it had thus been enabled to leave the state finances in a healthier condition than they had been in in 1809, it had left Consalvi with the problem of restoring the Church property whilst compensating its lay purchasers (the procedure usually adopted with buildings previously belonging to religious bodies) or else of

leaving the property in the hands of the lay purchasers and compensating the previous Church owners (as was often done in the
case of the lands). Either way the national debt was materially
increased.

It was increased further when Consalvi attempted to revive the
economy by direct state intervention. Action of some kind was
forced upon him, for the old guild machinery for regulating
agriculture, industry and trade – the *corporazioni d'arti e mestieri* –
had been destroyed by the French while Consalvi himself, as far
back as the year 1801, had abolished the over-all control exercised
by the ancient *università*. In common with other Italian governments, that of Rome was committed, by the time of the restoration,
to economic planning of a kind. Most immediately, it had to provide for a rather rapidly increasing population (that of Rome rose
from 117,000 to 128,000 in the two years 1813–15; in 1800 it had
been as high as 153,000) and one that was confronted in 1816 with a
more than usually severe failure of the harvest. To meet the immediate situation Consalvi prohibited the export of grain and paid
bounties on its import; looking to the future he tried to establish
smallholdings on the Roman campagna in the place of the big and
abandoned estates there, and he gave bounties to encourage the tex-
tile industry and to promote the culture of tobacco on the Adriatic
side of the Apennines. A new college at Rome was supposed to
undertake research into the scientific study of agriculture.[1] But lack
of capital crippled all his enterprises, and soon the cost of the police,
and of the army, smothered the few sparks of economic revival.
Subsidies were paid to prevent the savings-banks of the poor from
defaulting, while the department known as the *Buon Governo* continued to make payments to the mayors of impoverished townships
to enable them to pay pittances to the poor where they were
starving.[2] But the creation of prosperity eluded him, as it eluded his
successors. Agriculture and the crafts were not unhealthy in the

[1] Schmidlin, Vol. 1, Part 1, p. 196.

[2] The usual expedient, in time of flood or other disaster, was for the local
authority to raise a forced loan from the wealthier inhabitants and try to recover the
money later from Rome. And this it might hope to do, because the papal government was readier to produce money for charitable purposes than for most others.
During the French occupation the depredations and requisitions arising from the

legations, and in the valleys of Umbria; the religious and artistic demands of visitors were heard once more in Rome, and tended steadily to increase there as travel became easier; but the Patrimony on the western, and the Marches on the eastern shores, along with the hill places of the Apennines, became natural nurseries of beggars and brigands for whom useful employment seemed lacking.

In a task of great difficulty, but which only he held the serious hope of achieving, Consalvi failed. Even before the death of the Pope, in 1823, which carried with it the fall from power of the Cardinal, the signs of a terrible disease, symptom of bad government, were already apparent in the legations. Two cardinal-legates, Sanseverino at Forlì and Rusconi at Ravenna, were beginning to imitate the bad example of Naples by fostering the formation of voluntary bands of *Sanfedisti* into 'Centurions', to combat the opposition already forming itself in the lodges of the secret societies. Here was the beginning of a system of 'government' which would develop during the reigns of Pius VII's successors and would end by making a settled and progressive order in the Papal States impossible. A resistance movement born of war and revolution, the *Sanfedisti* had been in their natural element in the days when they rose behind Lahoz in the Marches in 1799 to help drive out the French and to overturn the Jacobin republic at Rome. But after the restoration there should have been no further need for them; their very existence implied that the government was not capable of governing. As an auxiliary and self-appointed police force, responsible to nobody, they came to behave in a violent and unruly way, and attracted violent and unruly men, becoming a reproach to the government which depended on them, but which could not control them, and a source of despair to good men of every opinion. In the view of Luigi Carlo Farini, the liberal historian of the Papal States, who lived through most of the episodes which he described, it had not been necessary for these cardinal-legates to have resort to

---

marching and counter-marching of armies produced a flood of special appeals which were handled by the *Delegazione di Pietro*, until that indefatigable cardinal was removed by Napoleon in 1810 (Vat. Arch. *Ep. Nap. It.*, Busta 1, Fascs. 1–6).

so desperate an expedient. Farini was a devastating critic of developments under the subsequent pontificates, but he admired Consalvi
and thought that the beginnings of trouble in his time were due to
the attitude of his opponents; he seems to have shared Metternich's
belief that the relative tranquillity of the Papal States in the period
1815–23 could be attributed to the comparative enlightenment
and clemency of Consalvi's rule, which had prevented the secret
societies from organizing movements on the scale which they
achieved in Naples and Piedmont. In Farini's view it was when
della Genga became Pope Leo XII in 1823, and still more when
his successor Gregory XVI allowed Cardinal Bernetti to turn the
Sanfedisti into the 'system' of the Centurions, that the way was
opened wide for the later disturbances.

Leo, as it will be necessary to notice in the next chapter, has much
to answer for. Yet the seeds of the future troubles were planted
before the good Pope died and before the great Secretary fell from
power. Too many exiles, too many proscriptions, too many priests
in positions of political control, too arbitrary a severity in dealing
with the Macerata incident by special legatine court, too much subservience in surrendering to Vienna those in the legations linked
with the Carbonari at Milan, and above all too wide a latitude
for the *Sanfedisti* – all these were in being before 1823, and were
noted by Farini.[1] Without an army, or even any adequate police
force, Consalvi had no means of enforcing his centralization, his
new codes, or his attempt to secularize more of the administration. The opposition was too much for him.

But Consalvi's most unfortunate legacy was the territories he
won. By his victory at Vienna he had saddled Rome with a problem she was never able to solve. It would have been better if the
legations, signed away at Tolentino, had never been recovered. If
Austria were to rule at Milan and Venice then Metternich was
correct – as well as interested – in believing that she should rule at
Bologna, because Bologna belonged with the Po valley. Under
Napoleon, at intervals under Metternich, and later, when the
French victories of 1859 gave her the chance, under Victor Em-

[1] *Stato Romano*, Vol. 1, ch. 1.

Metternich. (*By courtesy of the State Library of Vienna.*)

manual, she was so linked, politically; by contrast, Rome was powerless to give the Romagna anything that she wanted.

Arguments of this sort would, of course, have been quite unintelligible to the Cardinal. His business, as he saw it, was to defend the legitimate legal rights of his sovereign even where (as at Avignon) they had more evidently become anachronistic than they had in the legations. And if the Pope was to retain a substantial as distinct from a token temporal power then it was, indeed, necessary to try to retain the legations, since they were the only economically valuable part of his dominions. The outlook of the time was that the Pope had to be maintained, with his court and with Saint Peter's, in the manner to which he had been accustomed, and on a footing of equality with the other European sovereigns; it was supposed that if he were not kept on that footing those sovereigns would cease to take him seriously, and would therefore cease to take seriously the claims of the Catholic Church in their own territories. As Consalvi explained at Vienna, it was necessary that he should be given back 'at least the resources which would be furnished him by the recovery of the whole of his states'.[1]

How deep-rooted was this belief can best be seen by the fact that it was held even by the most clear-sighted political thinker in the Sacred College, Cardinal Giuseppe Sala, the diarist of the Roman Republic of 1798. Sala presented to Pius VII, soon after his election, a comprehensive plan for the reform of the Papal States, and after the restoration of 1815 he was invited to present a new edition of it. In this very radical treatise he listed the 'Defects of Our System'. In his view the papal government (1) had 'confused the sacred and profane', (2) had repeated too often the phrase: 'things have always been done in this way', (3) had made the mistake of reiterating 'let us be careful not to make things worse', and (4) 'had lost or forgotten the art of understanding men'. And the consequences which he deduced from these errors were (1) that the spiritual power should be separated from the temporal, (2) that custom should be ignored, (3) that an end should be made of fear and condescension, and (4) that an effort should be made to understand men and to

[1] Vat. Arch Segr. di Stato, Rub. 242, Busta 391.

R

provide not for persons but for undertakings.[1] Sala saw much more clearly than did his contemporaries the need to separate sharply the spiritual power from the temporal in the Roman government. He was profoundly shocked by the 'masquerade' of 'abbatism' ('abbés' who were not ecclesiastics at all) and by the wearing of the clerical collar by laymen which was something, he pointed out, that happened nowhere else. 'We have often confused the spiritual with the temporal, sacrificing the former in the endeavour to maintain the latter, and we have thereby lost them both.'[2] 'To obtain the desired separation of the spiritual from the temporal it is necessary to establish the principle that all jobs which are secular in character are entrusted to laymen . . . when the Supreme Pontiff acts as Head of the Church he speaks as Pope; when he acts as sovereign he speaks as Prince. . . .'[3] The spiritual function of the papacy is essential, being inherent in its character. The temporal function is only accidental and accessory.

Yet this clear-sighted critic, who saw into the roots of what was wrong, and who realized the terrible truth that the spiritual purpose was being frustrated by the weight of the mismanaged temporal care, seems to have been unable to take the next and logical step of pointing out that it was time to limit and reduce the temporal obligations of the Popes. Most oddly, he seems to think that, despite the damage it is doing, the temporal power is still essential. 'If, for many centuries, the position of Vicar of Jesus Christ was sufficient for the Pope to make himself respected and feared both by peoples and by kings . . . with time the veneration would have weakened and the powers proportional to the needs of the Roman Church would perhaps have become lacking without the glory and resources of the temporal sovereignty. . . . God is free to work miracles at His will but, in the ordinary way, the Pope will not be able to act as Pope if he has no State to enable him freely to exercise his Authority and to command that respect and that obedience which all the faithful owe him.'[4]

Possibly this passage was ironical. Or possibly Sala could say no

---

[1] *Scritti di G. A. Sala (Archivio della R. Società Romana di Storia Patria)*, Vol. 4, p. 55. In this volume his plan as a whole is on pp. 45–234.

[2] *Ibid.*, p. 60.   [3] *Ibid.*, p. 75.   [4] *Ibid.*, pp. 72–73.

less, in the Rome of his day, and after he had said so much that would upset the curia. At all events he went no further than to insist upon the need to free the clergy, the Roman congregations, and the Pope himself from temporal duties. By his plan the Papal States, instead of being a sort of enlarged papal household, composed of 'levites of the temple', as Newman called them, standing in an intimate relationship with the Head of the Church, would have become more like a farm looked after by a competent lay bailiff, producing useful revenues for the papacy but not distracting the Pope's attention or that of any other ecclesiastics. But all the nineteenth-century Popes would have regarded such an arrangement as the gravest dereliction of their duty. They were determined to be true sovereigns, temporal as well as spiritual, and although Pius IX would be compelled, for a few months, to try to act as part of a constitutional and secular temporal government, while remaining spiritually autocratic, the arrangement failed completely.

In short the Popes felt committed, by tradition, by principle, and by prestige, to the Papal States and to their theocratic government. Nothing could save them from their millstone save Napoleonic force. There had been a brief moment, during the struggle between Pius VII and Napoleon, when the possibility existed that they would be saved by that means – the moment when Count Lebzeltern had suggested to Pius VII, at Savona, that it would be best if he were to return to Rome as bishop, and as Head of the Church, but without temporal sovereignty. Pius had agreed that, if only Napoleon would show his goodwill by letting him have his spiritual freedom and the advisers of his choice, he should do so; he would not allow the loss of his temporal sovereignty to stand in the way. But unfortunately Napoleon had not been prepared to allow him his spiritual liberty.

So as matters turned out the prestige which Pius VII won for the papacy by his passive resistance, and the return to religion which characterized the early nineteenth century, were capitalized by Consalvi at Vienna in the form of the legations and the Marches. And in that too solid form the spiritual victory which the Pope had won found an unfortunate reward. For political principles were now being worked out in western Europe with which no theocracy, however enlightened, could come to terms; and the result would be that the Papal States would become not merely a distraction to the Popes but even the cause of some confused judgment on their part where the ethics of political questions were concerned.[1]

---

[1] Most notably in Gregory XVI's encyclical *Singulari nos* (1834) and in Pius IX's Syllabus of Errors (1864). The denunciations of democratic liberties contained in these documents were related to the fact that the extension of such liberties to the Papal States was incompatible with the theocratic government there.

CHAPTER SEVENTEEN

Political Failure in the Papal States

I n the long run the fate of the Papal States would be sealed by the fact that geography, politics, and the climate of opinion were to make it impossible to continue to run an independent theocracy in the centre of the Italian peninsula.

It is in the nature of human polities to be overtaken by the tide of history, and no particular discredit attaches to this polity by the fact that it was liquidated in 1860–70. Its tragedy was that its penultimate phase was lamentable, and barely to be redeemed by its ultimate one, that of Pio Nono, with its glimpses of imagination and its moments of heroism. When all allowance has been made for the passions and distortions of embittered Romagnuol exiles, who conducted profitable lecture-tours in England or America, and whose wilder observations coloured the comments of the liberal historians; when it has been pointed out that Naples, or Modena, were possibly worse governed; and when justice has been done to the personal probity of the Popes, it still remains necessary to notice that the Roman government failed fearfully in the period between 1823 and 1846.

It was on the fourteenth anniversary of Radet's attack on the Quirinal – July 6, 1823 – that Pius VII, losing his balance and falling, when he was alone in his study, broke his thigh-bone and brought on his last illness He was eighty-one years old, and extremely feeble; the doctors dared not operate, and neither their ministrations, nor the patent adjustable bed sent by Louis XVIII from Paris, nor the twenty-five bottles of his best tokay sent by the Emperor Francis served to do more than ease his sufferings. On August 20 he died, and Cardinal Pacca, as Camerlingo, performed the ceremony of tapping his forehead with the silver hammer, calling on him by his baptismal name, Barnaba, and taking possession of that Fisherman's ring which the dead Pope had had more trouble than most Popes in protecting.

A great pontificate was over. No doubt Pius VII was not the man after the restoration that he had been before it, and physically he had been feeble since a fall he had suffered in 1817. But since his long struggle with Napoleon he had never ceased to be a legendary figure, and for many years he would be looked back upon as 'the good Pope'.

And with his going went 'the great Cardinal', whose departure had been foreseen. Though both Vienna and Paris would have been glad to see him maintained in power, or even elected Pope, as some guarantee of moderation and good government at Rome, and though at sixty-seven he was at the right age for assuming the tiara, in the existing state of curial opinion nothing was more certain than his removal from high office. Not only did the cardinals hold his attempts at reform, and his exclusiveness, against him; he was now also being accused of leniency towards the secret societies in the Romagna, and of liberalism, and at the same time of subserviency towards Austria. *Zelante* opinion, the opinion of those who saw it as their duty to uphold the traditions of the Roman government against all foreign powers, as well as against any secular opposition at home, was united in its opposition. Besides, he had committed the unpardonable fault of being in power for too long.

The favour of the Conclave first fell on Consalvi's critic Severoli; but Severoli had been Nuncio at Vienna, and Metternich was aware of his deep-rooted opposition to Austrian designs in Italy; so against Severoli the Austrian Exclusive was entered.[1] From one enemy of Consalvi the cardinals then turned to another – della Genga, whom the Secretary of State had withered with his scorn at Paris in 1814; and della Genga they elected. Having assumed the name Leo XII, the new Pope proceeded to appoint the octogenarian della Somaglia as his Secretary of State. Consalvi was not wholly ignored; he was made Secretary of Briefs, and then Prefect of Propaganda; but these were neither of them positions from which he was likely to be able to have much influence over political policy.

---

[1] It was presented by Albani, and is printed in N. Bianchi *Storia Documentata della Diplomazia Europea in Italia*, Vol. 2, p. 389.

However, it all mattered little now, for by the twenty-fourth of the following January Consalvi, too, was dead. Most of the veterans of the napoleonic struggle were gone; di Pietro had died the year before Pius VII, and of the principal protagonists from the past there remained only Pacca. That tough fighter now settled down to write his memoirs, which remained, until the much later posthumous publication of the Consalvi papers in 1859, the principal narrative of the adventures of the papacy in the days of Napoleon.

Canova, too, had died in the year before Pius, so the Pope's memory was perpetuated by another hand, in the form of a too sombre statue, in Saint Peter's, carved by the Danish sculptor Thorwaldsen, and paid for by Consalvi. And the memory of the Secretary was honoured by the same artist on the gloomy walls of the Pantheon, with a monument paid for by his few friends. A great age in Roman sculpture and architecture was ending on a subdued note. And even as the Pope lay dying the most historic of the city's great basilicas, Saint Paul's without the Walls, was going up in flames.

Leo XII, to his credit, had not sought to be elected, as Clement XIV had; knowing the state of his health he had warned the cardinals that they were 'electing a corpse'. But that had not deterred them; indeed an incapacity for action seemed almost an asset in a Pope of whom they were asking chiefly that he should not carry out the policy adumbrated in the *motu proprio* of 1816. But Leo, though he nearly died soon after his election, was not yet moribund. And he had a policy of a kind. It was his belief that all would be well if there were a higher standard of morality in the Papal States, and this he tried to secure by direct governmental intervention, closing the Roman wine shops in 1824, and banning the waltz at the carnival in 1826. To these negative acts he tried to give a positive complement by encouraging missions and crusades of all kinds; in 1825 was held the first Holy Year which it had been possible to hold at Rome since that presided over by Pius VI in 1775. It was perhaps natural that his view of the character of the evils of the day led him to restore the judicial and administrative position of the higher clergy, threatened by Consalvi, together with the older methods of juridical procedure; for he was uninhibited by any doubts about the juridical or political understanding and efficiency of the priests.

During Leo's comparatively short reign – he died on February 10, 1829 – the discontent in the Papal States, and especially in the legations, grew more serious. The policy of using the Sanfedists, discouraged by Consalvi, was now encouraged from Rome, with a view to suppressing the activities of the secret societies. These were now generally called the *Carbonari* – charcoal burners – after the widespread but amorphous society of that name, or sometimes simply the 'liberals' or the 'factious'; the effect of inciting the Sanfedists against them was to increase their own coherence and activity. At the beginning of June 1825 Leo sent the intransigent Cardinal Rivarola (who had organized the Restoration of spring 1814 at Rome) to Ravenna, as Cardinal Legate; with the aid of information laid by the Sanfedists, and through the instrumentality of the emergency court and of the special powers conferred on him by the Pope, this Cardinal, by the end of August, had sentenced seven men to death, fifty-four to forced labour, six to life imprisonment, fifty-three to various terms of imprisonment, two to exile, 129 to police supervision in the first degree, and 157 to police supervision in the second degree.[1] An attempt to assassinate Rivarola, which killed the wrong man, led the Pope to send Mgr Internizzi with another special commission, who arrested a number of suspects at Ravenna and hanged them after summary trial, leaving their bodies on the gibbets as an example to others. Ravenna had become, as it remained, the most disturbed of the legations; but in all of them, as in Umbria and the Marches, there was now a running warfare between Sanfedists and *Carbonari*, with the latter always tending to escape across the Apennines into tolerant Tuscany, *refugium peccatorum*.

So Leo, by failing to recognize the reasonable limits of clerical authority, by his encouragement of the Sanfedists, by the severities of his special legatine courts, by the strict censorship which he imposed on the Press (all political topics were banned) and by individual acts of intolerance such as the reimposition of all the old

[1] Figures given by Schmidlin, Vol. 1, Part 2, p. 23.

restrictions on the Jews in the Roman ghetto, alienated the sympathies of his secular subjects in all classes, so that he was greeted in silence by the Roman crowds and mercilessly lampooned in the clandestine Press. So too the papal government, whose reputation had stood well in Consalvi's time, at least in comparison with the governments of Naples and Sardinia, began to acquire its evil reputation in France and especially in England.

Just how the *Carbonaro* organization developed in the legations during the brief reign of Leo's successor Pius VIII (March 31, 1829, to December 1, 1830) is a problem about which little is known. Evidently some careful plans were laid, for when the Conclave met to elect Pius VIII's successor, and the cardinal-legates were all away from their posts attending it at Rome, the *Carbonari* took the opportunity provided by risings in Parma and Modena to seize Bologna and thence to move outwards. By February 25 there was a provisional government at Bologna, to which not only the cities of the legations but almost all the cities of Umbria and the Marches had given their adherence, and a declaration was issued that the temporal power of the Popes was at an end. At Orvieto and Rieti, however, the papal garrisons held firm, and in Rome herself there was only a faint echo of the revolution.

These events, and their sequel, which have often been described,[1] need only be briefly summarized here. They were part of the Italian response to the French revolution of July 1830 and in particular to the assurances given by the ministers of the new King, Louis Philippe, that they would not allow foreign powers to intervene in disturbances outside their own territories 'to restore order'. It was in these declarations from Paris that the revolutionaries placed their trust, imagining, as they did, that they meant that France would not allow the Austrian army to move across the river Po; so when, in fact, the Austrians did move in, unopposed, and crushed the movement, the bitterness of the revolutionaries is understandable. It was put into words by Mazzini: *Les secours de la France! pauvres déçus! l'abîme qu'ils ont creusé sous vos pas ne se com-*

[1] Bianchi, *op. cit.*, Vol. 3, p. 44, etc. G. F-H. Berkeley *Italy in the Making, 1815–1846*, p. 90, etc. C. Spellanzon *Storia del Risorgimento e dell' unità d'Italia* (Rizzoli, 1934), Vol. 2, pp. 358–481.

blera que par vos cadavres. L'inertie – l'improbation – la défense à nos concitoyens de voler à votre aide – voilà les secours de la France![1]

Consalvi had told Metternich that the real guarantee of Italian security lay in the presence of an Austrian force, in strength, in Lombardy. But just as he had disliked its use in Naples, so he had had no intention that it should ever be used in the Papal States. The events of 1831 showed that he had been correct about the importance of the guarantee, for it was when the Austrian force was thought to have been neutralized by France that the trouble began. But the revolution also showed the existence of a dissatisfaction with papal rule which cannot wholly be laid at the door of his successors, and whose existence he had denied with too airy a confidence.

It has been said that the Conclave which was still trying to find a successor for Pius VIII when the revolutionary movement broke out at Modena was accelerated in its deliberations by the danger impending in the north and the need of having a Pope in being who could call in the Austrians at a moment's notice.[2] It may be so, but it would be wrong to suppose that, even in this crisis, the cardinals were willing to elect whomsoever would be most pleasing to Vienna. Had that been their aim they would have followed the lead of their most pro-Austrian colleague, Albani, who had been Pius VIII's Secretary of State, and who was leading the group which wanted to elect Pacca. Instead they followed Albani's rival Bernetti, who had been Leo XII's Secretary of State, and elected Mauro Cappellari, a Camaldolese monk, who was a theologian and philosopher, more obviously suited to the spiritual than to the temporal duties of his new position. Nevertheless, if he was far from being an 'Austrian candidate' he was also far from being a candidate

---

[1] *Une nuit de Rimini*, Mazzini, *Scritti*, Nat. Ed. Vol. 2, p. 3. What aroused Mazzini's special bitterness was the way in which the French authorities prevented the Italian exiles in France from going to the aid of the movement in the legations. At Lyon, in February 1831, he had witnessed this. 'One day I saw a crowd gathered to read a government notice fixed to the wall. It was a harsh declaration denouncing the Italian undertaking, a warning to the exiles to dissolve their organization, and a brutal threat to use the full rigour of the penal laws against anyone who attempted to violate friendly frontiers and to compromise France with the governments.' (Mazzini, *Note Autobiografiche*, ed. Menghini, Le Monnier, 1944, p. 33.)

[2] Cf. Bianchi, *op. cit.*, Vol. 3, pp. 41, 42.

unacceptable to Austria. He was an Austrian subject by birth, and as Prefect of Propaganda under the previous Pope he had shown his legitimist orthodoxy by opposing the Catholic revolutionaries of Belgium in their revolt against their Dutch Protestant sovereign.

Cappellari (Gregory XVI) was elected on February 2, 1831, and the revolution reached Bologna on February 3. Bernetti, whom Gregory appointed Secretary of State, began by making a desperate attempt to avoid an Austrian occupation by turning for help to France and to Naples, endeavouring to frighten both Louis Philippe and Ferdinand II with the pretence that the presence of the sons of Louis Bonaparte amongst the revolutionaries meant that the movement was really a Bonapartist plot to take over Italy. And he caused the new Pope to put out a conciliatory proclamation and to give Cardinal Benvenuti instructions, on February 14, to act as Legate *a latere*, with power to parley with the rebels and procure a pacification 'by those means of pardon and mercy which are so in accord with the cardinal's paternal heart'.[1] However, the provisional government interned Benvenuti, no help was forthcoming from Naples or from France, and one of the rebel generals, Sercognani, was preparing to march on Rome.

Bernetti had at his disposal a small force, mostly mercenaries whom he had himself collected in Leo XII's time, and if they had shown any resolution the spread of the movement might well have been stopped. It was the opinion at the time of Mastai-Ferretti (the future Pope Pius IX) who, as Archbishop of Spoleto, was geographically well placed to judge the strength of Sercognani's following, in the southern cities of Umbria, that it amounted to 'scarcely 500 men, without uniform, or leadership, or courage. . . .' 'Either the pontifical troops', he observed, 'have decided to fight, in which case they will win; or the pontifical troops are all corrupt,

---

[1] See A. Serafini *Pio Nono* (Vatican Press, 1958), Vol. 1, p. 477. This 1,760-page book, which is concerned with the life of Mastai-Ferretti before he became Pope, is based on the extensive materials collected to assist in the process of his beatification. It provides an unique body of documentary evidence concerning the conditions at Spoleto and Imola, in the eighteen-thirties and -forties, those being the Sees which he held successively. It also discloses the critical views of a fair-minded bishop about the Roman régime under which he was serving.

and in that case I leave the matter in the hands of the Lord and remain silent.'[1]

The second of the Archbishop's two alternatives proved to be correct. The only serious opposition offered to the rebels was the work of resolute local leaders, like the Archbishop's own brother, Gabriele Ferretti, at Rieti, who armed the citizens and successfully held the city. So on March 15 Bernetti, who had already been in touch with the Austrian army which had occupied Modena, sent a formal and urgent request, through the Nuncio at Vienna, for Austrian intervention.[2] By the 21st the Austrians were in the Legation of Bologna and the rebel leader General Zucchi was retiring on Ancona, taking the Pope's Legate, Cardinal Benvenuti, with him. By March 27 the provisional government had surrendered the city, making terms with Benvenuti for a safe-conduct for the rebel leaders and for a general amnesty. These terms were not honoured by the Austrians, who captured General Zucchi and his companions and imprisoned them, or by Bernetti and the Pope, who took the view that Benvenuti had negotiated under constraint.[3] But retribution was not on this occasion notably harsh. A

[1] Idem, p. 474. According to C. Spellanzon (op. cit., Vol. 2, p. 441), Sercognani had 2,000 men when he surrendered.

[2] The Austrian General Frimont was in full possession of Parma and Modena, as well as of Ferrara and Comacchio, by March 9 (see C. Spellanzon, Vol. 2, p. 439). But he would not advance on Bologna until he had had specific instructions from his own government – not merely emissaries from the Pope.

On one point of consequence A. Serafini, in the book quoted on p. 267, Note 1, takes issue with Spellanzon and with the traditional account of this uprising. It has usually been stated (cf. Spellanzon, p. 407) that the Legate, Cardinal Benvenuti, though ostensibly sent to negotiate terms, had received a secret letter from Bernetti telling him to 'provoke a counter-revolution'. It was certainly on the grounds that he carried such a letter that he was manhandled and interned. But this letter, though it has more than once been reproduced, does not seem to be available. In its absence all that can be said is that there seem some grounds for supposing, with Serafini (p. 477), that it may have originated with an *agent provocateur* rather than with the Secretary of State. Another allegation was that the cardinal distributed poisoned cigarettes, an allegation which angered Lamennais, in his *Avenir* (*Articles de l'Avenir*, Louvain, 1831, Vol. 3, pp. 252–53).

[3] In his encyclical of April 5, 1831, the Pope said: 'but it is self-evident, and only too well known, that an act of this kind, extracted by force from one who, as soon as he became a prisoner of the enemy, had immediately lost the powers which made him interpreter of Our mind, was null and void' (*Acta Gregorii Papae XVI*, Vol. 1, p. 13).

few leaders of the revolt, and notably Count Terenzio Mamiani (who would be one of Pius IX's prime ministers in 1848) and Count Pietro Ferretti (a cousin of the Archbishop) suffered exile, with confiscation of their goods. For the rest there was a general amnesty, though only after a long delay, and many became subjected to police supervision.

This uprising of the year 1831, which was much the most considerable political movement in the Papal States before the year 1848, made clear what was the nature of the leadership of the revolutionary movement. It was led by prominent laymen of good birth,[1] especially at Bologna and Ravenna, and it suffered seriously from want of support in the countryside, especially in the lower valley of the Tiber, and from lack of roots in Rome, where even the turbulent populace of the Trastevere demonstrated in favour of the Pope. The heart of it was the separatism of the Romagna and the anti-clericalism of the aristocratic and professional laymen. The papal government could only have met it by granting a wide measure of local autonomy, at least to the legations, and by removing priests altogether from positions of political, administrative, or judicial responsibility. Whether, after doing all this, Rome could have retained the sovereignty, without admitting elected laymen from the legations into a share in control over the central government in the capital (as was forced upon her in 1848) must be doubted; yet that would have meant the end of the theocracy. So long as she granted anything less she would have to continue to hold on by force; consent, in the towns, amongst enlightened and privileged laymen, was altogether lacking.

The revolt was followed by a conference of the ambassadors of Austria, Russia, Prussia and France, at Rome, with English and Sardinian observers. It drew up a memorandum of advice to the

[1] The leading members of the provisional government formed at Bologna were a lawyer, Giovanni Vicini, who was President; Count Terenzio Mamiani, who was Minister of the Interior; Counts Alessandro Agucchi (who had been at Vienna at the time of the congress), Carlo Pepoli, and Cesare Bianchetti; two professors; and the distinguished Marquis Francesco Bevilacqua. They were a gentlemanly group and, although they declared the authority of the papal government to be at an end, they rested their case, legalistically, on the agreement of the year 1447 between Pope Nicholas V and the city of Bologna, and they intended to reach an understanding with Gregory XVI.

papal government on how to reform the administration, laying stress on the need to introduce laymen, recommending a return to the greater independence enjoyed by the municipalities before the time of Napoleon and Consalvi, and pressing for a central junta to control finance in a more responsible fashion. No doubt this memorandum, which was the work of the Prussian ambassador de Bunsen, contained some good advice; but it was not advice which was calculated to satisfy men who were bent upon independence, or upon political power for themselves at Rome. The memorandum was a conservative document, which still envisaged priests in the more important positions. At the same time Metternich disliked it because it recommended elective municipal and provincial councils and he did not want to see these spreading to Lombardy.

The memorandum provided no real answer to the problem of the Papal States because it failed to face squarely the two basic issues, namely the separatism of the Romagna and the hostility towards the political control of the priests. And it was naturally resented at Rome, as unsought outside advice is generally resented. In the end all that happened was that Bernetti undertook, on July 5, 1831, to provide the legates (whom he increased to six) with small nominated councils, possessed of some real control over finance, and to set up nominated provincial councils, though these would be consultative only. Yielding to increased French pressure the Austrians withdrew on July 15, but only after undertaking to return in the event of trouble.

It soon came. During the early winter the disorder grew progressively worse in the legations, and Bernetti secured the approval of the four main continental powers to his sending the pontifical army there, under the control of Albani, who was given extraordinary powers. He had 5,000 men, and was operating only against scattered groups of students and civic guards, yet – perhaps because he was so strongly Austrophile – he called the Austrians back again, and they returned promptly enough. This time, however, the French reacted vigorously, seizing Ancona, so that a dual occupation was set up. It was not until the end of November of the year 1838 that these two armies in the trans-Apennine provinces, the one there to keep order on the Pope's behalf, the other there to maintain the French side of the balance of power in Italy, were at last able to agree sufficiently together to yield to the Pope's entreaty that they should both go. In 1849 they would both be back again, the French on the Tyrrhenian coast and the Austrians on the Adriatic. Never after that would Rome, even in outward appearance, be independent, for the departure of the French, after a further twenty-one years, would be the signal for the entry of the Piedmontese.

The events of 1831–32 and the continued unrest afterwards made the Papal States into a European Question with the widest publicity. This was partly because of the dangerous rivalry which the situation recreated between Austria and France and partly because, as the one remaining theocracy in an age which was largely anti-clerical, these states held, for western Europe, a fearful sort of fascination which was not exercised by régimes equally repressive but less unusual. This special character, belonging to this problem alone in nineteenth-century history, should no doubt be remembered by the reader of the contemporary critics as also of the historians who followed them. It is a factor which by no means invalidates their criticisms; it merely reminds us that they will criticize with a special animus.

To Catholics as well as to Protestants there is something particularly offensive about political misrule when it is in the hands of priests, and for the most part the contemporary rebels against the papal government were Catholics who sincerely hoped to see their religion purified by separation from temporal preoccupations. Such were the authors of the Manifesto of Rimini, drawn up as a result of the movement in that city in 1845, written with an eye to securing a European audience, and no doubt for that reason tending to repeat the arguments used in the memorandum of 1831. Such was Massimo d'Azeglio, whose famous pamphlet, *Degli Ultimi Casi di Romagna*, of 1846, condemned the 'multiple autocracy' of legates and delegates, the chaos of the legal system, the want of an annual budget or of publication of the state accounts, the refusal to build railways, the high customs dues whose collection was farmed out, the insolence of the Swiss regiments and irresponsibility of the Centurions, the summary jurisdiction of the extraordinary commissions. And such were the descriptions of the prisons given by those who had had the misfortune to suffer in them.

What all these declared opponents of the system had to say about it constitutes important evidence, but it is not the only evidence, and it has been heavily drawn upon. In some ways more interesting, and certainly less used, is the evidence of those critics who were honestly trying to work within the system, who were wholly loyal to the papal government, and whose only desire was to see it rid of its defects. One such, at an earlier date, had been Cardinal Giuseppe Sala; another, in the 'thirties and 'forties, was Archbishop Mastai-Ferretti, whose detailed observations, month by month, and sometimes week by week, have only recently become available.[1]

Mastai's criticisms were stringent; yet they came from a man who had little use for the programmes of the revolutionaries. To him the Manifesto of Rimini was '. . . that classic production – no Jesuits, no priests, no bishops . . . no Swiss, no Latin language, no censorship of immoral literature . . . in substance what is wanted is a government without the grace of God . . .'[2]; nor did d'Azeglio's pamphlet seem to him much better: 'Amongst many outrageous lies and calumnies he says some true things. He is not impious, since he says nothing against Religion, and protests he is a Catholic. He is merely excited by the Italian fever, and if those who think like him follow his lead there will be a good and a bad outcome. The good will be that we shall not have insurrection and sedition, which he condemns; the bad will be that we shall have a flood of writings protesting, criticizing, and condemning the government.'[3]

The interest which attaches to Mastai's own criticisms of the papal government arises from his intimate involvement with it. In the uprising of 1831, when he was still Archbishop of Spoleto, he had been particularly closely involved for, the delegate having disappeared, he had been obliged to take the responsibility of advising the mayor and magistracy of his city as to how they should behave towards the revolutionary authorities. Receiving no instructions or

---

[1] In Serafini's book (see p. 267, note 1). (This material had not, of course, been made available when I was writing a few pages on the same subject in my *Pio Nono* (Eyre and Spottiswoode, 1954), pp. 32–33.)

[2] Serafini, p. 1411.   [3] *Ibid.*, p. 1418.

Gregory XVI. (*Radio Times Hulton Picture Library.*)

advice from Rome he had decided to recommend them, for the sake of law and order, to obey the new régime. And after the Austrian occupation, and the armistice, it had been to Mastai, at Spoleto, as to somebody he could trust, that Sercognani had surrendered his troops on March 30. On April 3, which was Easter Day, having read a homily in his cathedral on the resurrection, with suitable references to the events of the past few weeks, he had written for the fourth time to Bernetti: 'Having had no reply to my last three letters I am greatly disturbed. Being without instructions to show me how I should deal with these very difficult matters, with which I am burdened, I am in real doubt as to what I should do. So I beg you to relieve me of my uncertainty.'[1] Then, taking heart from a commendation of his conduct which at last arrived from Bernetti, he sent to Cardinal Pacca, who was protector of Spoleto, an eloquent appeal for a full amnesty for all those at Spoleto who, though weakness might have led them to collaborate with the revolution, yet had never lost their devotion to the Holy See.

But this letter was written on the same day (April 5) as Gregory XVI published his disavowal of the Benvenuti armistice, and for months afterwards the fate of Mastai's flock remained in doubt. When he went to Rome to plead for them, and especially for the mayor and magistracy, Bernetti told him that, although the latter were not on the list of those to be tried, yet, if they feared that they might be on the list, it would be well that they should not have their fears removed. All those compromised by the recent events were to be closely watched. The Archbishop was now unable to meet many of his friends at Spoleto, because they were regarded as compromised, and it would give scandal to the loyalists if he did so. The gulf was thus widened.

Mastai was told by Rome that all would be well because Austria was willing to increase the size of her army of occupation; but experience had taught him what this meant. The marching and counter-marching of bodies of troops merely stirred up hostility and created an insoluble problem for those expected to provide for them. Thus on April 3, 1831, he had reported: 'General Resta sent to say that he had today despatched in our direction a column of

---

[1] *Ibid.*, p. 490

three or four hundred (pontifical) soldiers . . . likewise it is well known that the Emperor of Austria's army is advancing in this direction. There would be little enough with which to provide for the necessities of our troops, but how shall we supply these others as well ?'[1] He was compelled to send an urgent note to the Austrian commander to explain that the district was perfectly quiet, and loyal to the Pope; but the Austrians continued their advance.

Undoubtedly the Archbishop would have been very glad to see implemented the general amnesty agreed by Benvenuti. The year 1831 left him with strong convictions about the virtues of amnesties (those freed by the famous amnesty of the first year of his own pontificate were many of them the rebels of 1831). They also left him with a resentment against Austrian intervention. But most gravely was he disillusioned that a bishop, whose duties should be spiritual, should be called upon to concern himself so deeply with matters temporal. Except during those few weeks at Spoleto, when he was acting as 'Delegate Extraordinary', he was not in fact called upon to undertake the political duties which fell to a legate or a delegate; but being sent in 1832 as Bishop to Imola, in the Legation of Ravenna, he found himself in one of the more disturbed regions and was never able to free himself from political preoccupations.

These now centred around the newly established 'Pontifical Volunteers', a body which owed its establishment to a decree of June 1, 1833, issued by Cardinal Spinola, acting in his capacity as Extraordinary Legate for the four legations, and with the approval of Bernetti. They were formed with a view to meeting the constant complaints about the Centurions, of whom Mastai had said in March of the same year: 'Whether, indeed, the impact of the Centurions is likely to contribute to the reestablishment of order or to the fomenting of civil war I say frankly, and without affectation, I am unable to decide. What distresses me is that amongst the Centurions there are many of the common people who for various crimes have suffered the ordinary penalties of the law.'[2] The magistrates at Imola had been protesting to Spinola that the Centurions, 'secretly armed, and with no outward sign or device to distinguish them, dare to behave as though they are a legitimate force and were tolerated as such by the

[1] *Ibid.*, p. 491.   [2] *Ibid.*, p. 1233.

pontifical troops'. When the magistrates asked the Governor for a list of the names of the Centurions he declared he had not got one. Such a situation evidently needed regularizing, and Spinola's decree tried to achieve this by putting the Centurions into uniform, providing barracks for them, calling them Pontifical Volunteers, and insisting that they must not be drawn from those with a criminal record. But such reforms, welcomed by Mastai as tending to make the men better disciplined and more responsible, took time; and meanwhile, since the volunteers were usually the same men as had previously been known as Centurions, they were widely called the 'Patented Provincial Centurions' in spite, or perhaps because, of official edicts that they were to be given their proper name.

Mastai continues to give a picture of them as bands of men, about a hundred in each, with two bands to each small city of the size of Imola or Ravenna, unpaid but highly privileged, and still without uniforms or barracks. He seems to have been scarcely on speaking terms with those at Imola, resented their claim that they were the true pillars of the Church, and protested against the spasmodic violence in which they indulged. Soon Bernetti, who had enlarged the scope and privileges of the organization in July 1834, was taking Mastai to task for his attitude, and Mastai was replying (July 28) '. . . On account of some disorders which have occurred I have always believed it a duty to persuade the Volunteers to use control, not to abuse the use of force, and always to give the best possible example. . . .'[1] And on September 5, he told his friend Falconieri, Archbishop of Ravenna, '. . . Bernetti has said that, on the matter of the Volunteers, it is necessary that I should think again, and I have replied that I believe them to be very useful when they are disciplined.'[2]

For the rest, the matters which most worried the Bishop of Imola were the ferocious attitude of some of the police ('. . . the Commissioner of police, one of those Papalini who are fanatics to the point of folly, and would like to see fifteen people hanged every hour . . .'); the number of those under sentence, which he gives in 1845 as 20,000; the immense delays in the procedure of the courts;

[1] Ibid., p. 1247.　　　　　　　[2] Ibid., p. 1251.

and the great numbers of the unemployed and the robbers.
('. . . Robbers, and more robbers . . . how shall we find a quick
remedy since the great mass of the people is corrupt, at least in part,
and wants to live in an ease which nourishes a thousand vices? . . .
for lack of other occupation they infest the country roads, when
they are not recruited by politicians hostile to the government'.[1])
And he finds the educated classes equally disaffected: '. . . it is something very rare to find a young man . . . qualified in the practice of
medicine, or the law, or such matters, in whom the government
can place confidence; few, very few are there such. . . .'[2] His
sovereign remedies are first a return to religion; second a severe
warning (but not imprisonment) of those known to be plotting
conspiracies, so that they are made aware in advance that the
government knows of their activities and can frustrate them; and
third – youth organizations. 'In the cities, and also in the countryside, the young people . . . pass long and tedious hours on café
benches, poisoning the air with smoke and talk, unwilling to take
a part in social life, and unable to do so because uneducated.'[3] They
realize they are wretched, and could be reclaimed by the right use
of agricultural, literary, dramatic, or musical academies. As for the
remedies put forward by the liberals, the government is theocratic
and must remain so; but greater use should be made of laymen, and
their rewards and position should approximate more closely to
those of the clergy.

So much for the criticisms of a bishop who commanded enough
confidence amongst the cardinals to be elected Pope. The extent of
the problem was appreciated at Rome both by Bernetti and by the
cardinal who, in January 1836, succeeded him as Secretary of State,
Luigi Lambruschini. Yet neither Cardinal Secretary of State showed
any capacity for constructive reform.[4] They allowed the short-

---

[1] *Ibid.*, p. 1,367.   [2] *Ibid.*, p. 1,266.   [3] *Ibid.*, p. 1,401.

[4] In an effort to alleviate the burden of temporal affairs which was falling on the
Pope and the Secretary of State Bernetti, in February 1833, created the new office of
Secretary of State for the Interior. This post, which was subordinated to that of
Secretary for the Exterior, was held first by Cardinal Gamberini. Unlike the other
papal documents, the records of this department were taken over by the Kingdom
of Italy after 1870, and are now in the Rome State Archives. They reveal a meticu-

term objective of trying to prevent, year by year, another major disturbance, to obscure the wider consideration of more fundamental and humane changes of the kind that Mastai, and Sala before him, believed to be necessary. The action they took was that of desperate men, staving off disaster from day to day – first there were four legations, then six, then one; legates were appointed, shifted, replaced every year or two; extraordinary commissions were set up after every disturbance.

On the other hand, Bernetti and Lambruschini kept order of a kind. When Mastai became Pope, and began to introduce wider changes, they quickly led to disaster. Evidently the problem ran deeper than any of these cardinals realized. It had become, indeed, insoluble within the framework of the theocratic state.

---

lous administration handling, in Rome, personal applications for permits of all kinds, from the legations as well as from other parts of the provinces, and leaving the reader wondering how the supposedly semi-autonomous legates employed their time when they were not sitting on extraordinary commissions.

Claims for reimbursement of special expenses incurred on account of disturbances figure prominently. Special budgets were allowed to legates and delegates for police expenditure; they were heaviest in the legations, but also relatively large at Macerata and Ancona. (Rome State Archives, *Arch. del Ministero dell' Interno, Sicurezza Interna, Spese di Polizia*, Fasc. CLXIV, Busta 1145.)

The expenses of the extraordinary commissions became a heavy charge on the legates' limited funds. Cardinal Gizzi, Legate of Forlì, was complaining in June 1844 that the commission at Rimini had landed him with a serious deficit and application would have to be made at once to the Treasurer-General for a supplementary grant. (*Ibid.*, Busta 1146.) In 1845 he refused to admit an extraordinary commission at Forlì.

CHAPTER EIGHTEEN

The Condemnation of Liberalism

That the Popes, after 1815, should have proved themselves
unable to exercise temporal rule successfully over the restored Papal States is not really surprising since analogous
problems proved beyond the powers of many contemporary rulers,
large as well as small. But like all political failures it had its tragic
consequences for the governed and, in the special case of the Popes,
the repression was not confined to the ruler's political subjects. For
the position of the Pope as Head of the Universal Church meant
that the political influence of the papacy extended much more
widely than did that of most rulers; and because of the opposition
in the Papal States this influence was used everywhere against movements which appeared to the Popes to be analogous to those from
which they suffered at home.

Ever since it had debouched into Italy from France the Revolution had spelt nothing but disaster for the Popes. And since that
disaster had been spiritual as well as secular – a tossing aside of canon
law as well as of clerical privilege – it was not difficult for many at
Rome – though not quite all – to convince themselves, with de
Maistre, that the ideas of 1789 were intrinsically diabolical. The
tragedy consisted in the failure of the restoration papacy to compre-
hend the need of movement in social and political organization; in
its 'canonization' of the notion of legitimacy, which led it to give
its support to legitimate monarchs even when they oppressed the
Church. The Catholic Poles were told that they must remain
quietly obedient to their autocratic and foreign sovereign, the
Tsar, although he was denying the necessary liberties of their faith.
The Catholic Belgians were told to obey the Calvinist King of
Holland, although he was doing the same. The Catholic Irish were
told that they must not mind having their episcopal nominations
vetoed by a Protestant King in London. The French liberal Catholics

278

were silenced, and told to obey their Most Christian King, who in fact was an agnostic. Everywhere the first principle was legitimacy, and this generally meant absolutism because the monarchs of the time, for the most part, were absolute.

Yet in fact this policy of the restored papacy was not altogether in accord with papal tradition. Some of the Jesuits of the sixteenth and seventeenth centuries, such as Suarez, had recognized a right as pertaining, in the last resort, to any people to withhold obedience from a legitimate sovereign if he denied them the practice of their religion. And even in the days of their weakness, in the eighteenth century, the Popes had been prepared, on occasions, as we saw, to withstand the Bourbons and the Hapsburgs to their face when their enlightenment endangered the foundations of the Church. Little of this spirit of resistance to the Powers was apparent in the post-1815 period except – paradoxically enough – when Metternich tried to lure the Papal States into a collective security system. Then Consalvi bristled with indignation.

Of course revolution – except in the special circumstances which interested the seventeenth-century Jesuits – had always been regarded by the Church as a very evil thing. Even in the pre-Constantinian Roman Empire Christians had been reminded of Saint Paul's counsel that they 'obey the powers that be'. But Revolution is always an indefinite term, and it was a particularly ill-defined bogey after 1815 because the violence and drama attaching to the French Revolution and Napoleon had tended so to preoccupy men's attention as to make them think of all political movements as being 'for' or 'against' the Revolution. Intermediate terms between Revolution and Legitimacy hardly existed in the minds of governments in Germany or Italy; there were only two political ideologies. By the eighteen-thirties those who favoured the Revolution had come to be called liberals, but that did not make them seem any more desirable. It was a label which would later become respectable, but it certainly did not seem so to Gregory XVI or to his monarchical contemporaries outside Paris and London.

Yet in fact, by the eighteen-thirties, liberal theory existed over an enormously wide field of ideas, some of them more revolutionary, some of them less, but not necessarily all of them deserving to be branded as evil because they had been practised in the great French Revolution, or in the Roman Republic of '98, or in the Cisalpine, or because those régimes had been largely hostile to the claims of the Church. The cardinals sometimes realized this; but when they looked into the philosophy of the matter they always found the disquieting fact that sovereignty was held by the liberals to belong, in one way or another, with the people. And that struck them as absurd because they were quite sure it belonged with God, and that under Him it rested with the Church, in matters spiritual, and with the legitimate rulers in matters temporal. The latter might make concessions, even very considerable concessions – representative assemblies and the like – such as existed in England and France; but they were concessions. They could not exist of right, because the people had no sovereign rights against their rulers, unless their rulers denied them their religion, and even then it was wrong to insist on those rights if doing so meant unseating a legitimate ruler; and they thought it more absolutely wrong to do that than Suarez had supposed.

Restoration Rome had two inducements to reject the theory of the Sovereign People. One was her experience of that People in action, which was calculated to encourage her theologians to return to their Bossuet because they had found that the People not only lusted after the Church's property but tended to try to control religion even more closely than had the enlightened despots. The other was that the theory of popular sovereignty was inapplicable to the Papal States. No Pope – not even Pius IX in 1848 – ever seriously supposed that he could be permanently subjected to the control of an elective lay assembly. In theory it was perhaps not wholly inconceivable that the temporal and spiritual should become so separated that the Pope could be a constitutional monarch in one capacity while remaining an absolute sovereign in the other (as Lord Minto and Lord Palmerston later advised Pius IX to become), but it is very certain that such a possibility was never envisaged by anybody of any consequence at Rome and that in fact the spiritual and temporal aspects of the Roman government never sufficiently unravelled themselves to permit of it. And, since nobody orthodox had doubted, from the days of the Council of Trent, that the spiritual government of the Church was autocratic, both by necessity and by apostolic tradition, it followed that the government of the Papal States could not be democratic. Gregory XVI had not only the inducement of bitter experience, in his own states, at the time of his accession, to lead him to condemn the liberals; he had also the inducement that the liberal theory, by presupposing some form of popular sovereignty, appeared to him to be a false theory of government, and as such he was prepared to condemn it elsewhere – for instance in France, in the form in which Lamennais taught it.

Yet was it false, from a Catholic standpoint?

There was no necessary reason, resting on dogma or tradition, for regarding the alliance between throne and altar as sacrosanct, or for seeing thrones as a necessary part of the furniture of government. Suarez had never been condemned for saying that God gave political sovereignty to the people. Cardinal Chiaramonti had found difficulties, but not insuperable ones, in working in a revolutionary republic. England might, in Consalvi's words, be *ce pays tout-à-fait exceptionnel*, from which it was dangerous to draw political analogies, but he admired her, and he foresaw a future for the Church within her borders. America, it is true, was still regarded as a semi-barbaric outpost, but it could not altogether escape attention at Rome that the Church was maintaining her life there, as she was in the new South American republics. Evidently Gregory's condemnation of liberal principles was not intended to imply that they were unacceptable where they were established; only that they were not to be invoked elsewhere – especially by priests.

Gregory allowed his horror of what the liberals had sometimes done, and his correct appreciation of the insuperable difficulty about democracy in his own state to blind him to the facts that some of the liberties which Lamennais was advocating for France were valuable, and might help the Church to breathe there more freely; that the Church in Poland (as well as the Poles) would be likely to benefit by a successful Polish revolt against the Tsar; and that a successful Belgian revolt against Holland would probably do the same for the Belgians. Gregory, Bernetti, and Lambruschini, like Consalvi before them, believed that, even if it were true that

immediate spiritual advantages might be gained by revolt, or by
the introduction of liberal measures, the shock to the monarchical
system involved by such changes would be disastrous to the Church
and Society. Yet in Gregory's time the monarchical system meant
an anti-Catholic Tsar, an anti-Catholic King of Prussia, an anti-
Catholic King of England, a free-thinking King of France, and a
Josephist Emperor of Austria. Just why these bulwarks should have
been held to be indispensable to the support of the Catholic Church
is difficult to understand. No doubt Rome was prompted by fear
of chaos and by fear of the over-weening pretensions of popular
sovereignty as well as by fear for her own temporal position. But
her policy was one of despair.

It is true that the papal government showed a certain realism in
discarding the principle of legitimacy in the face of *faits accomplis*. If
she was in no hurry about recognizing the revolutions of the
eighteen-twenties in Latin America (there seemed, for some time,
a possibility that the Spanish and Portuguese monarchies might
recover their legitimate rights there) she was notably prompt in
recognizing the new régime at Paris set up by the revolution of
July 1830. The attitude of Pius VIII was governed on this occasion
by the speed and success with which the revolution was accomplished and with which the new government suppressed the more
radical movements. There was evidently not going to be chaos.
The Nuncio at Paris, Cardinal Lambruschini (the future Secretary
of State), was full of foreboding and opposed to any policy of
ralliement to the new régime. But since he had maintained to the last
moment that Charles X, the last Bourbon King, would ride the
storm, his prognostications did not carry weight. Pius VIII was prepared to listen to other advice – including that of Lamennais. This
wise, balanced, but short-lived Pope, who had been the friend and
pupil of Consalvi, refused to tie the fortunes of the Church in
France to the Bourbon cause. Just as his master had separated her
from Louis XVIII and tied her to Napoleon, so he would separate
her once more from the Bourbons and tie her to a new revolutionary government. He gave no countenance to the Gallican agitation,
sent back the émigré priests who were beginning to pour into

Italy, and told the French clergy it was their duty to support the established rather than the legitimate ruler.

What had peculiarly excited the French clergy, from Archbishop de Quélen of Paris downwards, after the French revolution of 1830, was the new government's decision to proclaim the religious 'indifference' of the State. Yet in practice this indifference meant little more than religious toleration. Church and State remained still closely associated in France. The King still nominated the bishops, and the stipends of the clergy were still paid by the government – two strong links with the State which Lamennais, who wanted to see a real separation, was urging should be severed. The Concordat of 1801 remained the basis for the relations between Church and State; and Louis Philippe, though he might be a free-thinker, thought much less and no more freely than had Napoleon. He was nominally a Catholic and – for diplomatic reasons – he was pleased to be addressed by the Pope as 'Your Most Christian Majesty', which had been the title accorded to the Bourbons. In short his position in regard to the Church was essentially the same as Napoleon's had been, and the realism shown by Pius VIII in promptly recognizing this French revolution of 1830 belonged in the sensible school of Consalvi and in the tradition of the Concordat – neither of which recommended it to the majority of the cardinals or to the French legitimist clergy.

Unfortunately Pius VIII, a sick man when he was elected, died on November 30, 1830, having reigned for only twenty months. Had he lived it is possible that Roman policy in regard to the movements for liberation in Belgium and Poland might have been less hostile.

Slow and measured in his approach to political problems, Pius VIII had not taken up a personal position in regard to the confused events in Belgium before he died. He had left it to his Secretary of State, Albani, to guide the attitude of the Papal Internuncio at Brussels, and this guidance had been given in the best legitimate tradition as that was understood by a very Austrophile cardinal.

There were special reasons for Rome to resent the Belgian revolution, although it was the revolution of a Catholic people against Protestant Dutch rule. As recently as June 1827 after long and hard negotiations, the Prefect of Propaganda (Cardinal Cappellari, shortly to become Pope Gregory XVI) had negotiated a Concordat with the Netherlands modelled on the Napoleonic one, though providing for the election of bishops by chapters and leaving to the Protestant King William a right of exclusion in advance against those whose election would be unwelcome to him. It also gave him a veto over episcopal appointments of the lower clergy. It was as good a settlement, from the Church's point of view, as Rome was obtaining elsewhere with Protestant rulers who were possessed of extensive enclaves of Catholic subjects; but it hardly allowed for the spirit of independence of the Belgian clergy, and in particular it failed to settle the vexed educational question. Influenced from France by Lamennais' movement, the Belgian clergy were demanding freedom in the field of education and the press; and in the matter of their own training they were unwilling to accept the efforts of King William's government to secure control over admissions to the seminaries, to make the course prescribed at his College of Philosophy obligatory, and to suppress the Catholic college of Louvain. These were the points on which the quarrel was in progress at the beginning of the year 1830 between the Belgian bishops and the Crown; and the Secretary of State, Cardinal Albani, in the interests of the Concordat and the principle of legitimacy, was urging moderation upon the Belgian hierarchy and describing their alliance with the liberals as 'monstrous'.

So when the revolution spread from Paris to Brussels in August 1830, Albani and Cappellari had little hesitation in taking the line that the clergy should show their loyalty to the King; nor would they give any support to the aspirations of the clergy when the movement became one for the independence of Belgium from Holland or when the Internuncio, Mgr Capaccini, began to speak of 'Calvinist fanaticism' let loose on a Catholic people, and of religious civil war.[1] Albani passed on the Internuncio's letters to Cappellari with the observation that they must be regarded as of little value,[2] and when Capaccini, trying loyally to obey Rome,

[1] Vat. Arch. *Paesi Bassi*, Internunzio, Busta 506, Fasc. IX.

[2] *Ibid.* On September 30, 1830, Cappellari strongly recommended to Albani that it was not the moment to take any action, and that the Internunzio's arguments be ignored.

had been compelled by the anger of both parties to fly to London, Albani wrote to him there to say that he hoped that a congress would soon settle the disturbance, in the Netherlands as elsewhere, and would 'establish in the surest way possible that the forces of the great states are applied to going to the defence of small states where-ever these are not strong enough to maintain the established order and public tranquillity in their own territories, and especially that it be open to any power to intervene by arms in the affairs of other states wherever the local government asks for it. To contest this right is to impugn the liberty belonging to every prince to ally him-self with others for his own defence.'[1] Thus spoke the cardinal who, in 1832, would call the Austrians back into the legations after they had withdrawn. In his view, if the Papal Internuncio had any role to perform in the Netherlands it was to intercede between the King and the Belgian Catholic leaders. It is right to remember that this was a 'correct' view, diplomatically speaking. Any open encourage-ment of the Catholic rebels by the Pope's representative must have been regarded by King William as an unfriendly act towards a friendly government, with which Rome had recently entered into an agreement, and so have lamentable consequences, even should Belgium achieve her independence, upon the Catholic minority remaining in Holland.

Similar considerations weighed with Rome in leading her to condemn the Polish uprising of 1830–32 against the Tsar. He was a sovereign whom Rome rightly regarded as a principal pillar of legitimacy; it would therefore be folly to affront him. It is true that relations between the two courts were not as cordial as they had been. Alexander had expelled the Jesuits in 1820; but since they had owed their survival to Russian protection against Bourbon and Roman persecution Pius VII had hardly been strongly placed in trying to defend them. Again, in 1821, Alexander had been affronted by Consalvi's insistence that it would be improper for Rome to help Vienna with her intervention in Naples. The logic of the Pope's position was not too clear to the Tsars; but in 1831 Alexander's successor Nicholas felt that if Rome thought it im-

[1] *Ibid.*, November 13.

proper for her to take her share, in the temporal order, in the maintenance of legitimate monarchy, she should surely at least help the
cause in which they were all agreed by restraining the clergy in any
region where they might be so misguided as to try to undermine it.
It is not difficult to understand the position of Nicholas, and of his
agent Prince Gagarin at Rome when they tried to persuade Gregory
XVI to tell the Polish clergy that it was their duty to preach
obedience to established authority and not to support the Polish
revolt which, in January 1831, had succeeded in capturing Warsaw
and turning itself into a war of liberation. And they had the
experience of the Roman attitude to Belgium to encourage them;
and still more the crisis in the Papal States.

On the other hand the Tsar Nicholas had proved to be very much
more inimical to the Catholic Church in his dominions than King
William had been in the Netherlands. Since his accession in 1825 he
had practically eliminated the Uniate Church (obedient to Rome),
absorbing it into orthodoxy, and had taken a series of steps designed
to bring the Latin Church in Poland as well as in Russia under his
own control. He had even removed the Primate of Poland and replaced him by an aged man on whom he could rely – all this without bothering to consult the Pope. Unlike his predecessor he was
making it his policy to strengthen his political authority by gaining
religious uniformity; and although there was little likelihood of his
undermining the religious allegiance of the intensely Catholic Poles
he could and did pursue a secularist policy in Poland, lifting
marriage and education out of clerical control, closing convents,
regulating seminaries, and forbidding the Catholic clergy to
receive converts.

So it was not self-evident that Gregory would comply with
Prince Gagarin's request that he should exhort the Polish clergy to
preach filial obedience to the Tsar's government. It might equally
be hoped that he would bargain with Nicholas for greater freedom
for the Polish Church, as Pius VI, for instance, had bargained with
Joseph II for greater freedom for the Belgian Church at the time of
the disturbances in 1790. But Gregory, the autumn before his election, when he was still Prefect of Propaganda, had discouraged the
Belgian clergy from entertaining any hopes of that kind; and now

Gagarin was pressing him at the moment when his own temporal subjects were in revolt against him. So in February 1831, the first month of his pontificate, he despatched a brief, *Impensa Caritas*, telling the clergy of Poland that the Church held in horror all violence and sedition. 'Everything which disturbs the tranquillity of a state she firmly forbids to the ministers of God, who is the author of peace and who came to bring peace to the earth. Bishops should therefore, with Saint Paul, preach obedience and sub-mission, and above all be on their guard against conduct which would be unseemly in the holy ministry and make it odious.'[1]

This douche of cold water seems to have missed its mark, for the Polish bishops appear never to have received it. It was a common experience for papal briefs sent to the Tsar's dominions to be con-fiscated, though it is surprising that it should have happened on this occasion. Possibly Prince Gagarin and the Tsar were hoping for something better; at all events in the end they got it. For in spite of an appeal by the Poles to Rome, in the form of a special mission under Count Sebastien Badéni from the provisional government, which described the grievances of the Polish Church and Nation and begged Gregory's assistance with the Christian powers, the Pope declined to lend his services;[2] instead, at the moment of their defeat, and when they were suffering the harshest reprisals and re-pression, the Polish bishops received the brief *Superiori Anno* (June 9, 1832).[3] In this they were told that submission to the Powers ordained by God was a principle which could never be varied or broken, save where such a power violated the laws of the Church; 'manufacturers of deceit and lies' who, under cover of religion, had opposed the legitimate power of princes were severely castigated; and a stern warning was given that it was the bishops' duty to direct all their vigilance and all their energy against 'the impostors and

---

[1] Leflon, p. 456.

[2] Gregory did, however, suggest to Metternich that he should approach the Tsar, see A. Boudou *Le Saint-Siège et La Russie*, Paris, 1922, Vol. 1, pp. 175–77.

[3] *Acta Gregorii Papae XVI*, Vol. 1, p. 143. Lamennais believed (*Oeuvres*, Pagnerre, 1844, Vol. 8, p. 109) that this brief was submitted to Gagarin for his approval, and that it was the price paid by the Pope for the promise of Russian military support in the Papal States. But his fears seem to have been unfounded (cf. Boudou, *op. cit.*, pp. 185–87, and A. R. Vidler, *Prophecy and Papacy*, S.C.M. Press, 1954, pp. 210, 211).

propagators of new ideas' with a view to safeguarding their flocks 'from the error of their doctrines and the falsity of their dogmas'. Their 'powerful Emperor' will show clemency towards them, and and the Pope will intercede 'for the good of religion.'

This was the brief which the Tsar brandished over the heads of a defeated people. The letters which Gregory sent to the Tsar personally, appealing for better treatment for the Polish Church, remained unpublished and unanswered; but even had they been generally known in Poland they would not have gone far to sweeten the bitterness of the Polish suffering, for they were confined to the Roman rights which Nicholas was violating and to the rights of the Church in Poland; they did not touch upon the political liberties of the Poles nor upon the independence of Poland.

These much wider liberties had become the concern not only of European liberals generally but also of the French liberal Catholics Lamennais, Lacordaire, and Montalembert, who were now crusading for an alliance between the Church and 'democratic freedom', a concept which they set over against the existing alliance between the Church and legitimacy. Lamennais had become widely known for his teaching about a free society, which should embrace freedom of speech, of the Press, and of religion, safeguarded by the separation of Church and State and an assembly elected by universal suffrage. He had attracted much attention in France, and also in Belgium; indeed his influence in the latter country had been one of the reasons why Cappellari had been so suspicious of the part played by the priests in the Belgian revolution. By the time the Polish revolution broke out he had begun his campaign in his paper the *Avenir* (October 1830 to November 1831) and he and his friends threw themselves into the Polish cause.

The *Avenir* rapidly became the recognized voice of religious revolutionary liberalism, seeking to explain to its readers the significance of what was happening in Poland and Belgium; it also took up the cause of Ireland, Montalembert, who had been there when he first received the paper's prospectus, contributing a vivid article on that country.[1] Catholic Emancipation in Ireland and England

[1] *Articles de l'Avenir* (Louvain, 1831), Vol. 1, p. 72.

(1829) the friends regarded as a conspicuous victory for their cause because it had been achieved in such a way as to separate Church and State, emancipating the Catholics from all political control. They knew that the matter might well have turned out differently, for the plan of 1814 had been for a Catholic Church in Great Britain linked with the State in the same way as she was linked in the Netherlands and in Prussia, and with a Protestant ruler exercising a veto over episcopal appointments and over communications from Rome. The Roman Propaganda had ruled in February 1814 that Catholics might accept such an arrangement with a clear conscience, and Consalvi's diplomacy, which set great store by improving relations between the Holy See and the Court of Saint James, had envisaged a settlement along those lines.[1] It was the uncompromising rejection by the Irish clergy of such a plan which defeated it, and secured for Catholics in Britain a complete separation from the State; and although this carried with it serious financial disadvantages Montalembert was profoundly impressed by the spiritual gain to Irish Catholicism.[1]

In the Roman view any alliance between the clergy and the liberals was 'monstrous', just as the alliance between the clergy and 'our dear sons in Christ', the legitimate rulers, was 'natural'. It is important to notice that neither kind of alliance was seen as merely tactical. To Rome the one was intrinsically wrong, the other was intrinsically right. To Lamennais and the liberals this position was reversed. To Rome the rulers stood for the essentially Catholic virtues of loyalty and obedience; to Lamennais the liberals stood for the necessary Catholic principle of freedom. Most of the liberal revolutionaries, it was true, had little interest in the Church other than to undermine her authority; while most of the more powerful

---

[1] See Bernard Ward's *The Eve of Catholic Emancipation* (Longmans, 1911), Vol. 2, pp. 79–91, and Appendix F, also John Tracy Ellis *Cardinal Consalvi and Anglo-Papal Relations* (Catholic University of America Press, 1942), p. 78. On February 15, 1814, Quarantotti, Vice-Prefect of Propaganda, sent two rescripts to Bishop Poynter, the Vicar Apostolic of the London district. One of them gave Roman approval to Catholic acceptance of the proposed measure of royal control over an emancipated Church. The other appealed to Poynter to use his influence with the Crown to secure British support for the return of the lost papal territories, in view of the friendly relations between the two rulers during the war.

T

sovereigns were not Catholics at all. Yet the principles stood, on both sides. Lamennais believed that only in an atmosphere of freedom, where all beliefs were equally tolerated, where there was freedom of the Press, where any group might educate children in its own principles, would the Church regain her soul. Gregory regarded it as impious to say that she had lost her soul, and the most evident dereliction of duty to leave her enemies free to attack her.

Lamennais' story is well known[1] and there is no need to enlarge upon it here. That he received no encouragement from Gregory XVI when he visited Rome with Montalembert and Lacordaire at the end of 1831 should not surprise anybody since he was the chief advocate of politico-religious principles precisely the opposite to those prevailing there. That his theories were subsequently condemned, in *Mirari vos* (August 1832) and in *Singulari nos* (June 1834) was also to be expected. A fatality hangs over the Lamennais drama which is one of its charms, dramatically speaking, and one of the reasons why it has attracted so much attention.

Yet Lamennais, till he drove her into pronouncing on him, was in better odour at Rome than he was with the French hierarchy. The cardinals might shake their heads over his liberalism, but they loved his ultramontane devotion; most of the French bishops, on the other hand, Gallican and royalist, found nothing to like about him at all. Pius VIII had resisted pressure from the French bishops that he should condemn Lamennais, and Gregory XVI similarly avoided passing judgement on the *Avenir* till its editor compelled him to do so. Possibly their indulgent attitude towards the man who was preaching political principles which Rome held in such abhorrence was influenced by another factor; for Lamennais, paradoxically, did not include the Papal States in his teaching about political liberty. This is one of the strangest things about the 'pilgrims of God and of liberty' as Lamennais and his friends called themselves: none of the liberties they were demanding as the very basis of truth and justice did they hold to be needed in the Papal States. 'The more the truly Catholic cause of the Belgians and the Poles calls forth our

[1] See especially the analysis of it in A. R. Vidler's *Prophecy and Papacy, cit.*

sympathy the more we are filled with horror by these revolutionaries of the Papal States who, plunging their country into the abyss
of disorder and misery, have no excuse for their action to put before
the world'.[1] Though Lamennais would later change his views
Montalembert would never change his; even under the Second
Empire, when he was courageously defying Napoleon III, in the
name of the democratic liberties, he still thought that the opposition
to the Pope's temporal power was merely perverse. These ultramontane liberal Catholics believed that the truth was given by God
to the people and expressed on their behalf by the Pope; the latter
could not tyrannize, because he and the people were one in the
truth; tyranny came from rulers (especially heretical and *incroyant*
rulers) and from aristocrats and other oppressors whose interests
and aims were selfish.

Lamennais' curious Christianizing of Rousseau's General Will,
while it led him to an unexpected verdict on the Papal States, and
one pleasing to the Curia, nevertheless came to cause the deepest
suspicion at Rome. Not on those terms would she be defended; her
authority came immediately from God and not mediately through
the People. Besides, the temporal order was one, and God had given
it to the legitimate princes. It was intolerable that the rulers of
Europe, even if they were not Catholic, should be threatened with
the upheaval which the *Avenir's* teaching implied; their ambassadors were making that point quite clear at the Vatican. So *Mirari
vos*[2] was despatched to Lamennais, on behalf of the Pope, by
Cardinal Pacca, now Dean of the Sacred College, together with a
covering letter of his own, in which he explains that what specially
distressed the Holy Father in the teachings of the *Avenir* were its
exaggerations about liberty of worship and liberty of the Press; it
might be necessary to tolerate these things, in certain circumstances,
but they could never be regarded as good in themselves. The Holy
Father, he adds, specifically reproves the doctrines about civil and
political liberty as tending to stir up sedition and revolt, and 'what he
has felt most bitterly is the act of union proposed to all who, "despite
the murder of Poland, the dismemberment of Belgium, and the con-

---

[1] *Articles de l'Avenir*, Vol. 3, p. 253.
[2] *Acta Gregorii*, Vol. 1, p. 169.

duct of governments that call themselves liberal, hope still in the liberty of the world and want to work for it" '.[1]

Having promised, in the *Avenir*, that he would obey the Holy See, whatever its verdict on that paper, Lamennais felt obliged to obey it when its verdict had been given, and to stop publication. But he did not accept, or pretend to accept, Gregory's ruling against the various democratic liberties, and when he found that his opponents supposed that he did accept it he wrote to the Pope on November 5, 1833, to say that, while he submitted to Rome in all matters of Church doctrine and discipline, he felt 'entirely free as regards his opinions, his words, and his actions in the purely temporal order'.[2] But this was not good enough for Gregory, who replied,[3] through Pacca, that he expected a 'simple, absolute, and unlimited' submission to *Mirari vos*. In other words he wanted unlimited acceptance of the doctrine of legitimist absolutism, or unlimited rejection of the democratic principles put forward by the *Avenir*. Nor did he expect this merely because Lamennais was a priest, and therefore bound by a special sort of obedience, for he had already censured Montalembert, the month before, for similar political views, and especially for translating into French Mickiewicz's passionate *Book of the Polish Pilgrim*, which was an apocalyptic exhortation to encourage the Polish exiles, and a litany to God to save Poland from her oppressors. This was the book which inspired Lamennais' *Paroles d'un Croyant*, in the following year which, in its turn, inspired Gregory's new denunciation in *Singulari nos* (June 1834).[4] Maintaining his distinction between spiritual obedience and temporal freedom Lamennais ignored the new encyclical while continuing to say Mass and to regard himself as an obedient priest. Before very long, however, he lost what could be recognized as Catholic faith. He was never excommunicated.

The aspect of the *affaire Lamennais* which is significant to us here

[1] Pacca's letter in Lamennais, *Oeuvres* (Pagnerre, 1844), Vol. 8, pp. 131–36.
[2] *Ibid.* p. 147.
[3] *Ibid.* p. 156.
[4] *Acta Gregorii*, Vol. I, p. 433. Lamennais' precepts were 'false, calumnious, rash, tending towards anarchy, contrary to the word of God, impious, scandalous, and erroneous'.

is the strictly political aspect. And that aspect of it provides the proper place at which to conclude this survey of the political affairs of the Papacy before the election of Pio Nono because it reveals the arguments used by Rome to justify the papal alliance with absolutism.

That the Pope should condemn anybody who seemed to be encouraging revolution was not only in accordance with Catholic tradition and teaching but may be felt to have been appropriate at a time when most of Europe was still licking the wounds inflicted by an era of revolution. In so far as Lamennais was inciting revolution (and it is arguable that the *Paroles d'un Croyant* did just that) Gregory's strictures are understandable. Yet even on the issue of revolution it could be said on the other side that the current revolutions (the Polish and Belgian) were directed against real tyrannies, and also tyrannies which were denying the liberties of the Church as well as other liberties. It was even arguable that those tyrannies amounted to a violation of the laws of the Church; and if that were so revolution would, on Catholic principles, be justified. Gregory, of course, knew this, and had said as much in his brief to the bishops of Poland of 1832; but he did not regard the Tsar as violating the laws of the Church in that sense.

More dismaying to liberal opinion than his attitude towards revolution was Gregory's denunciation of what were coming to be regarded as the 'democratic liberties'. In *Mirari vos* he denounced in scathing terms the liberties demanded by Lamennais, and especially that 'delirium' 'freedom of conscience' (freedom to choose between religious attitudes) to which the way was opened by 'immoderate liberty of opinion'. The 'stinking source' from which this error flowed was 'indifferentism'. No doubt it was in Lamennais' erection of these principles into absolutes that the root of his offence lay; but it is precisely as absolutes that they have since come to be widely accepted; nor was the Church herself later to rest content everywhere with the view that these liberties were only to be tolerated in certain unfortunate circumstances.

The revolutionary movement in Gregory's day was not the Jacobin anti-religious thing that it had been in the France of 1793 or the Italy of 1798. It was even, often, in alliance with religion. And on the political plane it had, at least as its ideal, principles not deserving of eternal reprobation. In these circumstances Gregory's identification of the interests of the Church and the good of society with absolute monarchy, and his explicit denunciation of Lamennais' liberties meant that the authority of the Supreme Pontiff was being given to political concepts which were dubious and dangerous. Even that staunch *zelante* Cardinal Pacca warned Gregory of the danger of pronouncing himself on political matters.[1]

Why did he do it?

No doubt, immediately speaking, on account of pressure from Metternich, pressure from the French hierarchy – other pressures. But why did he do it with conviction? No doubt it was chiefly because of the revolution in his own states and his knowledge that the Lamennais principles could not be applied there. They were incompatible with the theocracy, so that he had a strong inducement to regard them as false, just as Pius IX later had an even stronger inducement after he had introduced liberal changes at Rome and they had led to disaster.

Though it is true that the idea that God gave the temporal dominion to monarchs was an idea of long tradition, and one which since Bossuet had been generally held in the Church, and that de Maistre had reinforced it, it was not the only tradition and Chiaramonti, who disliked de Maistre, had sat light to it. The restoration Popes could have shown more tolerance for the liberal principles – but not in their own states; and since they were committed there to being absolute temporal monarchs it was natural that they should favour absolute monarchy elsewhere. It is not surprising that it was only after the temporal power of the Popes had been lost that Leo XIII felt able to give clear expression to the principle that Rome was indifferent to forms of government, urging the French to rally to their new republic. We have only to ask ourselves what would have happened at Bologna if Gregory XVI had used the same sort of language about government as Leo XIII used later to realize that he was committed, in his political opinions, by the existence of his temporal sovereignty.

[1] Schmidlin, Vol. 1, Part 2, p. 253.

It may not necessarily have been a misfortune that, in the period 1815 to 1846, the support of the papacy was lent to the monarchical cause. The misfortune was that Gregory made pronouncements on political principles in terms which implied that what he was saying had permanent validity when in fact what he was saying had, at best, a temporary and contingent validity and more probably was ill-judged. And this misfortune was greatly aggravated by the fact that he was so singularly unsuccessful in the government of his own states. Was he to be regarded as a good guide to the conditions of a well-ordered polity? Europe could not help asking that question.

So we have reached, in conclusion, a pontificate in some ways as unfortunate as the one with which we began. In some ways, but not in quite the same ways. Gregory's policy towards the rulers was not really appeasement because it never seems to have occurred to him that the interests of the Thrones, the Papacy, and the Church were not one. Clement had not been so blind as that, and the measure of his understanding was the measure of his fault. His failure had been a failure of courage. The weakness he had betrayed had been so serious because, with evident misgiving, he had deliberately sacrificed a branch of the Church at the instance of the temporal rulers. Gregory's failure was rather a failure of judgement, a nervous, all too natural fear about things temporal, a bondage to possessions, and an ill-conceived attempt to tie the Church and Europe forever to forms of government and society which in fact had had their day.

Jansenism and Richerism

It seems simplest to keep to the term Jansenist in talking about that movement amongst the lower clergy in France and elsewhere in Europe in the later part of the eighteenth century which had such important effects at the time of the French Revolution, although Jansenist teaching really only represents one element in the amalgam. By origin Jansenism was a theological and moral movement. But because the Pope and the Jesuits set their face against Jansenist theology, and the French bishops and the Bourbons commonly supported Rome, the later Jansenists, of the eighteenth century, were thrown into an alliance with the Paris *Parlement*, and also with the lower clergy, with whose cause they came to be identified. In this way they became merged with the Richerists, whose special object it was to assert the claims of the lower clergy and to improve their position. The link between Jansenist-Richerism in France and Febronianism in Germany and Italy was the common intent of both to reform the Church by attacking Rome and the Jesuits and by bringing in the secular power to achieve their programme. The schismatic Jansenist Bishop of Utrecht was their unofficial leader, and at the Synods of Utrecht and Pistoia they gave practical expression to their ideas. There were smaller synods of a similar kind in France in places where bishops might happen to have some sympathy with the movement, and there was vigorous pamphleteering. The most immediate aim of the curés was to secure for themselves representation at diocesan meetings and rights in the choice of vicars and in the nomination of bishops. The ultimate aim of their leaders was a General Council of the Church at which the lower clergy would be represented, *Unigenitus* would be quashed, and reunion would be effected with some, at least, of the Protestants and schismatics. On the whole subject of the relation of eighteenth-century Jansenism to the religious innovations of the French Revolution the fullest study remains that by E. Préclin *Les Jansénistes du XVIIIe siècle et la Constitution Civile du Clergé: le développement du richérisme. Sa propagation dans le Bas Clergé. 1713–1791. Paris. Librairie Universitaire. J. Gamber. 1929.* But it needs today to be qualified, especially by reference to M. G. Hutt's *The Curés and the Third Estate: the*

Ideas of Reform in the Pamphlets of the French Lower Clergy in the period 1787–1789 (Journal of Ecclesiastical History, Vol. VIII, No. 1) where we are reminded (p. 86) that the curés 'were obsessed by the problem of their status within the Church and this had long been the core of Richerist teaching'.

APPENDIX TWO

Napoleon's Speech at Milan, June 5, 1800

The version of Napoleon's remarks about the Church which was accepted by the editors of Napoleon's correspondence (No. 4884) and which was published at the time not only in Italy but also in France, till it was banned there by Napoleon's police, ran as follows:

'I regard you, who are the ministers of this [Catholic] Religion, which is likewise my own, as my dearest friends; and I declare to you that I shall know how to punish in exemplary fashion, and with the most drastic penalties, and if necessary with death, as disturbers of the public peace and enemies of the public good all those responsible for the slightest insult to your or my religion. . . . My express intention is that the Christian Catholic and Roman Religion shall be maintained in her full vigour and in the complete possession of that free and public expression which it enjoyed at the time when I first set foot in this happy country.

'Whatever changes, especially in regard to her discipline, occurred at the time when I was first in Italy did so in despite of me and against my will. Merely an agent of my government . . . I could not then prevent all those disorders . . . armed now with full power I am determined to put into operation all those measures which I know to be most timely and efficacious in defending and sustaining that same religion.

'Modern philosophers have tried to persuade France that the Catholic Religion is the implacable enemy of every democratic system and of every republican government. From this arose that fierce persecution which the French Republic launched against religion and her Ministers and from this were born all those errors of which that unhappy Nation found herself the victim so often for so many years.

'No small part was played in these disorders by the diversity of opinions which at the time of the revolution prevailed in France, divided as she was into various sects in the matter of Religion.

'Experience has disillusioned the French and has convinced them that the Catholic Religion is the one which more than any other is suited to every kind of government and that in a special way it develops the principles and sustains the rights of a Democratic and Republican Government.

'I too am a philosopher, and I know that in no society can a man be honest and just if he does not know whence he comes and where he is going. Reason is not sufficient to give him this light, without which every man is obliged to journey in the dark. The Catholic Religion alone, with its infallibility, confronts man with his beginning and his end.

'No society can exist without morality. There can be no sound morality where religion does not exist. . . .

'When I can meet the new Pope I hope I shall have the pleasure of removing all the obstacles which may still prevent an entire reconciliation between France and the Head of the Church.'

APPENDIX THREE

The French Concordat of 1801—Convention du 26 messidor an IX

Le gouvernement de la République reconnaît que la religion catholique, apostolique et romaine, est la religion de la grande majorité des citoyens français.

Sa Sainteté reconnaît également que cette même religion a retiré et attend encore, en ce moment, le plus grand bien et le plus grand éclat de l'établissement du culte catholique en France et de la profession particulière qu'en font les consuls de la République.

En conséquence, d'après cette reconnaissance mutuelle, tant pour le bien de la religion que pour le maintien de la tranquillité intérieure, ils sont convenus de ce qui suit.

Art. 1. La religion catholique, apostolique et romaine sera librement exercée en France. Son culte sera public, en se conformant aux règlements de police que le gouvernement jugera nécessaires pour la tranquillité publique.

Art. 2. Il sera fait par le Saint-Siège, de concert avec le gouvernement, une nouvelle circonscription des diocèses français.

Art 3. Sa Sainteté déclarera aux titulaires des évêchés français qu'elle attend d'eux, avec une ferme confiance, pour le bien de la paix et de l'unité, toute espèce de sacrifices, même celui de leurs sièges.

Après cette exhortation, s'ils se refusaient à ce sacrifice commandé par le bien de l'Église (refus néanmoins auquel Sa Sainteté ne s'attend pas), il sera pourvu par de nouveaux titulaires au gouvernement des évêchés de la circonscription nouvelle, de la manière suivante.

Art. 4. Le Premier consul de la République nommera, dans les trois mois qui suivront la publication de la bulle de Sa Sainteté, aux archevêchés et évêchés de la circonscription nouvelle. Sa Sainteté conférera l'institution canonique suivant les formes établies par rapport à la France avant le changement de gouvernement.

Art. 5. Les nominations aux évêchés qui vaqueront dans la suite, seront également faites par le Premier consul; et l'institution canonique sera donnée par le Saint-Siège, en conformité de l'article précédent.

Art. 6. Les évêques, avant d'entrer en fonctions, prêteront directement, entre les mains du Premier Consul, le serment de fidélité qui était en usage avant le changement de gouvernement, exprimé dans les termes suivants:

'Je jure et promets à Dieu, sur les saints Évangiles, de garder obéissance et fidélité au gouvernement établi par la constitution de la République française. Je promets aussi de n'avoir aucune intelligence, de n'assister à aucun conseil, de n'entretenir aucune ligue, soit au dedans, soit au dehors, qui soit contraire à la tranquillité publique; et si, dans mon diocèse ou ailleurs, j'apprends qu'il se trame quelque chose au préjudice de l'État, je le ferai savoir au gouvernement.'

Art. 7. Les ecclésiastiques du second ordre prêteront le même serment entre les mains des autorités civiles désignées par le gouvernement.

Art. 8. La formule de prière suivante sera récitée à la fin de l'office divin dans toutes les églises catholiques de France:

'Domine, salvam fac Rempublicam;

'Domine, salvos fac Consules.'

Art. 9. Les évêques feront une nouvelle circonscription des paroisses de leurs diocèses, qui n'aura d'effet que d'après le consentement du gouvernement.

Art. 10. Les évêques nommeront aux cures. Leur choix ne pourra tomber que sur des personnes agréées par le gouvernement.

Art. 11. Les évêques pourront avoir un chapitre dans leur cathédrale, et un séminaire pour leur diocèse, sans que le gouvernement s'oblige à les doter.

Art. 12. Toutes les églises métropolitaines, cathédrales, paroissiales et autres, non aliénées, nécessaires au culte, seront mises à la disposition des évêques.

Art. 13. Sa Sainteté, pour le bien de la paix et l'heureux rétablissement de la religion catholique, déclare que ni elle, ni ses successeurs, ne troubleront, en aucune manière, les acquéreurs des biens ecclésiastiques aliénés; et qu'en conséquence, la propriété de ces mêmes biens, les droits et revenus y attachés, demeureront incommutables entre leurs mains ou celles de leurs ayants cause.

Art. 14. Le gouvernement assurera un traitement convenable aux évêques et aux curés dont les diocèses et les cures seront compris dans la circonscription nouvelle.

Art. 15. Le gouvernement prendra également des mesures pour que les catholiques français puissent, s'ils le veulent, faire en faveur des églises, des fondations.

Art. 16. Sa Sainteté reconnaît dans le Premier Consul de la République française les mêmes droits et prérogatives dont jouissait près d'elle l'ancien gouvernement.

Art. 17. Il est convenu entre les parties contractantes que, dans le cas où quelqu'un des successeurs du Premier Consul actuel ne serait pas catholique, les droits et prérogatives mentionnés dans l'article ci-dessus, et la nomination aux évêchés, seront réglés, par rapport à lui, par une nouvelle convention.

APPENDIX FOUR

Papal Policy in 1814 towards Roman Collaborators with the French

The government was more severe with the priests than with the laymen. A layman might have been noted down as a 'liberal', and have co-operated fully with the French régime, but if he was 'honest' and 'conciliatory' he would be as likely as not to find himself included in the list of those who might be given government employment (cf. Vat. Arch, *Ep. Nap. It*, Busta VII, Fasc. 53, which contains a register of such men).

Not so with the priests. The crucial issue with them was the nature of the oath they had taken in support of the French government. As early as January of the year 1799, at the time of the Roman Republic, the Vice-Regent, Mgr Bonzi, had devised a form of oath which they might legitimately take in support of the new régime. This ran: 'I swear to take no part in any conspiracy, plot, or riot, aiming at a re-establishment of the monarchy and . . . fealty, loyalty and obedience to the Republic and the Constitution, saving the rights of the Catholic and Roman religion . . . (*Ibid.*, Fasc. 28). In the legations, after their recovery by the French in 1800, it remained legitimate to take the oath in this form, but in 1808, when Napoleon took over the rest of the states, the permission was not extended to the territories newly incorporated – another indication that the legations were regarded in a different light, or as 'lost' at Tolentino. Under Gabrielli's regulations in 1808 a priest in Rome, or the Marches, or Umbria, must not swear fealty to the new régime; that was regarded as involving much too close a loyalty; he might only undertake to obey 'in all which is not contrary to the Law of God and of the Church' (*Ibid.*, Fasc. 6). Moreover priests were not to accept posts which were likely to consolidate the new régime, nor to sing Te Deums in honour of its functionaries or their achievements, nor to offer public prayers for the Emperor (*Ibid.*, Fasc. 7).

The Pope, in his exile, continued to set the greatest store by a punctilious obedience in this matter. In March 1810 he expressed from Savona his astonishment that any of the priests were trying to take the oath in a different form (*Ibid.*, Fasc. 7), though matters were far from easy for the Roman clergy, especially when Napoleon, on May 4, 1812, made it a felony for them not to take the full oath as prescribed throughout his Empire (*Ibid.*, Fasc. 23).

However, the situation changed abruptly at the beginning of 1814 with the decline in the Emperor's fortunes, and by March of that year this change was reflected in instructions that non-juring priests and monks who had emigrated and were now returning were to be paid their stipends in full (*Ibid.*, Fasc. 24). After the Restoration we find a huge list of priests, most carefully compiled, from which it appears that upwards of 800 had taken the oath in the form prescribed by Napoleon and forbidden by the Pope (*Ibid.*, Fasc. 50). An order of July 5, 1814 (Busta VIII, Fasc. 14) took away their employment from the more important jurors, e.g. Vicars, or Superiors of Communities, but left the fate of the others to the discretion of their bishops.

Bibliographical Guide

1. DOCUMENTARY SOURCES

Vatican Archives

For the political papers of the period before 1814, i.e. before the over-all political responsibility of the office of Secretary of State had been clearly defined, it is necessary to consult a variety of catalogues, e.g. that for the Archives of the Congregation of the Propaganda or those for the papers of particular cardinals, such as Boncompagni, who was Pius VI's Secretary of State.

The papers bearing on the French revolutionary and Napoleonic period in France and Italy (apart from the important papal correspondence with the French bishops catalogued under *Vescovi*) are listed in catalogue 87 under the general heading *Epoca Napoleonica, Francia, Italia, 1798–1815.* Under *Francia* are those bearing on French affairs and this part of the catalogue has been reordered since 1946 and translated into French by J. Leflon and A. Latreille; the papers are contained in 25 folders. Under *Italia* are listed those documents bearing on Italy, and mainly on the Papal States, which are contained in nine folders without chronological arrangement. They suffered both damage and disorder from their burial in the Vatican gardens, after the kidnapping of Pius VII in 1809, and were only disinterred in 1889–90. They are mostly the papers of the Extraordinary Congregation *di Pietro* which, from 1792, handled critical domestic and international matters often (in Pius VI's time) giving orders to the Secretary of State which he was expected to carry out.

For the more settled period after 1814 the state papers are catalogued under *Segretario di Stato.* Foreign relations, ecclesiastical and political, are under *Segretario di Stato, Esteri,* and sub-divided by countries, except for certain salient topics, such as the Congress of Vienna or the Congress of Laybach, which have been collected into separate folders, still under the same general heading. The most important collection of diplomatic papers not catalogued under *Segretario di Stato* are the *Epistolae ad Principes* which are available in the Secret Archives.

Rome State Archives

In 1833 the duties of Papal Secretary of State were divided between a Secretary for External and a Secretary for Internal Affairs, with the result that the papers relating to internal affairs, from March 20, 1833, are now to be found in 100 folders in the State Archives (at present housed in the *Sapienza*) under the title *Segretaria per gli affari di Stato interni istituita da Gregorio XVI* in the *Archivio del Ministero dell' Interno*.

Biblioteca Vallicelliana at the Oratorian Chiesa Nuova (now run by the State)

Contains important papers for the period of the Roman Republic of 1798–99, especially those of Cardinal Leonardo Antonelli, who was acting as Delegate at Rome during the exile of Pius VI (Cat. of MSS, Appendix III, Vol 12).

British Museum

In the Manuscript room, under reference 18.288, there is a collection entitled *Papers relating to the Papal States, 1808–1811*. Many of these are contemporary copies of protests put out from the Quirinal in the months before the abduction of Pius VII which were later published in the various collections of such papers referred to below.

For guidance to the archives of the European capitals see Pastor, Schmidlin, Latreille, van Duerm, *op. cit.* below.

2. PUBLISHED SOURCES

(For papal documents up to the year 1836 see the *Bullarii Romani Continuatio* . . . , Prati, 1842 etc, and for the pontificate of Gregory XVI the *Acta Gregorii XVI*, Rome, 1901.)

CLEMENT XIV

The fundamental work is Vol 38 of L. von Pastor's *History of the Popes* (Eng. transl, Routledge and Kegan Paul, 1951). While Pastor is concerned to try to take a balanced view between the pro-Jesuits, who naturally decried Clement XIV, and the anti-Jesuits, who were for the Pope, he in fact ended up on the Jesuit side.

The fullest account is that of Augustin Theiner: *Histoire du pontificat de Clément XIV*, 4 vols, Brussels, 1853. As Prefect of the Secret Archives of the Vatican Theiner had access to Clement XIV's letters, though he found that those for the crucial year before the suppression of the Jesuits had been stolen. Theiner was an Oratorian. He had little love for the Jesuits and much of his work is taken up with attacking their defender, J. Crétineau-Joly, whose two books, *Histoire religieuse, politique et littéraire de la Compagnie de Jésus*, 5 vols, Paris, 1845, and *Clément XIV et les Jésuites*, Paris, 1847, certainly present the Jesuit case in a one-sided way, indeed with many absurdities. On the other hand extravagence of statement was not confined to the pro-Jesuit historians of the nineteenth century; it characterizes even the more moderate of the historian critics of the Society, e.g. A de Saint-Priest *Histoire de la Chute des Jésuites au XVIIIe Siècle*, Paris, 1844, or J. Huber, the Munich professor and friend of Acton, Friedrich and Doellinger, whose book *The Jesuits* ran into four French editions between 1875 and 1880. The most reasonable account of the suppression, from the anti-Jesuit angle, was that of L. von Ranke, in his *History of the Popes*, but even he was led by his sympathies into depicting the character of Clement XIV in rosy colours which hardly carry conviction (cf. English transl. of 1901, Colonial Press, Vol III, Sect. XVIII).

PIUS VI

The last two volumes of Pastor's *History of the Popes* (Vols. 39 and 40 in the English edition) are devoted to Pius VI the last, after two chapters on Germany, being devoted entirely to his relations with the French Revolution. Pastor here leans heavily upon the work of

J. Gendry: *Pie VI, sa vie – son pontificat*, 2 vols., Paris, 1905, which is detailed, and based on the documents at the Vatican and Vallicelliana, though rather pious in its approach.

Primary Printed Sources

For Roman relations with France and with the French clergy see the annotated index of Roman correspondence with the French bishops published by G. Bourgin: *La France et Rome de 1788 à 1797, Regeste des dépêches du Secrétaire d'État, tirées du fond 'Vescovi' des Archives secrètes du Vatican*, Paris, 1909 (No. 102 of the *Librairie des Écoles Françaises d'Athènes et de Rome*) and A. Theiner: *Documents inédits relatifs aux Affaires Religieuses de la France, 1790 à 1800, extraits des Archives secrètes du Vatican*, 2 vols., Paris, 1857.

On the Roman Republic of 1798–99 see the *Diario Romano degli anni 1798–99* by G. A. Sala which occupies the first three volumes of the author's *Scritti*, published by the *Società Romana di Storia Patria* in 1891. Besides the diary, Vol. 3 contains a number of the proclamations and other documents issued by the Republic.

On ecclesiastical affairs in Germany see especially the *Memorie Storiche di Mgr Bartolomeo Pacca . . . sul di lui soggiorno in Germania dall' anno 1786 al 1794*, Rome, 1832.

Amongst the letters and memoirs of particular relevance may be mentioned the following:

Correspondance Secrète de l'Abbé de Salamon avec le Cardinal de Zelada (1791–1792), publ. par le Vte de Richemont, Paris, 1898. Salamon was unofficial papal agent in Paris and Zelada Secretary of State.

Correspondance Diplomatique et Mémoires inédits du Cardinal Maury (1792–1817), 2 vols., Ed. Mgr Ricard, Lille, 1891.

Mémoires de Grégoire, ancien évêque de Blois, Ed. M. H. Carnot, 2 vols., Paris, 1837.

Mémoires Politiques et Correspondance Diplomatique de J. de Maistre, Paris, 1858, and his *Considérations sur la France*, Paris, 1853, which was written in 1796. Chapter 5 of the latter is entitled *De la révolution française considérée dans son caractère anti-religieux*.

Mémoires du Général Thiébault, 5 vols., Paris, 1894. Vol. 2 is

U

mostly descriptive of conditions in the Papal States and in Naples from 1797 to 1799.

Histories

For an introduction to the extensive historical literature of the period see the bibliographies contained in Pastor's *History of the Popes*, Vol. 35, pp. XII to XXXVII, and the Fliche et Martin *Histoire de L'Église*, Vol. 20, *La crise révolutionnaire, 1789–1846*, by J. Leflon, Bloud et Gay, 1951, pp. 7–14 and *passim*. But see in particular:

For Italy:

C. Spellanzon: *Storia del Risorgimento e dell' unità d'Italia*, Vol. 1, Rizzoli, 1933 (Bibliographies).

J. Leflon: *Pie VII*, Vol. 1, Plon, 1958. This is the first volume of a projected five volume study of the Pope and deals largely with the time when he was Archbishop of Imola under the Cisalpine Republic.

V. E. Giuntella: *La Giacobina Repubblica Romana 1798–1799* in *Archivio della Società Romana di Storia Patria*, Vol. LXXIII, 1950.

G. Racioppi: *Storia dei popoli della Lucania e della Basilicata*, 2 vols., Rome, 1889.

Benedetto Croce: *La Riconquista del Regno di Napoli nel 1799*, Bari, 1943. Prints the correspondence between King Ferdinand, Queen Maria Carolina, their Minister Acton, and Cardinal Ruffo. Preface by Croce.

A. Heriot: *The French in Italy, 1796–1799*, Chatto and Windus, 1957.

H. M. M. Acton: *The Bourbons of Naples, 1734–1825*, Methuen, 1956.

For France:

Of the classical French historians of the Revolution the two who were most concerned with the Roman issue were Louis Madelin (*La Rome de Napoléon*, Paris, 1906, and *La Révolution et Rome*, Paris, 1913), and Albert Mathiez (see especially his anti-Roman *Rome et* *le Clergé Français sous la Constituante,*Paris, 1911, and his briefer but more polemical *La Révolution et l'Église,* 1910).

Standard works are:

A. Sicard: *Le Clergé de France pendant la Révolution,* 3 vols., Paris, 1894–1912.

E. Préclin: *Les Jansenistes du XVIIIe Siècle et la Constitution Civile du Clergé,* Librairie Universitaire, 1929.

P. de la Gorce: *Histoire religieuse de la Révolution,* 5 vols., Paris, 1909–1923.

Recent studies include:

J. Leflon: *Crise révolutionnaire (cit.)* and A. Latreille *L'Église Catholique et la Révolution Française,* Vol. 1, *Le Pontificat de Pie VI et la Crise Française (1775–1799),* Hachette, 1946.

PIUS VII (to 1814)

The last pontificate recounted in Pastor's history is that of Pius VI. But after Pastor's death his work was continued on a comparable scale by his collaborator J. Schmidlin in his *Papstgeschichte der neuesten Zeit,* 3 vols., Munich, 3rd Ed., 1936, which covers the period 1800–1922. There is a French translation of the first volume, covering the period 1800–46 (Vitte, 1938) in two parts, Part 1 *Pie VII* and Part 2 *Léon XII, Pie VIII et Grégoire XVI.*

Primary Printed Sources

Roman anxiety that European political circles should be widely informed on the struggle between Pius VII and Napoleon led to a printing of the more important documents even while the Pope was a prisoner in the Quirinal; already in 1814 there was a fifth edition of these documents in French (*Correspondance Officielle de la Cour de Rome avec les agens de Bonaparte*), put out by Pogiolini at Rome, and in London an *Authentic Narrative of the Seizure and Removal of Pius VII.* The publication of these papers reached its fullest extent in 1833–34 with the appearance at Rome of the six volumes of the *Documenti relativi alle contestazioni insorte fra la S. Sede ed il Governo Francese.*

Apart from these official publications the most important collections of Vatican documents to be published were those printed by Ilario Rinieri at the beginning of the twentieth century under the heading *La Diplomazia Pontificia nel Secolo XIX* in volumes published by the *Ufficio della Civiltà Cattolica*. Vol. 1 (1902) covered the period 1800–1802, Vol. 2 (1902) the period 1802–1804, Vol. 3 (1903) the correspondence between Consalvi and Pacca of 1814–15 and Vol. 4 (1904) events leading up to and including the Congress of Vienna. Rinieri also published, in 1906, his *Napoleone e Pio VII (1804–1813)*, in three parts, printing a number of unpublished Vatican documents in parts 2 and 3.

The French documents have been to some extent published by the French historians, notably in the following books:

Boulay de la Meurthe: *Documents sur la Négociation du Concordat,* 5 vols., Paris, 1891. (Based also on the Vatican papers.)

Cardinal Mathieu: *Le Concordat de 1801,* Paris, 1903. Includes unpublished Vatican papers.

Abbé Feret: *La France et le Saint-Siège, Vol. I Le Premier Empire et le Saint-Siège,* Paris, 1911.

d'Haussonville: *L'Église Romaine et le Premier Empire,* 3rd Ed., 5 vols., Paris, 1870.

A. Latreille: *Napoléon et le Saint-Siège (1801–1808); l'Ambassade du Cardinal Fesch à Rome,* Paris, 1935. The author does not publish documents in full, but his book is based extensively on the hitherto unused personal papers of Cardinal Fesch in the Departmental and Episcopal Archives at Lyon.

A number of the important papers from the Vienna Archives bearing on the Conclave of Venice and on the Austrian attempt to influence its outcome were published by C. van Duerm in his *Un peu plus de lumière sur Le Conclave de Venise,* Louvain, 1896.

Of the letters and memoirs see especially:

Consalvi's Memoirs. First published in French translation by J. Crétineau-Joly (*Mémoires du Cardinal Consalvi,* Paris, 1864, 2nd Ed. 1866) the Italian text was only published at Rome, by A. Signorelli, in 1950 (*Memorie del Cardinale Ercole Consalvi*).

Cardinal Bartolomeo Pacca: *Memorie Storiche del Ministero, dei due viaggi in Francia, e della prigionia nel forte di S. Carlo in Fenestrelle,* Rome, 1830.

Memoirs of Cardinal Maury and of Bishop Grégoire and J. de Maistre quoted above.

E. de Lévis-Mirepoix *Un Collaborateur de Metternich, Mémoires et papiers de Lebzeltern,* Plon, 1949. See pp. 157–194 for Lebzeltern's mission to Savona and pp. 313–32 for his assistance to Pius VII in his restoration to Rome in 1814.

The official *Correspondance de Napoléon* (Paris, 1858–70), especially Vols. 11 and 12 (1805–1806) and Vol. XIX (1809); also L. Lecestre *Lettres inédites de Napoléon,* 2 vols., Paris, 1897.

Histories

For extended bibliographies see J. Leflon (*Crise révolutionnaire*) and J. Schmidlin (*Histoire des Papes*).

Of special use are:

P. de la Gorce: *op. cit.,* Vol. 5.

F. Masson: *Le Sacre et le Couronnement de Napoléon,* Paris, 1908.

Artaud de Montor: *Histoire du Pape Pie VII,* Paris, 2nd Ed., 1837. Employed by the French government at its embassy at Rome from the year 1801 the writer was closely in touch with Roman affairs and to some extent a witness of what he recounts.

Mayol de Lupé: *La Captivité de Pie VII,* 2nd Ed., Paris, 1916. A well documented and full account of the kidnapping and imprisonment of the Pope.

H. Welschinger: *Le Pape et L'Empereur, 1804–1815,* Plon, 1905. An account based on the documents in the Paris National Archives and in which use was made, for the first time, of the proceedings of the National Council of 1811 which were refused to d'Haussonville.

E. Celani: *I Preliminari del Conclave di Venezia* in Vol. 37 (1913) of the *Archivio della Società Romana di Storia Patria.* Surveys the various accounts of the Conclave, adds what is relevant from the Vatican Archives, and publishes Consalvi's letters to the Principessa Borghese.

A. Latreille: *L'Église Catholique et la Révolution Française*, Vol. 2, (Bibliography), Hachette, 1950.

A. Fugier: *Napoléon et L'Italie*, Janin, 1947.

J. Leflon: *Bernier*, Paris, 1938, 2 vols.

J. Leflon: *Pie VII*, Vol. 1 (*cit.*). Important for the Conclave of Venice because it demonstrates the vital role played by Mgr (later Cardinal) Despuig, an unofficial envoy of Spain, recorded in his diary (*Libro de viages*) for which see G. Segui: *El Cardenal Despuig y la Santa Sede, Analecta Tarraconensia*, Vol. XVI, 1943.

V. Bindel: *Histoire Religieuse de Napoléon*, 2 vols., Paris, 1940. A history of the Church in France under Napoleon.

THE RESTORATION PAPACY (1814-1846)

The fundamental work is J. Schmidlin *op. cit.* (French translation Vol. 1, Part 2; bibliography of documents in Part 1, of printed books in Part 2). But for the Papal States and their political context in Italy see also C. Spellanzon: *Storia del Risorgimento e dell' Unità d'Italia*, Vol. 2, Rizzoli, 1934 (Bibliographies).

Primary Printed Sources

Abbé Feret: *La France et le Saint-Siège*, Vol. 2, Paris, 1911.

C. van Duerm: *Correspondance du Cardinal Hercule Consalvi avec le Prince Clément de Metternich, 1815-1823*. Louvain, 1899. Published from the Metternich papers in the Vienna Archives.

M. Petrocchi: *La Restaurazione, Il Cardinale Consalvi, e la Riforma del 1816*, Le Monnier, 1941. The Consalvi-Severoli correspondence is published here with a commentary.

G. A. Sala: *Scritti*, Vol. 4, Soc. Rom. di Storia Patria, 1891. This volume contains (pp. 45-234) Cardinal Giuseppe Sala's plan for the reform of the papal government. It was analysed in G. Cugnoni: *Memorie della vita e degli scritti del Cardinale Giuseppe Antonio Sala* in Vol. XI (1888) of the *Arch. della R. Soc. Rom. di Stor. Patria*.

N. Bianchi: *Storia Documentata della Diplomazia Europea in Italia dall' anno 1814 all' anno 1861*, 8 vols., Turin, 1865 etc. A selective collection of papers, but still useful. Vols. 1-3 cover the period

1814–46. See especially those relating to the crisis in the Papal States of 1831–32 which are published in Vol. 3, pp. 345–94.

Carte Segrete e Atti Ufficiali della Polizia Austriaca in Italia, 3 vols., Tip. Elvetica, 1851. A curious collection of spies' reports of uneven value; in so far as they are concerned with the Papal States their special interest lies in the light they throw on the profound suspicion with which Vienna regarded the papal government even in Gregory XVI's time. She believed Rome was encouraging the revolutionary secret societies as a weapon against Austria.

A. Serafini: *Pio Nono*, Vol. (1792–1846), Tip. Pol. Vat., 1958. This detailed study (1,760 pp.) of the life of Mastai-Ferretti before he became Pope Pius IX has been written from the mass of documents collected by the author for the use of the Sacred Congregation of Rites investigating the Cause of the Pope's beatification. But it incidentally provides a unique body of information about the Papal States, especially in the period 1827–46, when the future Pope held the Sees first of Spoleto and then of Imola.

M. D'Azeglio: *I Miei Ricordi*, 2 vols., 3rd Ed., Florence, 1868. Occasionally relevant and interesting, e.g. his judgement of Consalvi (2. 212–16).

Degli ultimi casi di Romagna, 'Italia', 1846. The classic condemnation of the papal government.

L. C. Farini: *Lo Stato Romano dall' anno 1815 al 1850*, 4 vols., Le Monnier, 1850. (Eng. transl. W. E. Gladstone, 1851–54). A history by an important figure in the Italian Risorgimento.

Cte de Sainte-Aulaire: *Souvenirs, 1832–41*. (Publ. by M. Théibaut Paris, 1927). Recollections of the French Ambassador at Rome.

F. Bunsen: *A Memoir of Baron Bunsen*, 2 vols. (Longmans, 2nd Ed., 1869)Contains letters and papers of the Prussian Ambassador at Rome.

Articles de L'Avenir, 7 vols., Paris, 1830–32. Articles by Lamennais, Montalembert, and other liberal Catholics in 1830–31 on political events in Europe, especially in relation to the Church.

Cardinal Luigi Lambruschini: *La Mia Nunziatura di Francia, a cura di Pietro Pirri*, Zanichelli, 1934. The Papal Secretary of State's recollections, written 1831–36, of the France of Charles X, the

French Revolution of 1830, and the revolution in the Papal States of 1831.

Histories

G. Mollat: *La question romaine de Pie VI à Pie XI*, Paris, 1932.

F. Hayward: *Le Dernier Siècle de la Rome Pontificale*, Vol. 2, Payot, 1928.

A. Boudou: *Le Saint-Siège et La Russie*, Vol. 1, 1814–47, Paris, 1922.

B. Ward: *The Eve of Catholic Emancipation*, 2 vols., Longmans, 1911.

P. Hughes: *The Catholic Question*, 1688–1829, London, 1929.

J. T. Ellis: *Cardinal Consalvi and Anglo-Papal Relations, 1814–1824*, Catholic University of America Press, 1942.

H. Haag: *Les Origines du Catholicisme Libéral en Belgique (1789–1839)*, Louvain, 1950. Shows the influence of Lamennais and the Belgian liberal Catholics on each other

C. Terlinden: *Guillaume Premier, roi des Pays-Bas, et l'Église Catholique en Belgique*, 1814–30, Brussels, 1906.

R. F. Leslie: *Polish Politics and the Revolution of November, 1830*, Athlone Press, 1956.

A. R. Vidler: *Prophecy and Papacy*, S.C.M. Press, 1954. A documented study of the issue between the Abbé de Lamennais and Rome which elucidates clearly the religious and political issues at stake.

Index

313

Date Due

FEB 18 '81				
OCT 2 3 '62	CANISIUS			
JAN 3 0 '63	CANISIUS OCT 0 5 1988			
FEB 1 3 '63	CANISIUS			
SEP 8 . '63				
	DEC 1 1 1987			